Net Lessons:
Web-Based Projects for
Your Classroom

To my best teachers—my parents—who taught me everything worth knowing.

Net Lessons: Web-Based Projects for Your Classroom

Laura Parker Roerden

Net Lessons: Web-Based Projects for Your Classroom
by Laura Parker Roerden

Published by Songline Studios, Inc. and O'Reilly & Associates, Inc., 101 Morris Street, Sebastopol, CA 95472.

Series Editor: Melissa Koch

Editor: Sheryl Avruch

Printing History: March 1997:   First Edition.

Library of Congress Cataloging-in-Publication Data
Parker Roerden, Laura.
      Net Lessons : Web-based projects for your classroom / Laura Parker Roerden.
         p.   cm.
      Includes bibliographical references and index.
      ISBN 1-56592-291-3 (pbk.)
      1.   Internet (Computer network) in education.   2. World Wide Web (Information retrieval system)   3. Activity programs in education—United States.   4. Teaching—United States—Aids and devices.
      I. Title
      LB1044.87.R64   1997
      025.06'37—DC21   97-1439
                                                                                               CIP
                                                                                               Rev.

ISBN: 1-56592-291-3

Cover Design: Edie Freedman
Production Services: Thomas E. Dorsaneo   [8/98]

Contents

Part I — Theory

- ▶ Why Use the Web in Education?
- ▶ What Does the Web Offer Your Classroom?
- ▶ Pitfalls of the Web
- ▶ Is the Web Difficult to Learn?
- ▶ Basic Internet Tools at Your Disposal
- ▶ Where to Find Help
- ▶ A Note to Novices

- ▶ Using the Web in Your Classroom
- ▶ The Big Twelve: Web Activity Types to Try
- ▶ Can the Web Help?
- ▶ Applying the Big Twelve to Your Subject Area
- ▶ Interdisciplinary Curriculum
- ▶ Building Students' Skills
- ▶ A Word About Assessment

- ▶ First Steps First
- ▶ General Guidelines
- ▶ If You Are a Beginner
- ▶ If You've Already Tried a Few Projects
- ▶ If You Are an Advanced User
- ▶ A Framework for Success
- ▶ Administering Your Web Project
- ▶ Creating a Web Site
- ▶ Pulling It Together: Some Timely Tips from the Field

Acknowledgments

Writing a book is like falling in love. Too good to be true. More fun than you imagined. At times, more tormenting than you think you can cope with. But above all, well worth it!

Thanks to the folks at Educators for Social Responsibility, who've taught me more about good teaching than I could ever outline here. Thanks in particular to Larry Dieringer, Nan Doty, Bill Kreidler, and Carol Miller Lieber for providing patience, mentoring, and inspiration.

Thanks to my friends for putting up with my endless chatter and questions. I'm indebted to Val Quercia, Jane Clarke, Kent Werst, Sarah Hanselman, Jessica Hanson, Tom Boulet, and Chris Gawle in particular.

A special thanks to my reviewers—skilled and experienced teachers whose invaluable input stretched my ideas. Thanks to Jay Altman, Lisa Sjostrom, Tom Boulet, and Maureen Gannon. Very special thanks to Melissa Koch of Songline Studios, Frank Willison, and my editor at O'Reilly, Sheryl Avruch, who believed in this project and supported me in countless ways.

Most of all, thanks to the many teachers out there who so willingly shared their ideas and talents. In particular, I'd like to thank Sue Miller and Nancy Skomars Davis. Thanks also to Cynthia Addison, Donald Bourdon, Jon M. Brokering, Phil Cliffe, Judy Conklin, Desmond Connolly, Cindy Cooper, Beth Flickinger, Patty Foote, Tera Freedman, Janice Friesen, William J. Gathergood, Sharon Hayes, Linda Little, Allyson Y. Marsh, Harry R. Noden, John Patten, Marshall Ramme, Greg Smith, and Heather Swift. All of you are truly pioneers!

And lastly I'd like to thank my husband, Doug, who lent advice, computer help, even lesson plans, and—most of all—unfailing love and support. You are my bedrock.

Foreword

Teaching has been called many things: an art, a science, a calling, a way of life. Throughout history, teachers have taken up the tools at hand to help them teach—whether marking on clay with a stylus or writing on a blackboard with chalk. As new technologies, such as photography, filmstrips, radio, and television, have emerged, teachers have used them to extend the range of what they could teach, illustrate ideas in different ways, bring new materials to students, and motivate learning. The process of adopting new technologies has not been quick or effortless, however.

Today, computers and the Internet are unlikely to have a widespread impact on education unless they are effectively integrated into the objectives and activities of the classroom teacher. *Net Lessons* gives teachers a road map to success using Web-based projects. They can explore, navigate, and learn to integrate their knowledge of the Web using frameworks and strategies furnished by the author.

Educators are being asked not simply to utilize new equipment, but to fundamentally transform their institutional practices. This is a long steady process, but in *Net Lessons,* Roerden gives teachers the building blocks for using the Internet to bring real-world learning into the classroom, where the teacher serves as a guide rather than the dispenser of all knowledge.

As teachers, we hear so many ideas and even mandates from parents, the community, government, and business on how we should teach. But many of these suggestions or curricula fail to fit into real classroom situations. The lessons and curriculum design techniques presented in *Net Lessons* take into account the variables of student composition, diversity, differences in buildings, national standards, and curriculum approaches.

Teachers need to learn from other teachers; the classroom-tested lessons in this book address this need. In addition, this book offers design and implementation directions that allow teachers to create and produce their own lessons, an element missing from the majority of curriculum books.

Helping the 2.8 million teachers in public and private schools effectively incorporate technology into the learning process is one of the most important steps the U.S. can take to make the most of our investment in educational technology. We don't want students to be just competent users of technology, but to become more accomplished learners overall.

Bonnie Bracey
Teacher Member of the National Information Infrastructure
Advisory Council
Technology Teacher in Residence, Arlington Career Center
Director of Networks, The McGuffey Project

Preface

Net Lessons is for classroom teachers—Web novices and veterans alike. Anyone who cares about teaching and curriculum will find this book useful.

Teachers whose schools are connected will learn how they can start reaping the benefits of this new resource to meet their curricular goals. You will find more than 100 project ideas, curricular frameworks, advice from veteran Net users, lesson plans, and roadmaps for getting you and your class onboard.

Curriculum directors will find *Net Lessons* helps them think about the potentials and applications of the Internet to the classroom, providing practical frameworks that span K-12 classrooms and reach across standard curricula.

Academic technology coordinators will find this book supports them in their quest to help teachers work more effectively and use technology to serve their purposes—*not* the other way around. If you are a technology coordinator in a school, chances are you know a classroom teacher who you have hooked up to the Net, but who hasn't yet taken advantage of the array of resources available. This book will help you help them. Give a copy to all of your department heads or maverick teachers, and you will have planted an important seed that will hopefully take root through the community.

If you are new to the Web, a skeptic, or even a technophobe—relax. This book is not about gadgets. It's about education. What are the Net's potentials for the classroom? Can it help you meet your educational goals? If so, how do you design effective curricula? These are just a few of the questions this book answers.

If you are experienced with the Web, then you already know that it is not the magic elixir to solve all your problems. And you may also know that the Web is a potentially powerful tool for your classroom. Use the activity frames and assessment tools provided in this book to explore new ideas and design more effective Internet projects.

Net Lessons includes everything you need to begin to harness the Web's unique potential as an educational tool.

WHAT MAKES THIS BOOK DIFFERENT

Most books about the Internet in education focus on the tools. How do you FTP? What's a Gopher? How about your SLIP or PPP connection? An appendix or addendum in these books might offer some curricular ideas and a host of neat resources.

These books by and large were written before the explosion of the World Wide Web. They focused largely on the tools since that's exactly what you needed to learn before you could even begin to imagine how this tool might help your classroom. Now many of you are familiar with the tools and are already online. You've arrived, but you're not sure what to do now that you are there.

Net Lessons will help you plan your online journey. It focuses on curriculum development rather than telling you how to get hooked up, or what service provider to use. *Net Lessons* instead carefully considers how and when the Internet might help you meet your curricular goals. This book provides more than static lessons from a curriculum designer; these lessons, from a variety of disciplines, were designed and used by educators in the classroom. With the curriculum design and implementation plans, you can effectively tailor these lessons and create your own.

HOW TO USE THIS BOOK

Throughout this book I use the terms "Internet" and "Web." The Web is part of the Internet; it is one method for organizing information (both text and graphics) on the Internet. Because the Web, with its easy-to-use graphical interface, has made the Internet more widely accessible, and because this book focuses on using the Web in the classroom, I often use the terms Internet and Web interchangeably.

Part I, "Theory," lays the theoretical framework for your Internet curriculum. Chapter 1, "The Lay of the Land," introduces what is unique and potentially useful to your classroom about both the Internet and the Web and gives an overview of the tools that will help you. Read this chapter to familiarize yourself with the medium.

Chapter 2, "Designing Your Curriculum," examines all of the curricular implications of using the Internet in your classroom. When can the Web help you meet your goals? A handy assessment tool for answering that question is included. Twelve Web activity types (which correspond with lesson plans in Part II) will help you model successful Web projects. Frameworks by subject area are also presented, along with thoughts about assessment and tips for facilitating cooperative learning. Use this chapter to plan your curriculum.

Chapter 3, "Implementing Your Curriculum," features everything you need to know to start using the Web in your classroom. It includes roadmaps for beginners, intermediate, and advanced users; a framework for creating a successful project; tips from veteran Web users; suggestions for administering your project; a Web project implementation plan; and ideas for the one-computer classroom.

Part II, "From Theory to Practice," offers more than 100 K-12 lesson plans and ideas that utilize the Web in all subject areas. Many projects include tips for adapting the lesson up or down to different age groups. Lesson plans are presented at the beginning, intermediate, and advanced level. Most projects are integrated, serving many disciplines across the curriculum.

Use the information corner of each activity and the two-line descriptor to find a lesson plan that meets your needs and curricular goals. The information corner includes the subject area(s), activity type, activity level, time frame, and requirements for partnering for the lesson. This information is also gathered in Appendix A, "Lesson Plan Index," a detailed listing of lesson plans by subject, grade level, activity type, and activity level.

Introduction

WHY THE WORLD WIDE WEB?

"Let's go surfin' now, everybody's learning how, come on a safari with me."—The Beach Boys

Tales abound these days of trips taken on the information super-highway. People in supermarkets can be overheard talking about on-ramps and off-ramps to the Net. Some children now spend more time chatting online than on the phone. And businesses no longer publish just their address and phone number. Billboards and business cards alike are filled to the brim with contact information, including email and Web site addresses.

What does all this mean? And what are its implications for the classroom? Like it or not, the Internet is here to stay. The latest reports on Internet users rival the billboards at McDonald's: over 16 million served. Some compare the coming of the World Wide Web to the advent of television. Whether or not your school is hooked up, chances are the Internet has already affected your students.

▶ What Does the Web Mean for Schools?

▶ What Is the World Wide Web?

▶ Tales from the Classroom

▶ Making Connections

WHAT DOES THE WEB MEAN FOR SCHOOLS?

A recent report commissioned by the U.S. Department of Education estimates that 49 percent of public secondary schools and 35 percent of public elementary schools have access to the Internet. And the figure is rising daily. Since the advent of the World Wide Web, more than 3,500 schools have developed Web sites.

As teachers, we've all seen technological fads come and go. And most of us have been fairly cautious about jumping onboard. "Give me a chalk board and a piece of chalk," we say. Add a few students, and we make nothing short of sheer poetry happen in our classrooms.

While many of the tools we use daily in the classroom are dispensable, some make our lives easier and our teaching more effective. The Web, when used thoughtfully, is one of those tools.

WHAT IS THE WORLD WIDE WEB?

To understand the World Wide Web, you first have to understand its home—the Internet. Some people compare the Internet to an enormous library or collection of libraries through which you can access information and people. Instead of sitting on shelves, the information on the Internet exists on computers throughout the world that are linked through a series of phone lines, cables, and satellites. When you hook into the Internet, either via a service provider or through a direct link, your computer is just one more in the network—able to access information in millions of other computers.

Though the Internet has been likened to a highway system, it's really more like air traffic control. Information on the Internet is routed through central "hubs" or gateways and then passed on to its final destination. That's why a message you send to Tokyo is only a local phone call away. Your computer calls a local computer, which then calls another computer, and so on, and so on.

The Internet has gained widespread popularity relatively recently. The World Wide Web, with its easy-to-use graphical interface, is a major reason for this explosion in cybertourism. With the aid of a Web browser, you merely need to point your mouse and click on a graphic or word to navigate between linked Web sites.

A typical Web site might include anything from movies you can download, color photos and graphics, to music and audio clips. Many sites are interactive. MayaQuest (*http://www.mecc.com/ies.html*) brings students along for an archaeological adventure in Mexico. Central to the quest is to discover why the Mayan civilization flourished some 1,000 years ago. Students receive weekly progress reports from anthropologists, archaeologists, and explorers about their travels—complete with photos. Students then respond to questions of the week and post their own discoveries, sharing their insights and questions with kids all over the world.

There are Web sites for almost anything imaginable. You can access information from the U.S. Census Bureau or MTV, browse a database of lesson plans, or check out a boy's photographs of his toy dinosaur collection. Anyone can develop a Web site. All you need is space on a Web server, some tools to convert your document and link it to others, and there you are—wired into a huge network of other Web sites.

A unique feature of the Web (and the inspiration behind its name) is the way that information is linked between sites. Log onto a cyberspace art museum at a small university in Ohio, click on the "Renaissance Art" button, and find yourself instantly transported to the Louvre in Paris, where a photograph of the Mona Lisa awaits you. The image was pulled from the actual hallowed halls of the Louvre (or more precisely probably from some obscure room in the basement of the Louvre) where information awaits on a computer (called a server) for just such a request.

Once there, you can "navigate" your way back to the original site (through your browser, which allows you to retrace your steps) or choose between links that the Louvre site offers. One button at the Louvre might say "Other Art-Related Web Sites." Choose that and a list of about twenty sites will pop up, all linked to their respective sites (other museums or universities around the world). Click on the button that offers a site featuring "Cool Links to Museums" and off you go, transported. . . (expectant pause while the site downloads). . . back to that original cyberspace museum in Ohio. Groan. And around we go!

Navigating the Web can be like a walk through a hall of mirrors. Since large networks of information are tied together by links, you're never quite sure what you'll find behind a button. And though there are search engines to help you find what you're looking for, they are not nearly as easy to use or comprehensive as our good friend the card catalog. Surfing the Net, you are sure to stumble upon some very interesting gems, and restumble upon gems you've already discovered. In frustrating moments, the Web can feel like a huge ball of tangled yarn, requiring great patience to unravel. But once you know where you are going and what you can do when you get there, a world of possibilities opens.

TALES FROM THE CLASSROOM

The three stories that follow reveal the inspiring, real-life impact of the Internet. For more tales about the use of the Net in classrooms, see *NetLearning: Why Teachers Use the Internet*, by Ferdi Serim and Melissa Koch, published by Songline Studios and O'Reilly & Associates, 1996.

Walpole Island, Ontario—Walpole Island has had its share of problems with pollution. Located on the St. Claire river downstream from "Chemical Valley"—a proliferation of chemical and petroleum companies—the community's water intake valve is closed once a month. There were more than 45 chemical spills in one year alone.

Walpole Island elementary students wanted to respond to the problem. Through GREEN, a Web-based water quality testing program from the Global Rivers Environment Education Network (*http://www.igc.apc.org/green/green.html*) students in grades 2 through 8 tested seven sites of the watershed. The tests revealed high levels of fecal coliform, nitrates, and turbidity, and above-normal levels of heavy metals at the tap drain.

EcoNet
http://www.igc.org/igc/econet/index.html

An environmental membership network featuring interesting projects to join and other educational resources.

The children then posted their data on EcoNet and compared their findings with test results from other sites in the watershed, including those of Port Huron Northern High School in Michigan. Upstream from Walpole Island, Port Huron High students monitored the Black River just before it enters the St. Claire and passes through Chemical Valley.

Using email, the Walpole Island elementary students discussed their results with the students from Michigan. Together they analyzed the data, which helped them understand more about the overall health of the watershed, how water quality changes as the water travels, and the probable source of the pollution.

"What the teachers loved about this project was that it made science real for the students," said Walpole Elementary's computer teacher Arlene Gray. "It is difficult teaching concepts when they appear to be isolated bits of information with no use or validity in the realm of these students' lives. But when you can show them that what they learn about the water (how to test, what the test results mean) has relevance and importance to them on a daily basis, it has meaning."

The GREEN project picked the right topic to focus on. Water has great significance to this Native American community. Duck hunting, a major part of the economy and culture, is threatened by the increasing pollution. The island is also home to rich and diverse ecosystems, including oak savannas, tall-grass prairies, and wetlands.

All too often, it seems, such rich learnings are filed away only in the annals of our schools and the minds of our children. Not this time, however. The students' concerns were taken seriously by the adults in the community. A student congress was scheduled to close the GREEN water study project. The young students presented their findings about the watershed to a group of concerned parents, business people, politicians, and the media.

Woodville, Wisconsin—A teacher in Woodville found that a tool as simple as email could change his relationship with his students—and give a student a safe place to hone his communication skills. Here is Paul Hambleton's story:

I had a boy in my 7th grade English class, a sincere and diligent student. But he had very low abilities and was very shy. He rarely spoke in class, and when he did it was nearly incomprehensible. He struggled through 7th grade.

The kids were required to keep journals. They had to set a goal of three, four, or five pages per week to maintain a C, B, or A, respectively. This student always chose C. His idea of writing was to put one sentence at the top of each page.

The next year, I did not have this kid in class. But soon after we installed our email system, he began to write me. We share an interest in fishing, so fishing is what we wrote back and forth about—at least once a week. I would try to talk to him in the hall between classes, but he wouldn't say much. He wanted to email me about fishing—not talk about it. His email messages were far more lengthy and mature in sentence structure than what they had been in his 7th grade journal.

Another example is a girl in my 7th grade reading class—a terribly shy, small girl who flushed red every time anyone looked in her direction, especially me. At the beginning of the year, after the kids got online, I invited them to email me. She did after a month or so. We wrote back and forth a few times about the stories we were reading. I noticed that she spoke more in class and came up to talk to me after class. It's as if email got us going— kind of a safe way for her to approach me—and then she didn't need it anymore.

Quincy, Massachusetts—In Quincy, where many of the seeds for our nation's struggle for freedom were sown, middle school children at the Broad Meadow School are using the Internet in a campaign to free third-world children. It all began when a Pakistani boy named Iqbal Masih visited their school two years ago.

Iqbal was only four years old when he was sold into bonded labor to work in a rug factory because his parents were in debt. Through a translator, the twelve-year old told the children about his six years working long days weaving rugs until he was freed by Pakistan's Bonded Labor Liberation Front (BLLF).

Scholastic Network
http://www.scholastic.com
Check out the scholastic network and other resources available for teachers.

The students were so moved by his story and by others like him that they launched an awareness-raising campaign using the Scholastic Network. Through email they contacted other middle schools, educating them about child labor abuses and calling for legislature to end the importing of goods from nations without child labor laws.

What started as a small awareness-raising campaign, two years later—thanks to the ongoing committed efforts of the children and the support of English teacher Ron Adams—has exceeded the wildest imaginations of even the children themselves. Fueled by the untimely gunshot death (or possible assassination) of Iqbal in his home village, the students started a campaign to build a school in Pakistan in Iqbal's memory for children who would not normally receive an education. Using email, the students began to solicit $12 donations—in symbolic tribute to Iqbal's age at his death—to build the school. Along with the outpouring of support from schools, politicians (such as Senator Edward Kennedy), and others, came the offer of a Web site to support the cause.

Again the students led the way. With the help of Amnesty International volunteers, the students created the site (*http://www.digitalrag. com/mirror/iqbal.html*). Donations, poetry, letters, and faxes poured in from all around the world in support of the campaign (including a fax from the band Aerosmith). Not only did the students raise enough money to build their school in Pakistan, they established a permanent endowment to sustain it in perpetuity. At the time of the writing of this book, the opening of the school is forthcoming and a bill sponsored by Senator Tom Harkin is pending, calling for an end to imports from counties that do not uphold the child labor laws as put forth in the U.N.'s International Labor Convention.

MAKING CONNECTIONS

These stories illustrate the simple yet profound impact that the Web can have on our classrooms. The Web can connect us: student to student, student to teacher, small town to city, one culture to another.

Some even say that the Internet knocks down the classroom walls and brings the world to our door. Hyperbole? Perhaps. But the Web certainly affords us resources unavailable in traditional ways. Textbooks are outdated by the time they hit our desks. Lesson plans, up-to-the-minute news on the latest world happenings, databases of statistics, and many of the world's libraries are all at our fingertips through the Internet. And, perhaps most importantly, it's clear from the stories from Walpole Island, Woodville, and Quincy that the Internet can help serve to empower students—in small and great ways.

So what's the catch? I was surfing the Web myself recently when I ran across a site that offered 3-D glasses with which to view an interesting array of graphics and mathematical models. I was smitten, so I ordered a pair. A few weeks later they came in the mail. Next thing I knew I was staring at my computer screen wearing a pair of cardboard glasses, laughing out loud at myself. In the name of education?

I realized then and there that the Web is, in a way, not unlike 3-D glasses. A little trendy. Sort of gimmicky. Very quirky. Imperfect. But it offers a new lens—a three-dimensional view where the world comes into sharper focus or pops to life before your very eyes. The trick is in harnessing this tool to serve your purposes.

Part I

Theory

The Lay of the Land

1

This chapter looks at what the unique features of the Web offer your classroom and outlines some of the basic Internet tools available to you. Once you have a basic understanding of the Web and the other tools available to you on the Internet, you'll have the groundwork for bringing the Web into your curriculum and using it effectively in your classroom.

▶ Why Use the Web in Education?

▶ What Does the Web Offer Your Classroom?

▶ Pitfalls of the Web

▶ Is the Web Difficult to Learn?

▶ Basic Internet Tools at Your Disposal

▶ Where to Find Help

▶ A Note to Novices

WHY USE THE WEB IN EDUCATION?

"Technology is cool. Teachers are cooler." —Tom Snyder Productions

Every day you make hundreds of decisions in your classroom. Do I group students for this assignment? Should I lecture? Maybe there's a video that covers this. This needs to be a handout. How can I get students excited? That group in the back isn't contributing. How can I get their ideas included? What would be a good transition activity for after recess?

Teaching is like conducting a jazz orchestra. When you walk into the classroom, you choose among tools at your disposal. Some are simple and reliable. A piece of chalk, for example. Or a tried and true favorite activity. Or a video. Like the rhythm section in the orchestra, these tools are the foundation. Others you save for special occasions. They are the embellishments that make it fun or add depth. That horn line or drum kick. And then there are those times you just plain ol' improvise.

It takes practice to make music. "If I could just get the bass line out in front. Now add a little more trumpet. Yes. Right there. Excellent. If only those trombones practiced!" The World Wide Web is a valuable tool to add to your teaching repertoire.

WHAT DOES THE WEB OFFER YOUR CLASSROOM?

Any tool worth its salt adds something to the job. A new tool might:

- Do what you always did (replacing one tool with another)
- Do something better, cheaper, faster
- Change the potential of what you are able to do

When used properly, the Web is a tool that is best described by the last two points. Here's why.

THE WEB IS TIMELY

One of the most unique and valuable assets of the Web is its timeliness. Since the Web is a digital rather than a print medium, information is updated continually. While textbooks become outdated, resources available on the Web reflect the latest breaking news.

The Teachable Moment

The Internet is a great resource for harnessing the potential of a teachable moment. It isn't difficult to imagine the educational impact that such an immediate and visceral connection to world events can create for your students. When questions come up that are difficult to answer or a world event stops us in our tracks, the Web is a perfect place to turn to.

Harry Noden's middle school students in Hudson, New York, received letters via email from Israeli students two days after Prime Minister Yitzhak Rabin's assassination. These narratives included personal reactions from students who had attended the peace rally at which Rabin was shot (see "A Letter from Israel"). Noden's students published these letters in their online Web magazine "Middlezine" (*http://www.newreach.net/people/hnoden/*) so the whole world could share in the students' reaction to the tragedy. This material is used by permission of Middlezine Magazine, Copyright 1996 by Harry Noden.

A Letter from Israel

Rubin Alexandra at Ben Zvi Junior High School in Petach Tikvah, Israel, emailed these letters to us via *Newsday* two days after Rabin was assassinated. Comments by Israeli students Liran Zvibel, Shiri Gross, Jacob Avid, Nataly, Ilana, and Yael.

```
From: benzvi@kav4.trendline.co.il
To: All peace seekers
Subject: Yitzhak Rabin
From: Rubin Alexandra - Ben Zvi J.H.S Petah Tikva, Israel
Date: November 14, 1995

My pupils expressed their feelings after the
assassination of our beloved P.M. Yitzhak Rabin. The
following is one of their letters.

Dear Friends,
This letter has nothing to do with magic or elves. It
is only a story I want to tell to all of you brothers
and sisters of my soul. A story of great grief I have
to share, and I invite you to be the ones who share
it with me. To makes things clear, I first want to say
that the "il" in my address stands for Israel.
```

continued on next page

continued from previous page

And just to be sure you know (though I know it was broadcasted all over the world earlier this evening), our prime minister, Rabin, was murdered this evening by a right-winged extremist after speaking in a huge demonstration in support of the peace process. I want to tell this story.

In the afternoon we went to the demonstration. It was a happy event — not against anything, not to protest or fight, but to show support in our government for it's efforts in building a new era of peace in this wars-torn land. I don't know how many of you have ever been in such an event — the sense of power is awesome. And it was huge. I estimate there were about 150- 200 thousand people there. We were filled with a wonderful feeling of joy, of hope, seeing so many around us, great music, balloons, dancing, meeting friends. A festival. And when the prime minister entered the stage, he was greeted by a thunder of clapping hands. Not only because it was such a joyous event, but also to show this man, a man that was cursed and spit upon and called "traitor" by his adversaries time and again during the last few months, a man that is blamed by them for every terrorist attack (because he dares negotiate with the enemy), to show him people do believe in him and admire what he does.

I went home after he spoke, trying to avoid traffic, thinking the action was nearly over. Little did I know. About an hour after I got home, we heard the news — Rabin was shot. The first thing that rushed through my mind. . .was "Kennedy." I am sorry to borrow on your myth, Americans, but this is all I could think of. And then, "Oh God, please let it end differently." But it didn't. . .he died on the operation table an hour later. After a few phone calls, we went back to the same square where the

THE WEB IS A RESOURCE

Think of the Web as another library at your disposal. Not only does it offer access to many libraries, but it offers sites developed on topics of special interest. For those of us whose local or school libraries are

demonstration was held. People started to gather —
not as many as before, but they kept coming. Wearing
black, bearing candles and torches, engulfed in
smoke. And we just sat there, watching the white
candles dripping tears, the red torches dripping
blood. Crying, hugging, singing softly (you wouldn't
believe how many songs of war and peace we have),
shocked to our bones. It was warm at the
demonstration, but at two in the morning, it was
getting so cold.

Every death is a tragedy. And Rabin was not an easy
man. A hard man, and a solider to the bone, which
made him unpopular amongst both sides, pro and con of
the peace process. He was called "traitor" by both
sides (which only proves how well-fit he was for the
job). But he led this peace process stubbornly, with
full faith at heart. Being a soldier, he was hated by
many of the Arabs, but he also knew how much we need
peace. He has brought us to a point some of us see as
a miracle in being (my father, who fought in many
wars with our neighbors, is going as a tourist to
Jordan. You have no idea how deeply he is moved by
that). And for that I loved and admired him, even
though I didn't like many of the things he did in his
life. The peace process will go on. It cannot be
stopped, not by one murder. But this act will
definitely intensify the atmosphere of hatred that
divides my country. It is an act of violence that
will lead to others. It scares the hell out of me.

This is all. Tomorrow will probably be a day of
national mourning. Now all I have to do is take a
shower (after sitting in the middle of all that
smoke) and go to bed. But I keep seeing one picture.
In the middle of the square, someone used soul-
candles (candles put on graves, usually) to form one
huge word. "Why?"

small, this can be a boon of new sources of information. Sites are
available on almost every topic imaginable. The accuracy of some of
these sites, however, can be in question. (See "Researcher Beware,"
later in this chapter.)

TIP

Nancy Skomars Davis, a computer and English teacher at Advanced Technologies Academy in Las Vegas, says, "Our librarian is not buying magazine subscriptions anymore because most of what he'd buy is available online. The same goes for newspapers, reference materials, and some classics."

A Resource for You, Too

It's staggering to imagine all those lesson plans on Othello or acceleration or whales sitting in teachers' files across the world. If you could bundle all of those plans in one place, you'd have a great resource. The Web does just that. There are Web sites that offer lesson plans on almost any topic imaginable for grades K-12. Unfortunately, the lesson plans are spread across several sites and represent a wide range of quality. But when you're stuck at 2:00 am without tomorrow's plan (not that that ever happens to us!) or you're trying to redesign your curriculum, it's a gem of a resource.

Where to Find Lesson Plans	Education on the Internet *http://www.nceet.snre.umich.edu/edlinks.html*
	Collaborative Lesson Archive K-12 *http://faldo.atmos.uiuc.edu/TUA_Home.html*
	Teacher Talk Forum K-12 *http://education.indiana.edu/cas/tt/tthmpg.html*
	Lesson Plans from AskEric K-12 *gopher://ericir.syr.edu/11/Lesson*
	Classroom Connect *http://www.wentworth.com*
	Explorer Curriculum Browsing *http://server2.greatlakes.k12.mi.us*
	Teachers Helping Teachers *http://www.pacificnet.net/~mandel/*
	Houghton Mifflin's Education Place *http://www.eduplace.com*

THE WEB CONNECTS STUDENTS AROUND THE GLOBE

While not every country in the world has a presence on the Web, many do. Most first-world nations are represented, and many of the developing countries as well. This affords an unprecedented educational opportunity for students.

International communication that in the past would have been limited by time and expense is now available in an instant and at the cost of a local phone call. Not only does this mean that the international penpal system of days past has been updated to be "better, faster, cheaper," it also affords the opportunity to collaborate on a project with another classroom over great distances.

Jon Brokering in Japan used the Web with his students to compare how World War II is taught in other countries. Students from Germany, Japan, France, and the U.S. exchanged information about how their textbooks portray the conflict. Other teachers are using the Web to explore other ideas. For example, a question that can be illustrated through geography—such as how tides work—can be fully investigated through students from different latitudes exchanging data about the heights of their tides. Or a unit on Thanksgiving can be supplemented with student dialogues with Native Americans.

THE WEB IS A RACIALLY/CULTURALLY BLIND MEDIUM

Much discussion about the Internet has centered around its potential as a racially and culturally blind medium. While a certain measure of blindness is inherent in the medium, the jury is still out whether this is a positive or negative attribute. The truth probably lies somewhere in between.

Certainly, when it comes to students, much is gained by communication unmarred by seeing one another and making pre-judgments. Chances are that students who participate meaningfully in relationships acquired through the Web have been exposed to ideas and perspectives they never would have gained otherwise. These gained perspectives and voices from all walks of life are clearly invaluable.

But there are many equity issues raised by the medium. "Colorblindness" does not lead to appreciation of differences. It might open the door to someone's closed mind, but to truly refashion a stereotype one needs to confront it. To truly appreciate diversity, one needs to be able to see it—in its physical as well as its cultural expression.

The Internet also raises serious questions about access. For it to be a truly democratic tool, there needs to be a commitment to equal access for all so that it is not yet another case of the "haves" being separated from the "have nots." This has been addressed at least in part by telecommunications legislation. And corporate sponsorship of technology in underserved schools presents a promising step toward evening the score.

THE WEB FACILITATES SCHOOL REFORM

Ever since the time of John Dewey we have been re-evaluating the way schools do business. The educational system we now utilize was structured for the industrial age. The "factory model" required that large groups of people be educated in systematized ways. Short class periods, subjects broken into distinct areas, even the bell beckoning like a shift whistle are legacies of that outdated model.

The information age requires different skills. Students need to know how to think critically, synthesize large amounts of information, and apply concepts learned with a global perspective. Our economy is as dependent on what happens in Tokyo as on what happens in Michigan. Now more than ever, jobs require an ability to navigate differences and get along with others.

Many of the reform agendas that we have adopted in schools to achieve these goals are facilitated by the Internet. The Web is a great tool for:

- Student-centered education
- Project-based learning
- Cooperative education
- Integration of the curriculum
- Team teaching
- School-based management
- Teaching social skills such as cooperative problem solving, conflict resolution, etc.

One of the Web's most widespread applications is its use in project-based learning. The tools available afford a hands-on opportunity for students to explore a theme or question in a collaborative way. Since the information available through the Web is so comprehensive, it lends itself well to integrated, thematic units. For teacher teams looking for integrated curricula to bring into your classrooms, the Web is both a valuable resource for ideas and a valuable tool to execute those ideas. And since it connects people from all walks of life, it's a great milieu for exploring social themes.

Hundreds of studies have pointed to the benefits of cooperative learning.[1] Compared with more traditional individualistic and competitive classrooms, cooperative classrooms promote higher achievement and better relationships among teachers and students, among other benefits. The Internet affords countless opportunities to collaborate with students of virtually every avenue and walk of life. Students are afforded the opportunity to practice and apply important social skills when they work cooperatively, skills that will later be the cornerstone of a successful life—both personally and professionally.

Lastly, some school districts use the Internet as a sort of administrative glue between schools. Schools can share ideas, resources, and information in a much more streamlined fashion. The Internet may one day (if it becomes standard, like the telephone) be a place where schools can develop resources for their community, a child's homework can wait on a server until he logs on, or a deeper connection to parents can be fostered. Many schools today post homework and school activities for students, parents, and other interested community members. Some schools have taken this a step further by providing news on other important issues—local, regional, and state—for the benefit of the community.

THE WEB IS FUN!

When I was doing my teacher training I was in a group of other student teachers who would meet weekly to trade stories and emerging wisdom. I remember one woman talking about a very difficult time she was having with a class, where none of the students were in the least bit engaged. Then she had what appeared to be a breakthrough. She had developed a wonderfully elaborate game for the class where everyone participated, and students were for the first time enthusiastic. Caught up in the students' energy, she thought she had tasted the sweet nectar of victory, and turned some corner in her teaching. It wasn't until the bell rang and the class ended that it dawned on her that while everyone had had a great time, nobody had learned anything of substance.

---

[1] Johnson, D.W., and R. Johnson. (1989) *Cooperation and Competition: Theory and Research.* Edina, Minnesota: Interaction Book Company.

I remember that story because I hold it up for myself as a caution...and an inspiration. Finding a fun hook or playful gimmick can be just what a tired old lesson needs, as long as it's not at the expense of a genuine learning experience. (I've since learned that the two are not mutually exclusive.) The Web, with its fun graphics and playful (even gimmicky) persona can be a great hook for some students. Students accustomed to learning that is hard and serious have even said that they didn't realize they were learning when they first started using the Web, because they were having so much fun. That's a good problem to have.

What the Research Shows

Note: Adapted with permission from *NetLearning: Why Teachers Use the Internet*, by Ferdi Serim and Melissa Koch.

According to Telecommunications and K-12 Educators: Findings from the National Survey (1993):

- More than two-thirds of educators report that integrating telecommunications activities into their teaching has made a real difference in how they teach.
- The most highly rated incentives for using telecommunications with students include expanding students' awareness about the world, accessing information, and increasing students' inquiry-based and analytical skills.
- Communicating with other educators, accessing information, and combating professional isolation are the most highly rated incentives for using telecommunications as a professional resource.

The Web in Schools

For Teachers

- Find (and share!) lesson plans
- Collaborate with other teachers
- Find support and input for your ideas
- Discover other professional development opportunities
- Connect with parents or the larger community
- Research background information for a topic you are teaching
- Find primary documents to enhance your lessons
- Find a mentor!

PITFALLS OF THE WEB

I've sung the Web's praises. Now it's time to tell you about its limitations.

THE WEB CAN BE TIME CONSUMING

Sometimes trying to find information on the Web can feel like looking for a needle in a haystack. You'll think you've stumbled upon the perfect site, you click hopefully on a button that says National Violence Statistics, and what you find is soft advice and a few numbers about violence in Scandinavia. It takes time to learn how to narrow your searches, how to "sniff" out an answer, and which search engines to use for which job. For help learning how to conduct effective searches on the Web, consult *NetResearch: Finding Information Online*, by Dan Barrett, published by Songline Studios and O'Reilly & Associates (*order@ora.com* or 1-800-998-9938). But any way you slice it, you'll find there are times when you spend half an hour or more looking for information and come up with nothing.

Downloading graphics can also take quite a bit of time, depending on the speed of the modem at your connection. Many a time I've drummed my fingers waiting, and waiting, and waiting, for artwork to load. For these reasons, it's important that you try out a Web site you're planning on using in your lesson plan before going live. You'll also want to allow plenty of time for students to explore.

With Your Students

- Create a Web project
- Join a Web project
- Connect with students in distant places and from other cultures
- Research topics of interest to effectively use the research tools as you go
- Hear first-hand accounts about current world events
- Learn about different perspectives on an issue
- Connect students with mentors

THE WEB MAY NOT BE RELIABLE

The best technologies make everything seem so simple. My Mac Powerbook 5300, for example, on which I am writing this book, has been trouble-free since the day I bought it. It always works. It's simple to use. But it's a false sense of security at best. Just today when I went to access a Web site, my modem wouldn't work. Nothing. I was crushed. Despondent even. When did I get so dependent?

The same thing will happen with the Web. For some reason you'll try to log onto a site and you'll get a message that says that you have "an invalid DNS entry or the site is busy. Try back again later." Or your network will go down. Or you'll get to the Web site and there'll be a huge "Construction" sign. Nothing that you wanted to use is there anymore. As with all matters technological, when it comes to the Web, plan for the unexpected. Most veteran Net users know you should download or print the most important parts of a site, just in case you run into a glitch. Then you at least have something to use with your students and your fine lesson isn't wasted.

THE WEB IS NOT A SUBSTITUTE FOR FACE-TO-FACE CONTACT

Once you've mastered the Web, like a kid with a new toy, you'll want to use it over and over again. Be careful not to fall into the trap of gratuitous use of the Web, though. Consider local resources first before turning to the Web. Is there a person who can come into your class to talk about his or her experience? Are there local people you can pair your students with as mentors? Admittedly, sometimes it is best to go outside your local community. But consider all of your options to meet your curricular goal before making the choice to go online.

IS THE WEB DIFFICULT TO LEARN?

Now that you know the benefits and how to avoid the pitfalls of the Web, I bet you're wondering if it's hard to use. The answer is no. Within a few hours of jumping online you'll be wondering why you waited so long to try.

The Web's graphical interface makes using the tools intuitive. Or at least mostly intuitive. I was both a skeptic and technophobe when I first started out on the Web. I never used a book to help me (I have this annoying habit of not reading instructions), and I fumbled my way through it just fine. Depending on your browser (the software that "views" the Web) and your service provider, everything you need to learn the Web is provided. For the most part, buttons on the Web do what their name suggests. Help screens are also provided. But to make your journey as smooth as possible, here is a brief outline of the tools available to you through your connection and how they work.

BASIC INTERNET TOOLS AT YOUR DISPOSAL

ELECTRONIC MAIL

Electronic mail is one of the most basic and useful tools available to you through your Internet connection. Email, as it is known, allows you to send a written message via your computer to someone else who has an email account. You do not have to have your computer on to receive an email message. When you sign up with an Internet Service Provider or get an account through your school, you will be assigned an email address. Your email address allows you to receive mail online, just as your postal address enables you to receive letters in the mail.

Your email address has two parts separated by the @ symbol—the user's name and the domain where the user is known:

username@domainname

The domain name usually identifies the hostname of an organization, such as a network provider, a commercial or nonprofit organization, or an educational or governmental institution.

My address is *LPRoerden@aol.com*. *LPRoerden* is my username, and *aol.com* (American Online) is my Internet Service Provider.

Regardless of your address or the email software you use, you will be able to perform some very basic and handy functions. You will be able to:

- Compose and send mail
- Address your mail to multiple people
- Read a message
- Respond to a message
- Forward a message to another with an introduction

- Save addresses in an address book
- Send a "carbon copy" (cc) of your message to another
- Print a message
- Save a message (and file for later reference)
- Delete a message
- Attach a document from your computer

TIP

For a more lengthy discussion of the tools and everything technological about the Net, I recommend *Educator's Guide to the Web,* by Bernard Robin, Elissa Keeler, and Robert Miller (MIS: Press). It covers everything a system administrator would need to know in a fun and accessible fashion. Another excellent reference, with an array of valuable information about teaching and curricular implications of the Web, is *NetLearning: Why Teachers Use the Internet,* by Ferdi Serim and Melissa Koch, available through O'Reilly & Associates at 1-800-998-9938, or order it online at *order@ora.com.*

Most mail programs are quite simple to use, allowing you to easily send and receive messages. When you send a message, you will need to type in the recipient name(s), a subject, and the text of your message. Including a descriptive subject in the subject line helps your recipient identify and organize messages. You will also appreciate this courtesy when you have many messages to sift through.

In addition to sending a message, you can also attach documents from your computer and send them along with your email message. A few words of caution: Make sure you send the documents in a format your recipient can read. When in doubt, you can cut and paste the document into the body of your email message and send it. Also, be aware of the download time your attached document may require. If your recipient uses a modem, large files may cause waits that seem like an eternity.

Most mail programs allow you to save messages or discard them. There are also usually various ways to organize your mail, including the development of folders for quick reference and filing. Just like with real mail (referred to in the Net community as snail mail), you'll develop your own standards for what you keep and what you throw away.

How Email Helps You

There are virtually hundreds of ways that you can use email to make your life easier and your teaching more effective. Some of the more common uses of email include:

- Communicating with students
- Communicating with other teachers in your discipline
- Posting a question to a bulletin board or mailing list (see "Mailing Lists" and "Newsgroups" for more information)
- Developing a collaborative project with another classroom or many other classrooms
- Connecting students with mentors
- Connecting students with penpals (commonly referred to as key-pals)

Part II includes many projects that rely only on the use of email. (See Appendix A for a complete list of projects that require email only.)

MAILING LISTS

Does anyone have the recipe for Play-Doh? Any suggestions for teaching Othello to at-risk kids? Help, I'm in desperate need of funding for our technology program, any good leads?

Mailing lists are the electronic equivalent of bulk mail. They allow you to send a message to a group of people and receive messages sent by others in the group. Mailing lists (also commonly referred to as listservs) are organized by topic or interest. There are many good education mailing lists, serving all types of special interests from the general (early childhood educators) to the specific (media literacy). See Table 1-1 for a sample list of education mailing lists.

Some mailing lists are moderated, meaning that there is a person who sifts through the messages and makes sure that they are on topic before sending them. Others are unmoderated. Some mailing lists are discussion groups, others just offer information such as a newsletter sent out regularly. You subscribe to a mailing list just like you would subscribe to a publication. Until you unsubscribe, you will receive all messages sent within the group.

You'll only need an email account and some good judgment to make the most of mailing lists. Mailing lists can be a terrific resource. But the word on the street about them is to choose carefully which lists to belong to and to limit your participation to one or two lists at a time (unless you have tons of extra time on your hands). When I first found out about mailing lists four years ago, I immediately subscribed to six that sounded like they would be helpful. None of my friends at the time had email, so it was very exciting to log onto my computer and have mail waiting for me. I was going along merrily with about 25 messages a day (of which I probably read ten that sounded interesting) all summer. Then September came, and I went away for two weeks. When I can back, I had 1,700 messages waiting for me. School was back in session and the mailing list had heated up. Needless to say, I wanted out. But I had neglected to save the information about how to unsubscribe. I eventually figured it out and have since limited myself to no more than two mailing lists at a time.

In order to use mailing lists, you'll need to know:

- Where to find them
- How to subscribe and unsubscribe
- How to send and receive email

It's as simple as that!

Where to Find Mailing Lists

There are several ways to acquire a list of mailing lists. If you only have email, you can send a message to *listserv@iubvm.ucs.indiana.edu* with the words "List Global" in the message line. You'll automatically receive back a huge list of mailing lists. If you have Web access you can go to *http://www.tile.net/tile/listserv/index.html* to view lists organized by name, description, subject, and more. Another good source for education-related lists is *http://k12.cnidr.org:90/lists.html*.

When you respond to a general message on a mailing list, be aware that your response will go to the entire list. There are many times when it is more appropriate to respond directly to the person who posted the message (via an email address which should be included in the message). Always ask yourself before sending a message publicly: Would the entire list want to know this?

List Name	Description	Address
ADMIN	educational administration	*listproc@bgu.edu*
BIOPI-L	biology and education	*listserv@ksuvm.ksu.edu*
CHATBAC	special ed discussion	*listserv@sjuvm.stjohns.edu*
ECEOL-L	early childhood education	*listserv@maine.maine.edu*
EDNET	education and networking	*listserv@nic.umass.edu*
EDRES-L	online education resources	*listserv@unbvm1.bitnet*
ELED-L	elementary education	*listserv@ksuvm.bitnet*
IECC	cultural exchange	*request@stolaf.edu*
KIDSPHERE	general education related topics	*listserv@vms.cis.pitt.edu*
MATHSED-L	math in education	*listserv@deakin.edu.au*
MIDDLE-L	middle school education	*listserv@vmd.cso.uiuc.edu*
MUSIC-ED	music education	*listserv@artsedge. kennedy-center.org*
PHYSHARE	high school physics	*listserv@psuvm.psu.edu*
TAMHA	American history	*listserv@cms.cc.wayne.edu*
TAG-L	talented and gifted education	*listserv@vm1.nodak.edu*
UAARTED	art education	*listserv@arizvm1.bitnet*
WWWEDU	World Wide Web in education	*listproc@educom.unc.edu*

TABLE 1-1
Education Mailing Lists

Subscribing and Unsubscribing

The functions of subscribing and unsubscribing to a mailing list are done automatically. You will need to know two addresses: the one that you send your general messages to (the actual listserv itself) and the address to subscribe and unsubscribe. Generally, the mailing list's address begins with its name. To send a message to the Kidsphere mailing list, for example, you would send your message to *kidsphere@vms.cis.pitt.edu.* When you subscribe or unsubscribe, however, you would generally replace the mailing list's name with the name *listserv.* So, to subscribe (or unsubscribe) to Kidsphere you would send your message to *listserv@vms.cis.pitt.edu.* Then in the main body of the message you would write:

subscribe (or *unsubscribe*) *kidsphere yourfirstname yourlastname*

These conventions are usually followed, but there are exceptions. It's always wise to save the instructions you receive when you first subscribe to a list as it will include directions for subscribing and unsubscribing.

TIP

Many mailing lists feature archives of all the messages posted to the list organized by topic. This is an excellent way to check out whether a list might meet your needs before subscribing (it's also an additional source of information).

How Mailing Lists Help You

Mailing lists are the best way to network with other educators with similar interests. While your messages in response to a general posting will go to the entire list, you may wish to contact a person directly via email so that you can have an ongoing, private conversation. You can use mailing lists to:

- Subscribe to a publication
- Participate in discussions about education topics
- Locate resources in your discipline
- Share lesson plans
- Exchange ideas
- Make new friends

NEWSGROUPS (USENET GROUPS)

Think of newsgroups as one giant bulletin board, where educators from all over can post their messages. Rather than receiving mail directly in your email box, you can cruise the bulletin boards to find out if there is any information of value.

Like a bulletin board at a conference, newsgroups are organized by topic, such as "Positions Wanted" or "Requests for Proposals." Included with the original message are all of the responses (those that were publicly posted, that is). These "threads," as they are called, can be rather disjointed and time-consuming to read, but once you've sifted through and isolated a newsgroup or two that you like, the effort will be worth it.

How Newsgroups Work

You read newsgroups in one of two ways. Depending on your Internet Service Provider and browser, you might need to launch a program called a newsreader. A newsreader allows you to customize the list of newsgroups you want to read and post to. This way, you will not have to search through a large number of lists again, just to find a group that you like to read. It is also a way to censor groups that might deal with issues inappropriate to children. (Newsgroups are one of the areas of the Net where you'll find pornographic material. You needn't worry that you'll stumble into such a group, however. The name of the group usually makes it pretty clear!) Security systems such as NetNanny and CyberPatrol are available to filter unwanted material from your students.

With Internet Service Providers such as America Online and CompuServe, choosing a newsgroup is as easy as clicking on an icon. The browser Navigator (usually referred to by the name of the company that developed it: Netscape) also has a built-in newsreader. Regardless of your service, you'll be able to:

- Read messages
- Post messages
- Customize a list of newsgroups you want to read
- Mark things as "read"

How Newsgroups Help You

Newsgroups are yet another resource where there is a healthy exchange of ideas on topics of interest to educators. You can use newsgroups much in the way that you would use a mailing list. And newsgroups have the added benefit over mailing lists of not having mail pile up in your box.

| **Interesting Education Newsgroups** | See *http://k12.cnidr.org:90/usenets.html* for a more complete list and links to groups that may interest you. |

For Students

k12.chat.elementary	Informal discussion among elementary students
K12.chat.junior	Informal discussion among students grades 6-8
K12.chat.senior	Informal discussion among high school students
k12.lang.deutsch-eng	Bilingual German/English practice with native speakers
k12.lang.esp-eng	Bilingual Spanish/English practice with native speakers
k12.lang.francais	Bilingual French/English practice with native speakers
k12.lang.russian-eng	Bilingual Russian/English practice with native speakers

For Teachers

k12.chat.teacher	Informal discussion among K-12 teachers
k12.ed.art	Art curriculum in K-12 education
k12.edhealth-pe	Health and physical education K-12
k12.ed.math	Mathematics curriculum K-12
k12.ed.music	Music and performing arts in K-12 education
k12.ed.science	Science curriculum K-12
k12.ed.soc-science	Social studies and history curriculum in K-12
k12.lang.art	Language arts curriculum K-12
pnet.school.k-12	Discussion about K-12 education
pnet.school.k-5	Discussion about K-5 education

THE WEB

Through your Web browser you are able to view and navigate the Web. Your browser's graphical interface allows you to move from Web page to Web page by clicking on hypertext links that appear as graphics or underlined text. You can navigate the Web, traveling around the world, by following links and by moving backward and forward from one document to another. You can also use directories that organize Web sites and keep your own bookmarks to go directly to your favorite sites.

Different browsers have different features, but generally through your browser you'll be able to:

- Locate a Web site by using the site's address, or URL
- Retrace your steps as you navigate from site to site
- Mark favorite Web sites that you'd like to return to (called bookmarks or hot lists)
- Search by topic

What's a URL?

The confusing string of letters that you see everywhere these days (often beginning with *http://www*) is called a URL or Uniform Resource Locator. The URL is simply the Web site's address. Every Web site has a URL.

There are standard conventions for a site's URL. If the site follows the convention, the Web address will begin with *http://www*. The next word will usually specify the company or organization's name. Since names may already be taken, there is some creative license used here. But, for example, if you were looking for Apple computer, you could guess that the next part of their address might be … you got it! Apple.

Browser	A user tool that displays Web documents and launches other applications
Home page	The starting point for the set of pages available for a person, company, organization, or school; also, the first page your browser displays when you start it
HTML	HyperText Markup Language: the language in which World Wide Web documents are written
Image	A picture or graphic that appears on a Web page
Link	The text or graphic you click on to make a hypertext jump to another page
Search engine	Web software that indexes Web pages and allows you to search for terms you specify
Site	The location of a Web server
URL	The address that uniquely identifies a Web resource

TABLE 1-2
Web Terminology

The last part of their address tells us whether it is a company (*com*), a university (*edu*), or an organization (*org*). Apple's URL would then be *http://www.apple.com*. Since many addresses also include the domain name of their service or other routing information, it is virtually impossible to guess a Web site address correctly all of the time. But it's always worth a stab.

To go to a particular Web site, you enter the URL in a space provided by your browser, and off you go, transported to that site.

Your First Adventure

Let's say that you are studying the planets in your classroom. You could ask students in small groups to outline on a map of the Earth the regions that they think would be night and the regions that would be day at this very hour. After sharing their ideas in small groups and then with the class, you could use the Web to show students just how day moves into night.

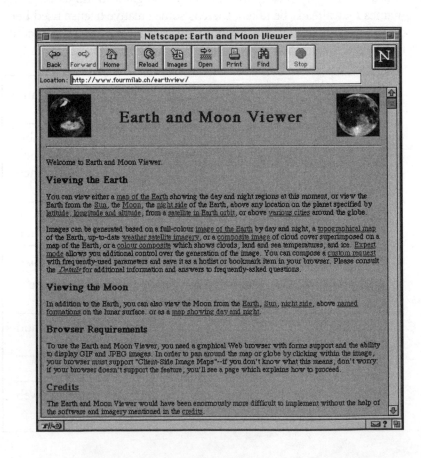

FIGURE 1-1

Earth and Moon View's home page (http://www.fourmilab. ch/earthview/)

Let's visit Earth and Moon Viewer, a Web site that allows you to view the Earth from different vantages (from the sun or the moon), at different times of day, even from different longitudes and latitudes!

To begin, you'll need to connect to the Internet and launch your World Wide Web browser. Depending on your browser, there will be a space somewhere on the first screen you see where you enter the URL for your site. Most browsers only require that you enter the address from *www.* on, but for this first adventure, let's put in the entire address. The URL for Earth and Moon View is *http://www.fourmilab. ch/earthview/*.

Once there, you will be greeted by Earth and Moon Viewer's home page (a home page is the first page of a site).

From here, let's check out the map of the Earth showing the day and night regions at this very moment, by clicking once on the text Map of the Earth. (Underlined text indicates there is a link, and clicking once will bring you to the described page.)

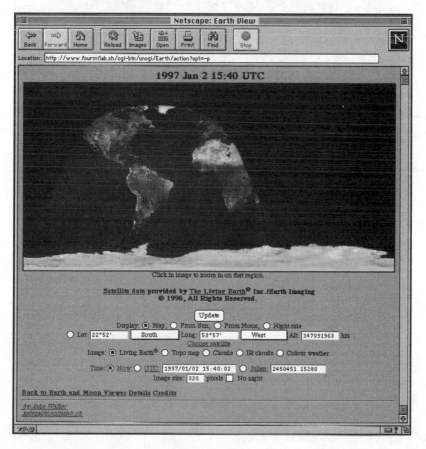

FIGURE 1-2
Map of the Earth (http://www.fourmilab. ch/cgi-bin/uncgi/ Earth/action?opt=-p)

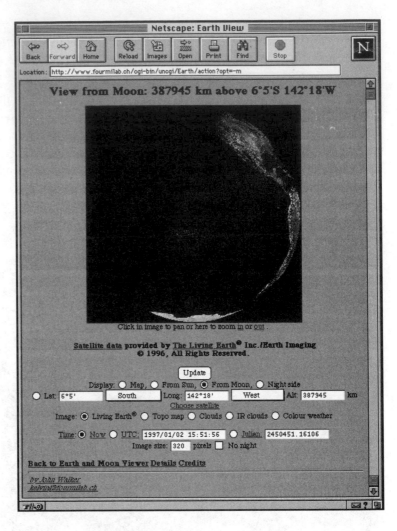

FIGURE 1-3

View of Earth from the moon (http://www. fourmilab.ch/cgi-bin/ uncgi/Earth/ action?opt=-m)

Now one of our options is to <u>Return Back to Earth and Moon Viewer</u> (located at the bottom of the page). Click once on this and you will return to the Earth and Moon Viewer home page. Now you can choose any other option to explore. Let's view the Earth from the moon.

From here you can again return to the home page and click on any additional resource that interests you. Congratulations, you've just completed your first Web journey!

As you can see, it's pretty simple to do. There's no telling where you ended up, but let's say that you'd like to go back to another page that you've already passed to try another option. Your browser will allow you to retrace your steps. On Netscape Navigator (the browser featured in these screen shots) the button is along the top menu. Simply click on "Back" and you'll retrace your steps screen-by-screen.

Bookmarks/Hot Lists

Along the way, if you find sites that you would like to return to at another time, you can create a bookmark for yourself through your browser. Think of a bookmark as a place holder. The URL of the desired site is stored for later use. When you log on, simply use your bookmark to find the site. Depending on your browser, this function may be referred to as adding the URL to your hot list. Whatever you call it, saving helpful URLs is an important habit to get into when navigating the Web. It's a bit like creating a roadmap for yourself to return to a favorite spot. To help you organize the Web sites you want to return to, most browsers will allow you to create folders where you can add and remove sites as needed.

Directories and Search Engines

Search engines and directories are the Web's version of the card catalog in a library. In some ways, the offerings for information retrieval on the Web exceed those offered by the card catalog. In other ways, they are far inferior. Your browser will probably include its own search engine or links to others. But at any time, you can use any of the search engines out there without charge, just by going to their address (see Table 1-3, "Search Engines," for URLs).

There are two types of search engines. Developers of a Web site can register their site under a particular topic. When you do a search under that topic, all the sites that have registered for it are pulled up. Other search engines, however, employ what are called robots—automatic search and retrieval devices that work off keywords found in the site. Robots comb the Web registering sites based on the text included within. As you can imagine, a robot search will typically yield many more matches than the searches you do in a library's card catalog. But this type of search can also be challenging. It takes practice to learn to refine your search to a narrow enough topic to yield truly helpful sites.

The Web has a wide range of different types of sites. Since anyone can create a site, you'll find sites developed by kids showing pictures of their pets; sites that feature people's favorite recipes; and some that just have seemingly random information about a person's life. If you are looking for information about MIDI computer gear for your music class, for example, using a typical search engine you are likely to encounter some fairly loose connections. One site I found from such a search included merely a list of all of the gear owned by a musician, among which was some MIDI gear. Your search will yield a list of sites all linked (they are underlined to show you that there is a link), so it is fairly easy to quickly check out a site to see if it meets your needs.

When I go through the card catalog at the Boston Public Library, I usually find a book that sounds as if it perfectly meets my needs. Then off I'll go to the stacks to retrieve my treasure. Once I zero in on the call numbers, though, I always seem to find a book that looks even more promising than the original—right in the general vicinity. I find the same to be true when doing a Web search. Often the site that you are led to does not meet your needs. But there might be great links from that site that far exceed what you had originally hoped to find. Allowing yourself the time to browse can really pay off.

Researcher Beware

The fact that anyone can have a Web site is both a blessing and a curse. Unlike traditionally published material, where information that is released has been verified, there are no such filters on the Web. You should consider the source of any information you find on the Web before you rely on it. Fortunately, there are many excellent Web sites developed by fairly reliable sources such as universities.

TIP

Have your students develop criteria for assessing the validity of information found on a Web site. Students can then apply that criteria when they use the Web as a research tool for a project.

Yahoo	*http://www.yahoo.com*
InfoSeek	*http://www.infoseek.com*
Lycos (robot)	*http://lycos.cs.cmu.edu/*
Excite	*http://www.excite.com*
Alta Vista	*http://www.altavista.digital.com*
Webcrawler	*http://webcrawler.com*

TABLE 1-3
Search Engines

WEB PUBLISHING

You might be surprised to learn just how easy creating a simple Web site has become. While you might not want to *begin* your Internet adventure with such a task, it is not unrealistic to expect that with some experience using the Web, you'll be ready to create your very own Web site.

Web sites at schools can serve many different purposes. Some sites are simple and created solely for a Web project, such as the publication of a magazine by and for adolescent girls or a site to post data about sightings of an animal along a migration corridor. Other sites serve the whole school. They might include the weekly lunch menu, notices about special events, profiles of faculty, and other information pertinent to the entire district. Still other school sites serve a wider community. They might include links to the local libraries' online services and address other community-wide concerns. Other innovative and comprehensive sites serve multiple schools across districts and even states, offering special elective courses through distance learning to all member schools.

What Do I Need?

To create a Web site you'll need some basic software and instructions:

- An Internet hookup
- Software for a Web server (that's the computer where the information for your site will live) or space on another Web server. The server must be a computer that can be left on 24 hours a day so that the information can be accessed when needed. Depending on your Internet Service Provider, you may be able to use space on their server. (America Online, for example, provides some limited space to their members.) Check with your school's system administrator for more information.

You'll also need to code your site in language the Web can understand. (HTML is the name of the code: it stands for HyperText Markup Language). You can learn the basic HTML commands you would need for a simple site fairly easily or you can skip this step completely by purchasing a software package that does this for you. This type of software is called Web page authoring software. Adobe's PageMill and Claris Home Page are two popular and relatively easy-to-use Web page authoring software packages under $100.

Fortunately, everything you need to create a simple site can be found on the Web. Web66 at the University of Minnesota (*http://web66. coled.umn.edu/Cookbook/*) is an excellent educator resource and features a Classroom Internet Server Cookbook that includes both the ingredients (software) and recipes (instructions) that you need to create your own Web site—for both Macintosh and Windows 95. Some of the software is shareware, meaning that it is available for you to try out for free. If you like it and want to continue using it, you are on the honor system to pay a (usually) small fee for its use. The Cookbook includes a tutorial and template that take you through the steps of creating a simple homepage using HTML. (For more information on planning the content of your site, see "Creating a Web Site" Chapter 3.)

OTHER TOOLS

The Internet tools that you'll use the most are your Web browser and email. These are the tools you'll want to begin your journey with. But there are some other interesting tools to draw on once you've gained some experience.

Chat

Internet Relay Chat (IRC), commonly known as Chat, allows you to carry on a conversation with someone online in real time. Instead of having to wait until the message is sent (as with email), Chat allows you to communicate with others just as you would in a phone conversation, except that in Chat you type your message instead of speaking it. Several people can participate in a conversation at once in virtual spaces set aside for this purpose, called Chat rooms.

For the most part, Chat is not used very effectively for education applications. However, it won't be long before there are more applications that could have significant educational benefits. Students could gather in a Chat room to cooperatively reconstruct a virtual dinosaur—given nothing but a pile of bones, a point-and-click tool that "constructs" the dinosaur, and the ability to communicate with one another about what needs to be done. Or students could meet to peer-mediate a conflict.

Some Chat rooms have gained the reputation as virtual singles bars (and not without reason!). There is a great deal that happens in Chat rooms that you would not want children to be privy to. There are, however, some Chat rooms for kids that have security measures in place. Kidlink (*http://www.kidlink.org/*) is one place you can safely send your students.

CU-SeeMe

Imagine being able to video conference with other schools over the Internet. Well, that potential exists—developed and available free from Cornell University (*http://cu-seeme.edu/*; also available commercially). CU-SeeMe (pronounced see-you-see-me) allows you to link up with other schools without ever leaving your campus. Video, audio, and text combine in near real-time (there is a several second delay). You must, however, have a video camera, digitizer, and a fast enough connection to the Internet to make it worthwhile (check with your school's system administrator for more information).

CU-SeeMe
http://www.cu-seeme.com
Everything you need to know to use CU-SeeMe.

FTP, Gopher, and Telnet

FTP, Gopher, and Telnet are tools that the Internet of yesterday depended on. For the most part, the Web of today takes care of these functions, without you even knowing that it is happening.[2]

FTP (File Transfer Protocol), however, is a handy tool that you may have occasion to use. FTP allows you to transfer files from another computer to yours or from your computer to another. In actuality, you are copying the files. For organizations or companies that do not yet have Web sites, this is one way to access information they have available. Or when you have a large file that you'd like to send to someone, FTP may be a more appropriate method than attaching it to email.

You can FTP directly from most browsers by putting the FTP address in the space usually provided for the URL. Instead of *http://* you'll use *ftp://*. To get a complete list of FTP site addresses, FTP to *ftp.ucsc.edu.*. FTP will often require a password. The convention is to sign on as username *anonymous* and use your email address as the password.

MULTIMEDIA TOOLS

Note: This section was provided by Douglas Parker Roerden, multimedia producer, Bedrock Barn Productions, Boston, Massachusetts (*http://www.bedrockbarn.com/pages/tools.htm*).

---

[2] If you are curious, you can find a detailed description of each of these tools in *The Whole Internet User's Guide*, Second Edition, by Ed Krol, published by O'Reilly & Associates (*order@ora.com* or 800-998-9938).

The *American Heritage Dictionary* defines multimedia as "the combined use of several media, such as movies, slides, music, and lighting, especially for the purpose of education or entertainment."

As of this writing, multimedia software run from personal computers can tap into two of our five senses—sight and sound—in just about any combination you would want. (Sorry, scratch-n-sniff computers aren't widely available yet.) You can annotate movies with text; add narration to a sequence of pictures; and put music behind just about anything. With the right hardware, you can even control lighting *outside* of your computer.

Like most evolving technologies, there are many different names and formats for very similar elements. And even more tools for accessing, playing, and recording those elements. Sound-related media is often referred to as "audio" and includes narration, music, and sound effects. Sight-related media can be still or moving and includes text, graphics, animations, and video. Like paint on a canvas, the dividing lines between media types become less distinct the more you combine them. For instance, if you string together a series of photographs, are you creating a slide show or a movie? Or is it a flipbook? An animation? While you can probably debate the matter until the day when scratch-n-sniff computers *are* commonplace, what matters now are the tools you'll use for multimedia and how you might need to refer to them. For up-to-date information regarding multimedia tools, see *http://www.bedrockbarn.com/pages/tools.htm*.

System Recommendations

To adequately employ the multimedia lesson plans in this book, you need the following computer equipment:

- 68030- or 68040-based Macintosh or Power Macintosh computer running System 7.1 or later
- 8Mb RAM
- Monitor that supports 640- by 480-pixel resolution and 256 colors

Optional:

- Scanner
- Digital still camera
- MIDI sound equipment
- Audio digitizing board
- Video camera and digitizing board

While it is certainly possible to run multimedia from a PC running Windows or one of its variants, it is infinitely more complex than doing so from a Macintosh. Chances are you'll spend a lot more time configuring your system than you will using multimedia. For a PC you'll need:

- Fast 80386-, 80486-, or Pentium-based PC or MPC running Microsoft Windows 3.1, Windows NT 3.5, or Windows 95 and DOS 5.0
- 8Mb RAM
- Monitor that supports 640- by 480-pixel resolution and 256 colors
- Sound card that supports MIDI

Windows System Recommendations

What Is MIDI?

MIDI (Musical Instrument Digital Interface) is basically a means by which a computer can control a (MIDI-compatible) musical instrument, like a synthesizer or a drum machine. Since the computer files that store MIDI information contain just the actions of playing a musical instrument—which note, when, how hard, and how long—they are very much like player piano rolls: you can play them faster or slower than they were originally recorded; you can play them on different instruments; and, far beyond piano-roll capabilities, you can even change key!

Until recently, you needed a MIDI-compatible musical instrument hooked up to your computer to play MIDI files. Now, with Quick-Time from Apple Computer installed, you can even play MIDI files from SimpleText…which is *only* a text processor!

What Is QuickTime?

QuickTime is a technology that enables software programs to work with multimedia. It comes with MoviePlayer, a program for playing and editing digital video and audio files. Web browsers like Netscape Navigator have incorporated QuickTime "plug-ins" so that you can play QuickTime "movies" from the Web without leaving it. QuickTime movies can contain any combination of video, audio, text, and graphics or simply one of these multimedia elements. You can find the latest version of QuickTime at *http://www.quicktime.apple.com/*.

While you can use MoviePlayer for cutting, copying, and pasting segments of QuickTime movies and for converting MIDI files, you'll use Apple Interactive Music Toolkit to combine and synchronize different media elements. You can find the latest version of Apple Interactive Music Toolkit at *http://www.amp.apple.com/imt/*.

Shareware and Freeware

Shareware refers to software—usually distributed across the Internet and other online services—that you can evaluate for a few weeks before purchasing. If you decide to keep it, you're obligated to pay the author or programmer for it. Each program is usually accompanied by a text file or some other means of communication to indicate how much you're expected to pay whom and whether you're entitled to free updates and how many. Some shareware authors may offer *additional* discounts to educators. I say "additional" because shareware fees are typically very low ($5–$30). Freeware is essentially the same, except you *never* have to pay for it.

WHERE TO FIND HELP

There are literally hundreds of publications devoted to teaching the basics and the inner workings of the Internet. The *Internet for Dummies* series is particularly good (and very easy to access). But one of the beauties of the Internet is the wealth of information available online. Nearly everything you need, including tools and software, is available by visiting a Web site.

The New York State Education and Research Network (NYSERNet) at *http://www.nysernet.org* has a 140-page guide for new users to the Internet (or FTP to *nysernet.org*).

The Clearninghouse for Networked Information Discovery and Retrieval (CNIDR) at *http://cnidr.org* is also a good resource on the Internet.

If you subscribe to America Online, see their help service. It includes great links to sites where you can learn HTML, find out about Web standards, and connect with other organizations that provide Internet assistance.

A NOTE TO NOVICES

Despite the weighty volumes written about how to use the Internet, you have nothing to fear when it comes to using the Web. The Web is so easy to use that most people learn the basics without ever needing a reference source. That's why this book can focus so much more completely on the curricular implications of the Web.

But like any new skill, it will take time to master the Web. Start out with realistic goals. You may not want to plan to take on a Web project until you've gotten well away from your training wheels. To start out, ask a friend or colleague who has used the Web to spend half an hour with you showing you the lay of the land (or try "Your First Adventure," earlier in this chapter). I guarantee you'll be relieved to find out just how easy it is!

Designing Your Curriculum

2

This chapter tells you how to design a curriculum that best utilizes the potential of the Web. The chapter includes:

▶ Using the Web in Your Classroom

▶ The Big Twelve: Web Activity Types to Try

▶ Applying the Big Twelve to Your Subject Area

▶ Interdisciplinary Curriculum

▶ Building Students' Skills

▶ A Word About Assessment

USING THE WEB IN YOUR CLASSROOM

"When the only tool you own is a hammer, every problem begins to resemble a nail." —Abraham Maslo

Creating a curriculum that utilizes the Web well is no different than designing any effective curriculum. It requires planning. What are my goals? What tools and strategies can I employ? How will those tools help me achieve my goals? How can I do it all in the time allotted (and still remain sane)? These are the questions that we teachers ask ourselves daily. The Web is just one more tool to consider when we reach into our magic bag of tricks.

Joan Todd, a 6th-grade science teacher in Massachusetts, was about to begin a unit on weather. In the past, she employed two strategies to teach the topic. During the first week, she lectured students about weather basics—identifying types of clouds; high pressure vs. low pressure systems; cold vs. warm fronts, etc. Then, as she continued on to other curriculum topics, she would start each class with a five-minute weather report. Students in small groups would present short- and long-range forecasts using a pull-down map of the U.S. to illustrate. This year, she wanted to improve the unit, integrating project-based learning and collaborative inquiry into her approach.

PLANNING YOUR CURRICULUM

Here is how Joan could approach her planning for the unit, exploring whether or not the Web might help her better meet her curricular goals.

Identify student outcomes/skills to be achieved by your unit/lesson

Joan's goals for her weather unit were as follows:

- Students will be able to identify cloud types.
- Students will understand high/low pressure systems, the effect of wind currents, warm/cold fronts, and other standard indicators.
- Students will be able to predict weather.

Create a curriculum web of the topics to be covered to achieve your goals

How will you make connections between topics? Where will you start? Where will you end up? Your curriculum web will help you think through important details such as scope, sequence, and any important connections you want to be sure to make.

Identify the strategies that are best to employ

Since different students respond to different types of strategies, Joan considered the various options she had available to her, including simulation, collaborative inquiry, lecture, etc. She decided that in order to help students better understand weather, she would begin the unit with a collaborative inquiry. This would require students to find answers to the broader question: What causes our weather? A collaborative inquiry process would allow students to form their own questions—questions for which they now cared to find the answers. She knew this approach would increase student retention of the

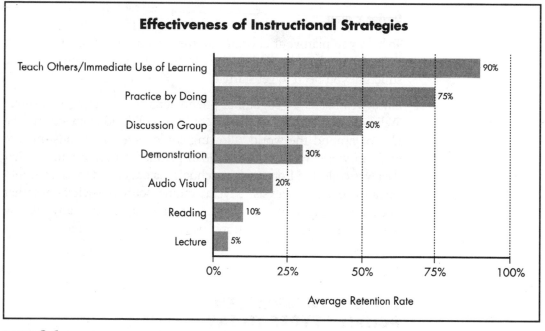

FIGURE 2-1

Effectiveness of Instructional Stategies
(Used with permission from NetLearning: Why Teachers Use the Internet, *by Ferdi Serim and Melissa Koch. Published by Songline Studios, Inc., and O'Reilly & Associates, Inc., 1996. Percentages for the graph courtesy of the National Training Laboratories, Bethel, Maine.)*

information, and motivate some students who otherwise might not be engaged in the lesson.

Assess your goals and strategies: what tools should you employ to meet your goals?

(See the sidebar "Can the Web Help?" for an easy-to-use assessment tool when considering using the Web to meet your educational objectives.)

In designing a collaborative inquiry to teach weather, Joan decided that her students could effectively explore weather through looking for trends in a data set that included daily temperatures, rainfall averages, and wind direction at various locations throughout the U.S. This would allow them to see how weather moved west to east via the prevailing westerly winds, and to identify regional differences in terms of rainfall and temperature. And she knew it would spark their curiosity about why such differences occur, the perfect lead-in to a deeper look at weather. But where would she find such a data set and what would be the "hook"?

Devise a plan

To help you plan your curriculum, the section "The Big Twelve" and the sidebar "Can the Web Help?" in this chapter will give you the structure you need to get started.

Since weather is a geographic phenomena, it is a topic with great Web potential. In this case, data could be collected from around the U.S. or around the world, allowing students a real, hands-on case study in world weather trends. Joan planned a unit where weather data was collected from partner schools via email and integrated into spreadsheets for analysis. Several online sources such as weather satellite imaging Web sites were also employed to fill in any missing information. Student questions were directed to a meteorologist available through email.

THE BIG TWELVE: WEB ACTIVITY TYPES TO TRY

Once you've decided that the Web might be a helpful tool to accomplish your curricular goals, it's time to start filling in the details of your plan. What type of activity or project will best address your goals? Would a simulation exercise be best, or should you consider publishing your students' ideas to a Web site? Just where will those statistics on job placement rates for welfare recipients come from? How can you devise an interactive way for students to learn about the Arctic region?

Most good homegrown Web projects fit into one of the strategies described in the following section. To begin, familiarize yourself with each activity type. Which strategy seems likely to help you accomplish your goals? What would each strategy look like employed in your classroom? (For examples of each activity type in your subject area, see "Applications of the Big Twelve to Your Subject Area.") Like all good pedagogy, different educational goals require different instructional strategies.

KEYPALS

This is one of the simplest activity types available to anyone with access to email. Students are partnered to communicate with another person—perhaps a student, a senior citizen, a professional in a field of interest, etc.—in a techno-spinoff on the old penpal activity.

How to Use

For best results, provide students with:

- A goal for their partnering
- A designated time frame for the partnering
- An outline of expectations (number of communications per week, length of communication, etc.)

Studies (and experience!) show that when undirected, students use online time for socializing only. Require students to draft a plan including a directed activity or questions they will address with their partner.

When to Use

- To link students to someone with whom they can mutually benefit
- An excellent application for practicing a language with a native speaker or learning about another culture

Benefits

- Allows for quick communication on timely topics

Pitfalls to Avoid

- Plan carefully to avoid unstructured communication

WEB MENTOR

Students are paired via email with experts or knowledgeable folks in the field they are studying. Mentors need not be limited to experts in a field. Pairing a child with a senior, an older student, or a person with a special interest in the field can be just as, if not more, effective than drawing on experts. Mentors can be a powerful addition to your teaching repertoire.

How to Use

- As with all Web activities, draw on local resources first. There may be someone in your community who could fill the role in person.
- Clearly outline expectations with the mentor (number, nature, and time of communications, etc.).
- Have students peer-review questions before they go to the mentor (to hone and focus).
- Plan your curricula carefully, so you know exactly when you'll be needing expert help. (Experts are very busy. Depending on what resource you are drawing on, you may have a small window of opportunity for reaching the desired person.)

When to Use

- Great for complicated topics where students are after depth rather than breadth
- To answer random questions you do not have answers for and your library does not address
- To develop relationship-building and communication skills
- Appropriate for any discipline and age

Benefits

- Students benefit from perspectives and information from experts and others more knowledgeable.

Pitfalls to Avoid

- Plan carefully to avoid unfocused communication

TIP

You can find experts from all sorts of fields (astronomer, biological scientist, economist, meteorologist, mathematician, etc.) at *http://www.askanexpert.com/askanexpert* and *http://njnie. dl.stevens-tech.edu/curriculum/aska.html*. To find a scientist, also see *http://www.cedarnet.org/aska/scientist/index.html*. See the teachers and writers collaborative at *http://www.twc.org/tmmain. htm* to find professional writers.

WEB RESOURCE

This activity type takes advantage of the Web's potential as a research tool. In addition to accessing such traditional library resources as books and periodicals, Web sites featuring resources not normally available in schools (such as interactive simulations, sophisticated databases, etc.) are also invaluable enhancements to your curriculum.

How to Use

- Teach students the basics about using search engines (see "Directories and Search Engines" in Chapter 1 for more information).

- Qualify a search with students before they embark on their research. What would be good parameters for your search? Limit the time for each student's search. (When first beginning to use online search engines, students will take a lot of time to answer basic, easy questions. This will improve over time as they become more familiar with the tools and can limit their searches to topics likely to be included.)

- Identify two or three good resources for students as a backup. Student searches may not be successful.

- Teach students how to carefully consider the validity and source of their information. (See "Researcher Beware," Chapter 1.)

- Design a treasure or scavenger hunt linked to your curriculum so that students can practice finding information. Gratuitous searches, while teaching the tools, are a lost opportunity to tie the effort to your student's content learning.

When to Use

- When students need access to information not readily available in your local or school library
- Best used with older students—upper elementary and beyond
- To find lesson plans or curricular resources such as primary documents to supplement your lesson plans

Benefits

- Access to timely, up-to-the-minute information

Pitfalls to Avoid

- Not all sources of information are reliable

TIP

If you are new to using email and the Web to research, try to simplify your project. If you have a class of 30 students to coordinate partners with, choose 6 students who will receive online partners. Then team each of the six with four other student researchers from your class who can divide up the research. (From William J. Gathergood, teacher, Columbus, Ohio.)

WEB COLLABORATION

Schools partner via email or meet virtually at a Web site to execute a project. Some projects work best when two schools are partnered, with each child in the class paired. Others involve many schools sharing resources, information, and/or responsibility for the project.

How to Use

- Be sure that there is a compelling reason for your partner(s) to participate. Equal partnerships where all parties share and use the collective information work best.
- Clearly identify the goals and timeline of the project. Create guidelines of participation for all partners.
- Post a general message looking for participants six to eight weeks in advance of the project launch.

- Send frequent reminders of upcoming milestones in the project.
- Help students learn to work effectively with others. (See "Tips for Teaching Students to Work Well Together," Chapter 3.)
- Promote interdependence in your project by structuring it to depend on each party of the group's resources.

When to Use

- When students can benefit from another perspective (such as when dealing with controversial issues, creating a work of art, etc.)
- When your topic can be best illustrated by data collection at different geographical locations (such as certain earth science, biology, and ecology topics, etc.)
- To create a sense of community in a venue that would not be possible in person (around diversity issues when your school is racially homogenous, etc.)
- To address issues of difference and diversity
- To reinforce problem-solving, conflict resolution, and communication skills

Benefits

- Allows students to practice collaborating and to learn from different viewpoints

Pitfalls to Avoid

- Without frequent and clear communication, partner contribution may diminish

WEB SURVEY

Students create and post a survey publicly (either through a Web site, listserv, or through securing partner classrooms) to find out information for a project.

How to Use

- Secure partners or participants six to eight weeks in advance. Allow two weeks for response.
- Offer to share the data and any lesson plans you've developed around the data with participants (the participants must also benefit from the survey to be motivated to join).

- Create a deadline for the survey. Allow two weeks for the response. Send a reminder to all participants a week in advance of the deadline.
- Have students outline the goal of the survey.
- Have students create the survey and analyze the results.
- Discuss bias in polling. How can you construct an unbiased survey? How is information from polls used? What are the ramifications for democracy?

When to Use

- To support a student initiative to the administration with quantitative data (i.e., 70 percent of schools offer seniors open campus)
- When your project can benefit from qualitative data but you need a larger or more diverse sample size than is presented by your school
- To identify common concerns or issues to be addressed in a Cooperative Challenge activity (See the following section for more information about the Cooperative Challenge activity type)
- To compare cultures, values, etc., as part of a social studies unit

Benefits

- Teaches students the uses and potential misuses of polls

Pitfalls to Avoid

- Plan in advance so you get a large enough sample for your survey

COOPERATIVE CHALLENGE

This activity type is based on Project Adventure's work. For more information about adventure programming and the role of challenge, contact Project Adventure at P.O. Box 100, Hamilton, MA 01936 (508) 468-7981.

Students work together to meet a challenge or solve a problem. Students can work via email, meet virtually in a Chat room, or gather in groups in your classroom. The challenge can range from solving a difficult math problem set (the Problem of the Week genre) to resolving a real conflict between two people or completing a virtual obstacle course.

How to Use

- Work with students to identify a challenge they wish to address. Students need to be invested for a cooperative challenge to work. (Have options available if they are having difficulty identifying any.)

- Help students learn to work effectively with others. (See "Tips for Teaching Students to Work Well Together," Chapter 3.)

- Explore themes of cooperation vs. competition across your curriculum (literature, history, science, and even mathematics present excellent opportunities to discuss the benefits of cooperation vs. competition).

- Begin with "Kisses for Everyone?", an activity provided here that helps students explore themes of cooperation and competition before delving into other cooperative challenges.

- Make sure the challenge is difficult enough! Stretch students to a new level.

- Gradually increase the difficulty of the challenge over several projects. Remind students of where they started and how far they've come.

- (Optional) Learn how to use such helpful tools as IRC (Internet Relay Chat) and other multimedia authoring tools to increase your repertoire of interesting activities.

When to Use

- When students are having difficulty working together
- To build confidence and a sense of success in students
- To bring students to a new level of difficulty and mastery of a concept
- To teach students when and how cooperation may be a viable option for responding to problems and conflicts

Benefits

- Stretches students beyond their old habits and ways of seeing
- Encourages cooperation

Pitfalls to Avoid

- Set up students for success so that a sense of failure is not more deeply engrained

KISSES FOR EVERYONE?

Subject:
Conflict Resolution

Grade level:
Grades 6-12

Activity type:
Cooperative Challenge

Activity level:
Beginner

Time frame:
1 class period

Partners:
None

Materials Needed

- 1 bag of Hershey's chocolate kisses (M&Ms, raisins, or nuts also work)
- Timer

Students in pairs "arm wrestle" for Hershey's chocolate kisses and explore themes of cooperation and competition.

OBJECTIVES

Students think critically and problem solve.

Students explore cooperation vs. competition.

PREREQUISITES

None

PROCEDURE

1. Pair students according to ability. Aim for students of similar physical strength to partner.

2. Clarify the rules (repeat):
   - Students must face each other with hands clasped and elbows on table (similar to arm wrestling posture). NOTE: Do not call it arm wrestling, though the positions are the same!
   - Partners may not talk.
   - You will receive one chocolate kiss each time your partner's hand touches the desk.
   - You will track your own kisses earned.
   - You will have 30 seconds.

3. Time students for 30 seconds. (Most students will begin arm wrestling. Be on the lookout for a pair that cooperates rather than competes by letting each other press the other's hand to the desk quickly, thereby amassing a large number of kisses that they can divide.)

4. Check in with pairs. How many kisses did each student win? (NOTE: If you have succeeded in evenly matching students, most students will have won a small number of kisses. If one pair has won a large number of kisses via cooperation have them describe to the class how they did it.)

5. Give each student the kisses that he or she won.

6. Tell students they will have one more chance to win kisses. If everyone competed rather than cooperated, ask, how could you approach this to get the maximum kisses? Challenge the students to think creatively about how to approach this activity.

7. Once someone has come up with the cooperative approach and shared it with the class, begin the activity again cooperatively, giving partners 15 seconds to earn kisses.

(Adapted with permission from Educators for Social Responsibility, 800-370-2515.)

8. Hand out the earned kisses to each pair.

9. Debrief with the group. Which way (competing vs. cooperating) gave you more kisses? What made you compete? What was the goal? Did the other person's gaining mean that you lost? What did you stand to gain by competing? Are there other situations where we compete without thinking? What does the media tell us to do? When might it be appropiate to compete? When it is best to cooperate?

Explain to students: There are times when it's best to use the muscle of your mind rather than the muscle of your arm to get what you really want. There can be much to gain by cooperating. Studies show that when given the opportunity to compete or cooperate for a resource, those who cooperate do best in acquiring the resource. The studies also show that one person needs to initiate cooperation first and then the other(s) will respond.[1]

KISSES FOR EVERYONE?

SOCIAL ACTION

Students identify a problem and address it through a service learning project. Students may or may not work with other students from other schools. Minimally, they use email or the Web to research their topic and gather support.

How to Use

- Work with students to identify a problem they wish to address (a Web survey is an effective way to identify an issue that is of global concern).

- As the saying goes, think globally and act locally. Encourage projects that address a global concern, but affect your own backyard. (For example, address students' universal concern about global warming through a local public service poster campaign in public places.) If, however, students live in the U.S. and insist that they wish to save the rain forest in Costa Rica, suggest that they partner with Costa Rican students for their project. Justify the Costa Rican involvement: it's difficult to know how to address a far-away problem without local input.

- Be sure to follow through on addressing the problem. Research shows that students experience a sense of disempowerment when faced with large-scale world problems. Turning that sense to one of empowerment is a simple matter of allowing students to take positive action to address the concern.

- Look for opportunities to connect social action projects to your curriculum.

[1] Thanks to Nan Doty, former senior program associate, Educators for Social Responsibility, for her help with this activity.

When to Use

- To teach problem solving skills
- To teach democracy in action
- When students have identified an issue that concerns them

Benefits

- Students develop a sense of empowerment when faced with problems

Pitfalls to Avoid

- Be sure that students follow through on their plan to address the problem

COMMUNITY CONNECTION

Students use the Web to create a stronger sense of community in their school or town. Projects could include a Web site profile of WWII veterans in your area as part of a Veterans Day celebration; an online collaborative magazine for girls and their mothers; or a Web site profile on careers for students, featuring interviews with community members.

TIP

It's important to include your administration when planning a community connection activity. What are your school's goals and values around connecting with community? What activities does it already do? What activities would it like to do? Then try to find ways that your Web activity might meet the school's goals (see "Creating a Web Site" in Chapter 3 for additional advice).

How to Use

- Look for opportunities to help your administration meet its goals (and garner support for your Web efforts!) by involving your administration in the planning process.
- Design projects that require students to talk to community members in person. Then use the Web to profile them.

- Be mindful of equity issues when choosing to feature information on a Web site. If you must include critical information in your site, be sure to use more traditional methods of communicating the information as well.

- Do not invest your time and your students' time in a Web site to connect with your community until your public library has access for community members. No one should be left without at least this one way to participate.

When to Use

- When you are trying to gather grassroots support for your efforts (such as during your district's budget-passing time!)

- When connecting community links with your curriculum

- To increase the sense of pride and ownership that your community has for your school

Benefits

- Allows you to bring people "together" who might not otherwise be connected

Pitfalls to Avoid

- The Web is not a substitute for face-to-face contact. Don't fall into the trap of thinking that you won't need another parent-teacher conference now that you have that comprehensive Web site.

SIMULATION

Simulation activities require students to use their imaginations to recreate an event or a process. For example, groups of students can represent different viewpoints (environmental groups, local government, and labor unions) on a hot topic such as building a dam, or student groups could represent parts of the body to illustrate how the body fights disease. Partnering with others via email and the use of interactive sites available on the Web (featuring simulations of frog dissections, archaeological digs, etc.) are the most popular uses of the Net for simulation activities.

How to Use

- Plan your simulation so that it maximizes the Web's unique features. Nothing is worse than a contrived simulation. (Simulations require a leap of faith on everyone's part. Starting out with a good idea is essential.)

- Only use an email simulation if it allows you access to people who would have a vested interest, different stake, or unique position on the issue illustrated by your simulation. (For example, southern schools and northern schools could simulate an event from the Civil War.)

- Look for interactive Web sites that illustrate a concept from your curriculum in ways you could not easily duplicate in class.

When to Use

- To illustrate an historical event (using players representing all sides of the issues)

- To explore a controversial issue (again using players representing all sides of the issues)

- To illustrate a complex concept or solve a problem

- Simulations are particularly effective with elementary students. (For example, link to your reading curriculum by asking another classroom to join you in a journey with a character from the book. Then have students write messages to that character.)

Benefits

- Allows access to different perspectives

- Requires researching on the part of the students

Pitfalls to Avoid

- Do not overuse this activity type. Consider all available resources for stimulating a concept or activity before turning to the Web.

WEB PUBLISHING

Students create a Web site and publish their original material on it. Material may be solely created by your classroom, collected through a collaborative project with other classrooms, or downloaded from the Web. For more information about the technical requirements, see "Web Publishing" in Chapter 1. For advice about planning the content of your site, see "Creating a Web Site" in Chapter 3.

How to Use

- Create a team of student editors for your Web publication. Invite a few key administrators to serve on your editorial board.

- Establish editorial guidelines for your publication.
- Teach writing, editing, and design skills to students while they build their site. Implementing these skills will reinforce what the students have learned.
- Have students develop criteria for a good Web site and then assess other Web sites before beginning construction on their own.
- Teach a few reliable students the basics about HTML before beginning. Plan on them becoming your production team.

When to Use

- When students have written a great deal around a topic or theme
- To create an international presence for your school
- To culminate a project or unit
- When you might otherwise use a journal
- When students finish a research project, they can create a reference source for other students

Benefits

- Students' writing and/or research is taken seriously. Higher standards are the result.

Pitfalls to Avoid

- Don't be too ambitious on your first try. Plan for upgrades over time. Update your site on a fairly regular basis.

MULTIMEDIA

These activities utilize multimedia tools available through the Web for hands-on interactive activities. Multimedia activities combine two or more media, including graphics, music, video, photographs, and text. Some activities of this type involve creating an interactive, multimedia Web site. For more information, see "Multimedia Tools" in Chapter 1.

How to Use

- Keep it simple. While the bells and whistles of multimedia are enchanting, they alone can make your site unmanageable for some visitors. Keep high downloading time in mind when choosing what files to include (video, audio, and graphic files can take a long time to download).

- Be clear about your curricular goals before beginning. The seductive nature of multimedia tools makes it very easy to design a project with little educational punch.

- Familiarize yourself with the various multimedia tools. Leave plenty of time for your learning curve in your first projects.

- Be aware that audio and video files come in many different flavors (or formats) and depend on the platform you are working on—be it Mac, Windows, or UNIX. See *http://www.bedrockbarn.com/pages/tools.htm* for updated software for your platform.

Can the Web Help?

	yes	no
- Do you need or would your lesson/unit be enriched by an outsider's perspective?	☐	☐
If so, who? _____		
Is an appropriate person(s) from your community *not* available to participate?	☐	☐
Might an appropriate person(s) be accessible via the Internet?	☐	☐

Web Activity Types to Try: Keypal, Web Collaboration, Web Survey

	yes	no
- Are geographical or cultural/racial differences an issue in your lesson/unit?	☐	☐
Could these differences be illuminated through partnering with another school from another part of the country or with a different student body profile?	☐	☐
If so, who? _____		

Web Activity Types to Try: Community Connection, Web Collaboration, Keypal, Web Survey, Web Resource, Web Simulation

	yes	no
- Would your students' inquiry into the topic require or would it be enriched by working with others?	☐	☐
If so, who? _____		
Is an appropriate person(s) from your community *not* available to participate?	☐	☐
Would an appropriate person(s) be more accessible via the Internet?	☐	☐

Web Activity Types to Try: Community Connection, Web Collaboration, Keypal, Web Survey, Web Resource

	yes	no
- Can you illustrate your topic through a simulation?	☐	☐
Would the simulation be more effective if it employed others?	☐	☐
If so, who? _____		
Is an appropriate person(s) from your community *not* available to participate?	☐	☐
Might an appropriate person(s) be accessible via the Internet?	☐	☐

Web Activity Types to Try: Simulation, Multimedia, Web Collaboration, Web Survey, Web Resource

When to Use

- When a concept is best illustrated by interactive activities, but you have none available
- To promote creativity in students
- For music and art applications

Benefits

- Can help illustrate complex concepts

	yes	no
■ Does your lesson/unit require or would it be enriched by an expert?	☐	☐

If so, who? _____

Is an appropriate person(s) from your community *not* available to participate? ☐ ☐

Web Activity Types to Try: Web Mentor

- Does your lesson/unit rely on or would it be enriched by access to current or additional information? ☐ ☐

If so, what type of information? _____

Do you need access to another library source for that information other than your local or school library? ☐ ☐

Web Activity Types to Try: Web Resource, Web Survey, Keypal, Web Mentor

- Would your students benefit from publishing the results of their work? ☐ ☐

If so, can the published work be augmented by other students' input? ☐ ☐

Can the published work be contributed to on an ongoing basis? ☐ ☐

Does the published work serve a need? ☐ ☐

Web Activity Types to Try: Web Publishing, Multimedia, Web Collaboration

- Does your lesson/unit identify a real-world problem that students might be able to address? ☐ ☐

If so, would students benefit from working with other students on the design of a solution? ☐ ☐

Would students benefit from working with an expert on addressing the problem? ☐ ☐

Web Activity Types to Try: Social Action, Community Connection, Cooperative Challenge

- Is information gathering or dispersal a major part of your lesson/unit? ☐ ☐

Web Activity Types to Try: Web Publishing, MultiMedia, Simulation, Community Connection

For each question that you answered "yes," review the "Web Activity Types to Try." Are there activity types that are suggested multiple times? Choose the Web activity type that best meets your curricular goal.

Pitfalls to Avoid

- Avoid gratuitous use. Be sure to make your project have educational meaning.

STUDENT-CREATED PROJECTS

What could be more student-centered than student-created projects? Encourage your students to come up with their own ideas for projects that utilize the unique resources available through the Web.

How to Use

- Require student projects to meet clearly defined criteria and goals.
- Have students outline project guidelines for participants.
- Have students use the assessment tool provided in the next section to establish whether or not they need to use the Web for their project.
- Help hone and refine the project before it goes live.

When to Use

- Whenever students have good ideas for projects that meet your goals!

Benefits

- Students are invested in the project

Pitfalls to Avoid

- Without teacher input, projects may be unfocused and ineffectual

A WORD ABOUT MULTIPLE INTELLIGENCES

As Howard Gardner's work with multiple intelligences confirms,[2] students have different innate strengths and talents. It's important then to offer a curriculum that features something for everyone. While a multimedia activity may play to one student's strengths, a Web survey will play to another's. Be sure to offer a great deal of variety in teaching strategies you employ. Offer students several options reflecting different learning modes for each assignment.

---

[2] See *Multiple Intelligences: The Theory in Practice* by Howard Gardner. New York: Basic Books, 1993.

APPLYING THE BIG TWELVE TO YOUR SUBJECT AREA

The pedal hits the metal when you apply the Big Twelve Web Activity Types to your classroom. Given the strengths and weaknesses of the medium, however, not all applications are equal. That is, some activity types lend themselves best to one subject area and perhaps not at all to another.

The following sections discuss the application of the Web to each subject area, offering suggestions to make the most of the medium. The activity types that most readily lend themselves to that subject area are explored, offering examples of possible applications. Use these ideas not as a prescriptive outline, but as inspiration to get your creative juices flowing. The featured activity types for each subject area are the *best* activity types for that subject area, not the only ones that apply. Once you get started, try applying all activity types to your subject area.

And remember: the Web should be serving *your* goals, not the other way around.

THE WEB AND SOCIAL STUDIES EDUCATION

The Web has great potential for social studies applications. Perhaps more than any other discipline, the goals and pedagogies employed in social studies play to the Web's unique strengths. The medium's timeliness and ability to navigate distances and differences opens up a world of possibilities. Using the Web, students can research current events, hear first-hand reactions to pressing issues from a global community, and even ask questions to a native of a culture they are studying.

Consider the Web as a resource anytime you wish to:

- Access current information about a social issue
- Have students interface with people from other viewpoints or cultures
- Give students a global perspective on an issue
- Teach U.S. or world geography

While the Web can be a boon in studying social issues or geography, applications for the study of history are less promising. When studying history you are best using the Web for simulations or to connect students to people from countries studied, rather than as a research tool. The sites that do feature interesting historical data or primary documents are few and far between. Often the information available is incomplete, serving a particular professor's line of research or another buff's special interest. It's unlikely, for example, that you could find anywhere near as much information about the American Revolution on the Web as you could in your own school or public library. You might, however, stumble upon an interesting site that features an opportunity to talk to Benedict Arnold or experience Paul Revere's famous ride.

One interesting feature of telecommunications is the potential it carries to link students from diverse backgrounds and viewpoints. Students in a rural community in Montana can receive letters from students in Bosnia about the peace process or from South Africa about the end to apartheid. A native Australian living in the bush can become friends with an African-American living in Manhattan. Bobbie in Boston can carry on a relationship with Kenji in Tokyo for months before it even comes up that her full name is Roberta and she is a girl. Or 3rd graders from Tokyo, Sydney, Peoria, and Atlanta can meet at a Web site where they team together to resolve a conflict.

Certainly, this contact affords a learning opportunity for students. The world becomes a bit smaller, and perhaps a measure more friendly. But how is the learning affected by the medium? Does a "colorblind" medium really serve to dispel stereotypes and close divides or could it reinforce them? Does something change between Kenji and Bobbie when he discovers she is a girl? Can you celebrate differences that you can't see? These are the questions the medium raises and ones that would be fruitful to explore with your social studies students.

One thing is for sure, though. As powerful as building virtual communities online can be, it is not a substitute for in-person contact. In planning your social studies curriculum, consider your local resources before turning to the global community.

Social Studies Framework

Advantages: Study social issues in "real" time on a global scale

Limitations: Not a very complete or reliable source of historical information

---

MECC Interactive Explorer Series

http://www.mecc.com/ies.html

The MECC Interactive Explorer Series includes MayaQuest, where students explore ancient ruins while connected with classrooms around the world, and Oregon Trail Online, a six-week online experience where classrooms—set up as wagons—team up across the country to traverse the trail.

I*EARN

http://www.igc.apc.org/iearn

The International Educational & Resource Network hosts a variety of international projects for elementary and secondary students. I*EARN believes that the more kids know about the world and each other, the more obtainable the goal of world peace becomes.

Activity Type	Possible Applications
Web Resource	<ul><li>Interview major players in a current event or those affected, i.e., interview elders about Social Security, Israelis and Palestinians about the peace process, etc.</li><li>Access news accounts from major media.</li><li>Inquire into government processes through public documents such as the Senate or House records, U.S. Census report, etc.</li><li>Investigate and report on controversial issues using primary documents.</li><li>Analyze economic indicators and statistics.</li><li>Reference historical documents via the Library of Congress, etc.</li></ul>
Web Collaboration	<ul><li>Study for AP exam, with students from all over.</li><li>Study World War II with classrooms from each country involved.</li></ul>
Web Survey	<ul><li>Survey political issues locally or globally.</li><li>Investigate biases in polling.</li><li>Compare cultures, i.e., work ethic, values, resource allocations, etc.</li><li>Identify problems that need to be addressed (see Cooperative Challenge).</li></ul>
Cooperative Challenge	<ul><li>Join others in investigating and designing a solution to a problem that students care about, i.e., pollution of a shared waterway or the lack of funding for the arts in your school district.</li><li>Join forces to take political action on a current issue, i.e., an online letter-writing campaign to key government officials.</li></ul>

- Join others to investigate alternative solutions to a problem or question from history, for example, how could the Cuban Missile Crisis have been avoided?

Social Action

- Design a fund-raiser for a social cause and gather support from around the world.

- Create a public service campaign complete with educational resources on your Web site.

- Plan a simultaneous celebration or social act, i.e., a moment of silence on the anniversary of the dropping of the A-bomb or tree planting on Arbor Day.

Community Connection

- Interview and profile war veterans on your Web site for Veterans Day.

- Create an online survey about a controversial issue in your district. Publish the results in your local newspaper.

Simulations

- Virtually visit another country or culture through keypals and Web site searches.

- Mimic an historical event online with representatives from the respective countries or states of all the major players, i.e., Nuremburg trials, Camp David accords, etc.

- Create a model United Nations with representative classrooms from as many countries as possible.

- Assign roles across cultures in a real or imagined conflict.

- Hold an online debate with players who have a stake in the issue, i.e., debate health care reform with an insurance company representative, etc.

- Chart the progress of a fictitious journey taken around the country or the globe.

Web Publishing

- Create a "suggestion box," a site where students can express their ideas and address an issue of concern.

- Research and design a site dedicated to an historical event.

- Around elections, create a virtual voting booth, where students around the world can cast their ballots.

- Publish a newsletter or magazine devoted to social issues and featuring students' writing.

THE WEB AND SCIENCE EDUCATION

Some of the most promising educational opportunities available on the Internet today are in the domain of science. There are interactive Web sites where students can virtually dissect a frog. Leave your parka behind when you log on to investigate the Arctic ecosystem, analyzing actual data sets of surface temperature, ice concentration, near-surface winds, ice velocity, and cloud cover. Or link up with the space shuttle during an historic docking with Russian cosmonauts and ask questions of the astronauts on board.

Other sites allow students to try out "real" science. Schools along a shared waterway can collect and analyze water quality data and then make recommendations for its cleanup. Or students can track the progress of migratory animals as they move across the country, helping ecologists identify critical corridors for the species protection.

Since there are so many exciting and well-designed science projects sponsored by such reputable organizations as NASA and PBS, you might want to limit your development of home-grown projects—at least at first. Joining an already established project can be an excellent way to get ideas for your own projects.

At present, there appear to be more projects to join and interesting sites available in the biological than the physical sciences. I believe that this will change as multimedia tools become more fully utilized on Web sites (and the tools are further developed). Since biology lends itself to collecting observable data, there are many sound educational projects available that employ very simple tools, such as email and the creation of a database. These types of projects are relatively easy to duplicate in your classroom. Physical sciences,

Arctic Project
http://ics.soe.umich.edu/ ed712/IAPIntro.html

Explore the Arctic alongside famous explorers.

however, are often best expressed in interactive sites. You might want to rely predominantly on existing projects and sites to teach physical sciences.

While many applications of the Web for science have much educational merit, this domain can also be dogged by gimmicky applications that, while they do have some really neat bells and whistles, do not necessarily teach. Hours can be wasted waiting for memory-hogging video to download, only to find a three-second look at a whale breaching out of the water or other information that could just as easily be found in a good old-fashioned encyclopedia or better presented in a National Geographic video.

But there are unique advantages to using the Web for science that the best applications out there exploit. When designing your own science projects utilizing simple tools such as email and resources available on the Web, there are some things to keep in mind. For best results on your home-grown telecommunications projects, design your project around:

- Concepts that are best illustrated through the comparison of data across regions or latitudes and longitudes
- A shared ecosystem
- The scientific method
- A Problem of the Week (a science challenge to be solved)

Frog Dissection
http://george.lbl.gov/ ITG.hm.pg.docs/dissect/
See a virtual frog dissection from every angle imaginable.

Students Become Scientists

Since the Internet lends itself so well to inquiry-based learning, questions from students can lead to real scientific inquiry. Look for opportunities to turn serious questions into online collaborative projects. Have students design the protocol for your online project. Then have them follow the scientific method. What data should you track? Who would be good partners? What is their hypothesis? Students can then use the Web to search for background information on their topic. Have older students finish the project by writing up the results in research paper format.

Science Framework

Advantages: Students can follow a line of scientific inquiry using some of the same tools professional scientists use.

Limitations: Some science-related Web sites are plagued by gimmicky, time-wasting applications.

Activity Type	Possible Applications

Web Mentor

- When students finish a major experiment, have a scientist available for questions, to help them interpret their data.

- Ask a scientist to help you outline your unit. What is the latest breaking question in the field? Begin an odyssey with your students to address that question.

Web Resource

- Interview major players in a current science event or those affected, i.e., interview astronomers about the implications of finding life on Mars.

- Access data kept by government agencies.

- Access Web sites that feature interactive learning opportunities (online frog dissections, etc.).

Web Collaboration

- With other classrooms, create a library that explains the physics of everyday phenomena (for example: sports).

- Track data on an endangered or rare species (such as loons) across the country.

- Research the health of an ecosystem with schools that share a common ecosystem, i.e., assess the water quality of a shared waterway.

Web Survey

- Survey students or others internationally about environmental or ethical issues raised by science (such as recycling habits, genetics research, etc.).

- Survey schools on sightings of migratory animals across contiguous countries.

- Identify environmental problems that need to be addressed (see Cooperative Challenge).

Cooperative Challenge

- Create a cooperative game at your Web site around a science concept. (For example, using IRC, have students from all over join in teams to solve physics problems or answer biology questions. Offer progressively more difficult questions.)

- Have your AP students create a site where students can practice taking a sample AP test.

- Create a simple Internet science scavenger hunt for young students. (How many dinosaurs can they find on the Net?)

- Have students design and moderate a science Problem of the Week.

Social Action

- Join forces to take political action on a current environmental issue, i.e., an online letter-writing campaign to key government officials.

- Organize a statewide cleanup or other major effort.

- Create a public service campaign complete with educational resources on your Web site.

Multimedia

- Study the Arctic environment using the fully interactive CD-ROM from SEDAAR Educational Research (*http://sedaar_edu. ciesin.org/*) available for previewing.

- Create a demonstration of a physical science phenomenon, utilizing multimedia tools and publishing to a Web site. (For example, create a demonstration of acceleration by videotaping a ball drop and through slow motion analyze it frame by frame. Calculate the acceleration based on the frames per minute.)

Simulation

- Animate a science concept for younger children. (Have your middle school class write a script for younger students to illustrate photosynthesis using a fictional character.)

THE WEB AND ENGLISH/LANGUAGES EDUCATION

In the earliest days of the Internet in the classroom, some popular applications served English and language instruction. Keypals were the rage, as students lined up for their electronic penpals. Students could practice virtually any foreign language with native speakers or simply practice writing. While keypals certainly still serve their purpose, applications to the language arts have branched into promising directions.

A middle school in New York working with classrooms across the world has created a collaborative virtual jackdaw for the book *Letters from Rifka*. Using the Internet as a resource, students collected and pooled primary documents and background information about Russia in the early 1900s to use as a reference source. Another elementary class collected poetry from classrooms around the world, publishing it in an anthology called *Around the World in 80 Poems*. And a classroom in Germany linked with native English speakers worldwide to study Shakespeare's *Macbeth*.

Many of these projects utilized the simplest Net tool available— email. While a critic may point out that email offers no greater opportunity than the U.S. Postal Service, these examples suggest to me that email just might make the difference. Would a German student's interest in *Macbeth* be held while she awaited mail from the U.S.? As is often the case, timing is everything. When directed toward a purpose, email can afford the perfect opportunity for students to practice communicating.

But how has the Web changed English instruction? One interesting feature of the Web are sites that feature books online. While I for one firmly maintain that computers will never fully replace the printed word, online books afford an opportunity not previously available to those of us who prefer the printed form. Students can readily manipulate the text online. Whole sections can be cut and pasted and keywords can be searched for. Just how is "art" portrayed in Auden's texts? A simple search and students can retrieve all of the references to a particular topic. A few cuts and pastes later and the student has a complete compendium on the topic. For critical analysis, this is obviously a very useful tool.

In terms of its value as a research tool, however, the Web still has a great distance to travel before it is of much use to English teachers. While there are several sites that do a nice job of covering elements of style, grammar, and usage, the sites for younger children and for

Books Online
*http://www.cs.cmu.edu/
Web/books.html*

A full complement of books
available online.

literature are limited. Since many of the best sites are developed by universities, they reflect the particular specialty or area of dissertation of the developer. If you happen to be covering Emily Dickinson, Shakespeare, or Jane Austen, we've got you covered. If you're reading Marquez or Hurston, it might be a different story.

But some of the literature sites are exemplary. They may include valuable background information on the era the writer was working in, personal letters, photos, and even an author's complete works. While most of the information assembled on the site is available elsewhere in books, it would be difficult to find it anywhere so comprehensively organized. In this case, the Web affords one-stop shopping, if you will.

Another promising usage of the Web for English studies is to publish students' writing. We all know the value of putting our students' thoughts formally on paper in the form of a publication (evidenced by the many hours we've spent advising the school newspaper or literary magazine). But what if your readership could be tripled or if your magazine could feature articles from students from other countries? There are many excellent student-produced publications on the Web. Nowhere else can students find such an audience for their writing or such a world community with which to collaborate.

Designing Your Own Project

While there are some projects offered by established organizations and commercial endeavors, by and large most opportunities for projects to join in the English and languages domain are home-grown. If you are interested in creating your own project, model some of the projects offered by Web veterans. The most promising projects out there include:

- Connecting students for a directed activity where communication or writing is key
- Publishing students' writing to a Web site
- Using the Web for background information on a topic (either through author sites or through connecting with someone who can provide context for a book)
- Utilizing the advantage of hypertext linked books online
- Taking advantage of the global community

English/Languages Framework

Advantages: Allows you to publish students' writings

Limitations: Not a very effective historical research tool

Activity Type	Possible Applications
Keypals	■ Link students with native foreign language speakers for directed activity or study.
	■ Peer editing with a twist: connect students to peer editors who have specialized knowledge or background about their topic.
Web Collaboration	■ Study a book from another culture with a classroom from that culture.
	■ Collect book reviews from peers around the world for a book review database.
Web Resource	■ Learn more about an art form from another culture, such as haiku.
	■ Access news accounts from major media for writing assignments.
	■ Get reactions to major breaking news from stakeholders for journalism activities.
	■ Access interesting information about an author or work through a Web site.
	■ Research a theme or topic in an author's work using books available online.
	■ Gather background information on cultures represented by world literature.
Web Survey	■ Identify recommended reading. (Students love to know what their peers think.)
	■ Get background information or statistics for a journalism project.

Community Connection	■ Profile grandmothers, mothers, and daughters from your community on your Web site. Include an advice columnist that helps girls through adolescence.
	■ Profile different careers of community members on your site for your career office.
	■ Create an online survey about a controversial issue in your district. Publish the results in your local newspaper.
Simulations	■ Assign roles for major characters in a novel. Have students role-play a new ending for the book.
Web Publishing	■ Publish a newsletter or magazine featuring students' writing. Solicit articles from the larger world community.
	■ Assign students to research a topic and make the results available to others via a Web site (on Elizabethan England, for example).
	■ Have students write PSAs for issues they care about and publish to a Web site.
Multimedia	■ Have students work with the music department to score their creative writing, then publish to a Web site.
	■ Have students combine artwork and music they found on the Web for a slide presentation.

THE WEB AND MATH EDUCATION

Most applications of the Web to mathematics rely on the medium's ability to connect students in collaborative problem-solving groups or for projects that rely on applied math. But there are many potential uses for the Web in math education, including:

■ Teaching basic statistics through polling

■ Practicing basic computations

■ Illustrating a concept via an applied math project

- Collaborative problem solving
- Mentoring
- Locating problem sets

The majority of the homegrown projects currently available to join on the Web are targeted to the elementary or middle school math level. They often involve integrated math/social studies polling projects, where students do quantitative research on a topic and then analyze the results (after computing mean, median, and mode, or making conversions from international measurements to U.S.). These projects, while valuable, do not draw on higher level math concepts for the most part.

The most interesting applications of the Web to math education are:

- Use geographical differences to illustrate a concept
- Draw on experts
- Involve collaborative problem solving

While there may not be a plethora of such activities, geometry, trigonometry, and calculus concepts can be well illustrated in an online project. For example, a project where students compare the angle of the sun across regions at a particular time of the day can rely on the application of the inverse trangent function.

Several of the more established projects and/or services that support math education include excellent problem sets, where students are asked to work collaboratively and can draw on experts (usually math professors at colleges) to answer their questions. Such a function, however, could easily be duplicated in your classroom without use of the Web. (In fact, one could argue justifiably that that is exactly what goes on in most math classrooms every day!) The value added by the Web, however, is the ready access to problem sets on virtually any topic, and access to math professors to address questions or problems that you alone may not be able to answer.

Math Framework

Advantages: Online projects that rely on geographical differences and data collection can draw on many math skills.

Limitations: Not as many homegrown projects available to join at secondary math levels

The Math Forum
http://forum.swarthmore. edu/

This site features a Problem of the Week, an ask-an-expert forum (Ask Dr. Math), an Internet hunt, and has great additional resources.

Activity Type	Possible Applications
Web Mentor	■ Have a mathematician available to answer complex questions.
	■ Pair students with professionals who use math at work (for interesting applied math problems from a real-world context).
Web Resource	■ Access interesting data for students to use in statistics problem sets.
	■ Find problem sets for all age levels.
Web Collaboration	■ Collaborate with other classrooms on a polling project.
	■ Collaboratively problem solve across age levels (the younger students will learn from the older, the older will find teaching a concept reinforces it).
Web Survey	■ Survey schools for any quantitative research project.
Cooperative Challenge	■ Have your students design and then moderate a Problem of the Week collaboration.
	■ Create a cooperative game at your Web site around a math concept. (For example, using IRC, have students from all over join in teams to solve math problems. Offer progressively more difficult questions.)
	■ Have your AP students create a site where students can practice taking a sample AP test.
	■ Create a simple Internet math scavenger hunt for young students. (Count the number of dinosaurs you can find on the Net.)

THE WEB AND ART/MUSIC EDUCATION

Leave it to the creative arts to take advantage of a new medium. More than five years ago, among the Internet education pioneers were teachers using the Internet to serve the purposes of art and music education. The applications were simple—world art shows organized via email (and circulated via snail mail) or a music teacher downloading guitar tablature for lessons—but nonetheless, art and music teachers were taking advantage of precious Internet resources available to their traditionally resource-starved disciplines.

Like everything on the Net, music and art resources (and their applications to education) have become increasingly more sophisticated over time. More and more, music and art teachers are using the Web to:

- Present students' work to the larger world
- Make cross-cultural comparisons/collaborations
- Access multimedia tools (download software)
- Access digital media (graphics, MIDI files, video etc.) (Note: See "A Word About Copyright Law and Fair Use," Chapter 3)
- Access music archives and virtual art museums
- Link students with professional artists

Some of the most exciting applications take advantage of the Web's access to the world community and to resources not readily available elsewhere. A music teacher presenting a world music unit, for example, can link students studying traditional Indian music with native musicians from India and download examples of both Hindustani and Shankar styles. It's difficult to imagine a typical school library or your average music budget accommodating such specialized needs.

Multimedia is yet another envelope the Web is pushing. Music and art teachers have access via the Web to an array of tools that make it possible for students to apply their creativity and emerging skill to a multimedia production (by definition an integrated curriculum project!). Slide shows scored to music on a topic covered in science class can be made available digitally to the world community via the Web. A world student art show no longer need be circulated via snail mail (or be limited to graphics only). An art show available via the Web can combine music, video, and graphics. (See "Multimedia Tools" in Chapter 1 for more information on multimedia applications.)

ClassicalNet
http://www.classical.net/
An introduction to classical music, containing biographies, history, and guides to classical recordings.

Another interesting aspect of the Web is the way that large amounts of information can be found in one spot. Virtual art museums like the online Louvre in Paris bring together works of art not commonly available other than in the actual location.

You should use discretion, however, when using music and art resources available via the Web. Titian's colors or Monet's dancing light do not translate adequately when displayed on a 256-bit color monitor. If you have resources available in a more appropriate format—such as a slide or large format color book—then by all means use them. Use the Web to maximize your resources.

Publishing students' art or music on a Web site or viewing art displayed in a Web site is, of course, not a substitute for a live event. A local performance or art show should, if possible, be incorporated into any Web publishing of students' work that you do. Live events offer unparalleled opportunities to bring together parents, students, and others for a celebration of community. Publishing the work to a Web site after the event serves to widen the audience.

Artserv
http://rubens.anu.edu.au/

An award-winning site from the Australian National University, Artserv includes more than 16,000 images, as well as art tutorials for students. Best for the secondary level.

Art/Music Framework

Advantages: Access to resources not readily available in most school/local libraries or through most music and art budgets

Limitations: Not a substitute for live events or more appropriate resources (slides for works of art, etc.)

Activity Type	Possible Applications
Keypals	■ Pair students from different cultures for cross-cultural art/music comparisons.
Web Mentor	■ Pair students with professional artists.
Web Resource	■ Access multimedia authoring tools.
	■ Access digital media (graphics, MIDI files, etc.).
	■ Access music archives and virtual art museums.
Web Collaboration	■ Join with a classroom from another culture to create a collaborative work of art.
	■ Create an international art or music showcase.

Web Publishing

- Feature students' art or music on a Web site.

- Publish art or music reviews to a Web site (these can be added to by the world community).

- Present a multimedia production on a Web site.

Multimedia

- Create a multimedia production using tools and digital media available on the Web. (See lesson plans with multimedia activity types in Part II.)

INTERDISCIPLINARY CURRICULUM

Web projects by their nature lend themselves well to integrating across the curriculum. The clusters presented in Table 2-1 outline subject area combinations suggested by a particular activity type. For example, you might design a Web Resource project that integrates English, social studies, math, and science. Or perhaps create an integrated social studies/science project as part of designing a Social Action project.

You are not limited by these groupings, of course; they are merely suggestions. Begin by choosing any activity type and then listing the disciplines that you hope to integrate. Surely an appropriate project will suggest itself!

BUILDING STUDENTS' SKILLS

All of the Big Twelve Web Activity Types can be useful in building skills with your students. While a Web mentor's primary role may be to help your students master a particular subject area, there are secondary skills being built with each encounter. Students are learning about relationship-building with an adult or person from a different background. They are practicing communicating their thoughts and needs in writing. Your students are probably even building vocabulary.

Table 2-2 outlines the Web Activity Types that build each skill. Use this to help you choose an Activity Type that will meet your skill-building goals for your students.

Activity Type	Subject Area
Keypals	Art/Music English/Languages Math
Web Mentor	Math Science
Web Resource	Art/Music English Science Social Studies
Web Collaboration	Art/Music English Math Science Social Studies
Web Survey	English Math Science Social Studies
Cooperative Challenge	Math Science Social Studies
Social Action	Science Social Studies
Community Connection	English Social Studies
Simulation	English Science Social Studies
Web Publishing	Art/Music English Social Studies
Multimedia	Art/Music English Science
Student-Created Projects	Art/Music English Science Social Studies

TABLE 2-1

An Interdisciplinary Approach: Some Activity Type Clusters

Skill	Activity Type
Collaboration	Keypals Web Collaboration Cooperative Challenge Social Action Community Connection
Communication	Keypals Web Mentor Web Collaboration Cooperative Challenge Social Action Web Publishing Community Connection Simulation
Conflict Resolution	Web Collaboration Cooperative Challenge Social Action
Critical Thinking	Web Mentor Web Resource Web Collaboration Web Survey Cooperative Challenge Social Action Simulation
Creative Expression	Keypals Simulation Web Publishing Multimedia
Problem-Solving	Web Collaboration Cooperative Challenge Social Action
Researching	Web Mentor Web Resource Web Survey

TABLE 2-2
Teaching Skills: Top Activity Types to Meet Your Goals

A WORD ABOUT ASSESSMENT

The latest educational research favors performance assessment over more traditional student tests and measurements. In performance assessment students demonstrate what they know by applying that knowledge in an exhibit, demonstration, video project, science project, etc. A Web project may be just the thing to draw on when looking for an appropriate performance assessment for your class.

The best performance assessments require:

- *You* to clearly outline criteria for success to students
- *Students* to demonstrate what they have learned in a real-life context

Finding a real-world application for the skills and knowledge gained in our schools is sometimes nearly impossible. But the Web can open up your options. The Web not only brings the world to your doorstep, it presents students with the opportunity to actively contribute to the real world. For example, students might collect data on migrating animals using many of the tools available through the Web, and then share their results with scientists and the larger community. So consider planning a Web project as performance assessment for your unit by looking for opportunities to approximate or simulate real-life applications of your students' knowledge using the Web.

TIP

Plan your Web project to benefit your local community. Write a press release about your project for your local paper or have an event that you can invite parents to. Donate the book you created cooperatively to your local library or senior center. The possibilities are endless.

When assessing a Web project, here are some common tips to keep in mind:

- Assess students for both their individual and group work. This will help promote interdependence.
- Have students peer-evaluate each other's performance using the criteria for success outlined at the beginning of the project.

- Have students self-evaluate their performance based on the criteria for success outlined in the beginning of the project.

- Include effective group work as a criterion for both their individual and group grade. (Be sure, however, to discuss and practice effective group work. See "Tips for Teaching Students to Work Well Together," Chapter 3.)

Finally, the Internet itself may be a major catalyst for changing the face of assessment. W. Ross Brewer and Bena Kallick[3] present a vision of assessment that, while it sounds futuristic, may be around the corner. Via the Web, parents, community members, and politicians may one day have access to digital reporting on a school's performance. The school's portfolio, if you will, might include digital examples of students' work or science fair projects shot in 3-D video views. Parents might log on to the school's Web site to access portfolios of their child's work—giving them frequent and current information about their child's progress. Teachers and administrators across districts and even states could collaborate on establishing consistent standards for assessment without attending countless hours of meetings. And likewise, districts could quickly compile reports on performance across schools.

While the need for many of these futuristic visions already exists, the execution may depend largely on widespread Internet access and school reform.

[3] See "Technology's Promise for Reporting Student Learning," by W. Ross Brew and Bena Kallick in the ASCD's *Yearbook, 1996*.

Implementing Your Curriculum

3

Chapter 3 includes plans, worksheets, and tips you need to begin implementing your Web curriculum. The guidelines and strategies in this chapter address the needs of both novices and experienced users. The chapter covers the following topics:

- ▶ First Steps First
- ▶ General Guidelines
- ▶ If You Are a Beginner
- ▶ If You've Already Tried a Few Projects
- ▶ If You Are an Advanced User
- ▶ A Framework for Success
- ▶ Administering Your Web Project
- ▶ Creating a Web Site
- ▶ Pulling It Together: Some Timely Tips from the Field
- ▶ When You Have Only One Computer
- ▶ Tips for Teaching Students to Work Well Together
- ▶ A Note Before You Go

FIRST STEPS FIRST

"Well begun is half done!" —Aristotle, *Politics*

You and your 4th graders have an idea for a Web project that sounds fun and educational. You've just begun a unit on whales and would like to simulate a year in the life of a whale, collaborating with classrooms along the humpback's migration route—from the breeding grounds of the Dominican Republic up the eastern seaboard to the feeding grounds of Maine. You've never done this project before, but everyone seems game. Where do you begin?

Well, that depends on whether or not you have ever done a Web project before. If you are new at using the Internet in your classroom, you will want to begin by laying the groundwork with a simple project, gradually moving on to more complex ones as you and your students gain valuable experience. The following Web Road Maps outline sequenced projects using the lesson plans from Part II of this book for the beginner, intermediate, and advanced user.

GENERAL GUIDELINES

The Big Twelve Activity Types presented in Chapter 2 generally build and draw on different skills. Progressively build skills by using the Big Twelve in the following way:

1. Teach basic skills and etiquette of using email with Keypals and Web Mentor activities.

2. Teach basic use of World Wide Web browsers and search engines with Web Resource activities.

3. Apply and practice the above skills with Web Collaboration, Web Survey, Cooperative Challenge, Social Action, Community Connection, and Simulation activities.

4. Learn advanced skills such as Web site and multimedia authoring through Web Publishing and Multimedia activities.

IF YOU ARE A BEGINNER

Begin by familiarizing your students with the basic tools of email, your Web browser, and search engines.

While you can construct activities at all levels for each of the Big Twelve, the following schema is one way to think about implementing your Internet curriculum.

	Beginner	Intermediate	Advanced
Keypals	•		
Web Mentor	•		
Web Resource		•	•
Web Collaboration		•	
Web Survey		•	
Cooperative Challenge		•	
Social Action		•	
Community Connection		•	
Simulation		•	•
Web Publishing		•	•
Multimedia			•
Student-Created Projects	•	•	•

TABLE 3-1
The Big Twelve Activity Types by Level

TIP

Teach the children the basics of email etiquette:

- Introduce yourself
- Check spelling and grammar
- Re-read for multiple interpretations
- Be polite

Pair students and have them practice writing introductions about themselves to later use as their first message to participants.

Beginner Web Road Map (K-6)	1. *Reflective Writing* (Chapter 5): Introduces the skills and etiquette for using email.
	2. *Letters from Felix* (Chapter 8) or *Weather Week* (Chapter 7): Applies the skills of email.
	3. *The Kids' Korner* (Chapter 5): Introduces and teaches navigation of the World Wide Web.
	4. *Lunches Around the World* (Chapter 8): Applies the skills of email and Web navigation. Teaches beginning Web searches.
	5. *A Global Service Project* (Chapter 8) or *Pass the Torch* (Chapter 5): Shows children the power of the Internet to create positive social change.

Beginner Web Road Map (7-12)	1. *Reflective Writing* (Chapter 5): Introduces skills and etiquette for using email.
	2. *A Bird in the Hand* (Chapter 7) or *The Gen(ie) in the Bottle* (Chapter 7): Applies the skills of email.
	3. *The Kids' Korner* (Chapter 5): Introduces and teaches navigation of the World Wide Web.
	4. *Find Your True Home* (Chapter 8) or *Navigating News* (Chapter 5): Applies the skills of Web navigation and teaches beginning Web searches.
	5. *A Global Service Project* (Chapter 8) or *Pass the Torch* (Chapter 5): Shows students the power of the Internet to create positive social change.

TIP

Searching the Web can be frustrating and time consuming for elementary students. Janice Friesen, a teacher at Russell Boulevard Elementary School in Columbia, Missouri, suggests you begin by providing students with a list of what they are looking for. Then prepare a list of URLs on index cards or directly on a Web page stored on your local computer for students to begin their search with. Include sites that have interesting links to other sites.

IF YOU'VE ALREADY TRIED A FEW PROJECTS

Continue applying the tools of email, your Web browser, and search engines to progressively more complex projects. Add Web Publishing, if you desire.

1. *Global Connections* (Chapter 8) or *Origami Outing* (Chapter 4): Students practice limited Web searches and collaborate with other students. 2. *The Animal Project* (Chapter 6): Students practice more open-ended Web searches and collaborate with other classrooms to raise awareness about a problem. 3. *Baking Bread* (Chapter 7) or *The Paper Chase* (Chapter 4): Students do extensive Web searches and collaborate with another classroom. 4. *A Whale's Tale* (Chapter 7): Students do extensive Web searches, collaborate with other classrooms, and simulate an event.	**Intermediate Web Road Map (K-6)**

1. *Great Expectations* (Chapter 5) or *Taking Stock* (Chapter 6): Students practice limited Web searches. 2. *Fantasy Hoops: Mathematics and the NBA* (Chapter 6) or *A Nation Torn in Two* (Chapter 8): Students practice limited Web searches and collaborate with other students. 3. *World War II History Textbooks Project* (Chapter 8) or *A Perspective on Bosnia* (Chapter 8): Students practice more open-ended Web searches and collaborate with other classrooms to raise awareness about a problem. 4. *U.S. Immigration* (Chapter 8) or *A Kids' Consumer Price Index* (Chapter 6): Students do extensive Web searches and collaborate with another classroom. 5. *PrimeTime* (Chapter 6): Students do extensive Web searches, survey other classrooms, and begin to use multimedia tools in the classroom only to present their data.	**Intermediate Web Road Map (7-12)**

IF YOU ARE AN ADVANCED USER

Explore more advanced Web site authoring and multimedia tools such as Pagemill, QuickTime, and MoviePlayer to tap students' creativity and develop technical skills. Begin with Web publishing and gradually move into multimedia tools.

Advanced Web Road Map (K-6)	1. *Things That Are Red: The World Wide Web Colors Book* (Chapter 4) or *A Thumbnail Quilt* (Chapter 4): Introduces basic paint programs and Web publishing.
	2. *Middlezine Magazine* (Chapter 5): More advanced Web publishing requiring ongoing updates.
	3. *What You Should Also Know* (Chapter 5) or *Listen to These Pictures* (Chapter 4): Introduces tools of QuickTime and MoviePlayer and the concept of multimedia.
	4. *And the Winner Is…* (Chapter 4): Applies the tools of QuickTime and MoviePlayer and publishing on a Web site.

Advanced Web Road Map (7-12)	1. *Family Project Center* (Chapter 8): Introduces Web publishing.
	2. *Our Village* (Chapter 8) or *The Homework Home Page* (Chapter 5): More advanced Web publishing requiring ongoing updates.
	3. *What You Should Also Know* (Chapter 5) or *Listen to These Pictures* (Chapter 4): Introduces the tools of QuickTime and MoviePlayer and the concept of multimedia.
	4. *A History Rap* (Chapter 4): Students apply the tools of QuickTime and MoviePlayer and publish on a Web site.

TIP

Partner elementary students with middle school students for these activities. Leave most of the technical aspects to the older students. The elementary students will develop familiarity with the concepts and readiness, all while having fun!

A FRAMEWORK FOR SUCCESS

Having identified a Web activity that reaps the unique benefits of the Web and meets your educational objectives is half the battle in designing a successful project. Now you need only plan out the details of your project to make your idea a success. Use the Web Project Implementation Plan (see Figure 3-1 later in this chapter) to outline the key elements in your project. You'll need to know:

1. Your educational goals
2. Who you would like to partner with*
3. Your partner(s)' role*
4. What your partner(s) will gain*
5. Where you will find partner(s)*
6. Project guidelines
7. Activity type
8. The project timeline
9. Resources (Web resources and others)

1. YOUR EDUCATIONAL GOALS

Clearly outline your educational objectives. How do these objectives link to your curriculum? Taking the time now to write out your goals will help you refine them and re-evaluate whether a Web project is the best way to meet your objectives. You'll also want to share these objectives with your partners (see "Administering Your Web Project").

Do a search on the Web for information on your topic before outlining the details of your project. You may find resources that will suggest a different twist or angle on your original idea.

2. WHO YOU WOULD LIKE TO PARTNER WITH

If you are planning on having partners in your project, you'll want to answer two questions:

- With whom specifically would you like to partner?
- How many partners would make for an effective project?

Does your Web project require partners? If so, who? The best Web collaborations are those where your partner is bringing a unique perspective not available to you at home. Does your partner need to live in a different latitude or hemisphere? Do you want someone from a particular country? Or a classroom from a community that might

---

* Necessary only if your project requires partner(s)

have a specialized economy (from a logging or fishing community, for example)? Perhaps you don't want to partner with a classroom at all. Maybe your students would like to interview jazz musicians or professionals who work in health care administration. You'll know you have a great idea for a Web project when you have very specific requirements for whom you would like to partner with.

TIP

Try to limit the number of participants in your project to the bare essentials. If you are doing a Web Survey for quantitative research, you will need a large enough sample to be statistically viable. (Upper high school students can practice statistics by doing the calculations!) If you are using Web Collaboration, you may find that you only need a few classrooms to meet your needs.

---

3. YOUR PARTNER(S)' ROLE

What do you expect from your partners? Are they full partners in the project (that is, will they be doing the same project you are, alongside you), or will they be used as a resource? What will they be required to contribute? Is there a culminating activity you can design that will be enhanced by your partner's participation? Be sure to construct a mutually beneficial relationship when partnering. What can you learn from one another? Outline your partner(s)' role and include this in your project guidelines (see "Project Guidelines").

4. WHAT YOUR PARTNER(S) WILL GAIN

Outline what your partner(s) will gain from participating in your project for later inclusion in your project's Call for Collaborators (for further information, see "A Call for Collaborators").

5. WHERE YOU WILL FIND PARTNER(S)

If your project relies on partner(s), you'll want to post a Call for Collaborators for your project on one or more of the sites outlined in the sidebar "Where to Find Web Projects and Participants."

The following Web sites feature project registries where classrooms can announce projects for which they seek participants. Use these sites to find Web projects to join or participants to join your project.

Where to Find Web Projects and Participants

- Intercultural Email Classroom Connections
  http://www.stolaf.edu/network/iecc/
- International Education and Resource Network
  http://www.iearn.org/iearn/
- Global SchoolNet Foundation
  http://www.gsn.org/gsn/gsn.projects.registry.html
- Hilites (also on Global SchoolNet Foundation)
  http://www.gsn.org/gsn/proj/hilites/index.html
- Electronic School House (ESH) on America Online
- GrassRoots on Canada's SchoolNet
  http://www.schoolnet.ca/grassroots
- Classroom Connect
  http://www.classroom.net

---

6. PROJECT GUIDELINES

Here you'll want to fill in all the details of how the project will unfold. What needs to happen? What are participants/students expected to do? What milestones will there be in the project? What handouts will you want to give your students?

7. ACTIVITY TYPE

Choose the appropriate type—Keypals, Web Mentor, Web Resource, Web Collaboration, Web Survey, Cooperative Challenge, Social Action, Community Connection, Simulation, Web Publishing, Multimedia, or Student-Created Projects.

8. PROJECT TIMELINE

Outline your project timeline, including the following:

- When your Call for Collaborators will go out (if you seek partners)
- Your project registration deadline (if you seek partners)
- Deadline for submissions (for any partners and your students)
- Target dates for major classroom lessons, etc.

9. RESOURCES

Finally, you'll want to consider all of the resources that you have available for your project. Generally ask: What resources might help your students better understand the subject matter? Then consider all of the possible resources, including:

- Your school library
- Your local library
- Your community (people, organizations, etc.)
- The Web

ADMINISTERING YOUR WEB PROJECT

There are several tricks of the trade for administering your Web project to maximize its educational impact while minimizing its drain on your time.

TIP

A mailing list is simply a list of people's email addresses that you can reach by sending email to only one address. For a comprehensive guide to setting up mailing lists, see *Managing Internet Information Services*, by Cricket Liu et al. (O'Reilly & Associates, Inc., 1994).

If you are partnering with others, good communication is key to the success of your project. To partner successfully you'll need the following:

- A Call for Collaborators
- A group mailing list of all participants (also known as a listserv)
- Form letters for all general communication: acknowledging registration, reminders of upcoming deadlines, thank-yous to participants, etc.
- Any necessary handouts, such as the project schedule or resources available online
- Help administering your project

Project Name: _____ ✔ _____

Project Description: _____ ✔ _____

Educational Goals: _____ 1 _____

Participants Wanted: _____ 2 _____
(target number/special requirements)

Addresses for Call for Collaborators: _____ 5 _____

Project Guidelines and Partner(s)' Roles: _____

Benefits to Participants: _____ 4 _____

Activity Type: _____ 7 _____

Project Timeline (include major deadlines): _____ 8 _____

Web Resources: _____ 9 _____
(if any)

Additional Resources: _____ 9 _____

Project Coordinator: _____ ✔ _____ Contact Info: _____ ✔ _____

FIGURE 3-1
Your Web Project Implementation Plan

A CALL FOR COLLABORATORS

Your Call for Collaborators is the first communication the world sees about your project. You want to be sure that the impression you make is good. And you want to be sure that those participants who would like to join you are able to meet the requirements of your project. To meet these goals, your Call for Collaborators (see Figure 3-2) should include:

- A brief description of your project
- An outline of the educational objectives of the project
- A project registration form
- Your project's timeline
- Details about whom you wish to partner with
- The project director's contact information

Figure 3-3 shows a sample Call for Collaborators for a humpback whale migration project.

NOTE: Some project registries have their own templates which you will need to use to post your project.

Project Name: _____ Date Posted: _____

Respond by: _____

Project Description: _____

Partners Wanted: _____

Objectives: _____

How Partners Will Benefit: _____

Project Timeline: _____

Requirements: _____

Project Coordinator: _____

Contact Information: _____

- -

PROJECT REGISTRATION FORM[1]

Teacher's Name: _____

School: _____

Subject(s) / Grade: _____

City, State, Country _____

Global Address: _____

(Latitude and Longitude—Degrees and Minutes)

Email Address: _____

Please include a short introductory paragraph about your students and their expectations for doing this project. (This information will be forwarded to the other participants.)

Send registration via email to the project coordinator:

FIGURE 3-2
Call for Collaborators Template

[1] From Cindy Cooper, teacher, Mt. Ulla and Hurley Elementary School, Mt. Ulla and Salisbury, North Carolina.

PROJECT NAME: A WHALE'S TALE   Date Posted: November 1
Respond by: December 15

PROJECT DESCRIPTION: Students will re-create a year in the life of a humpback whale named Hugh—including its migration from the breeding grounds of the Dominican Republic to the feeding grounds of Maine. Students begin by researching humpback whales in their area using various sources, including the Web. Each participant school will be assigned to research and write a virtual postcard describing a month in Hugh's life in their area. Their postcard must include:

- Where Hugh is (locally)
- What month it is
- What Hugh does daily
- Where Hugh is going to be next

The postcards will then be sent to all participants. Each classroom will then compile all the results in:

- A timeline to be posted in the classroom
- An illustrated storybook entitled "A Whale's Tale"

SUBJECT/GRADE LEVEL: 4-6 Science/English

PARTICIPANTS WANTED: Ten 4-6th grade classrooms along the Atlantic Ocean from the Dominican Republic to Maine

OBJECTIVES:

- Students will research the life of humpback whales locally.
- Students will learn about the life history traits of a humpback whale.
- Students will learn how to use the Web and other research tools.
- Students will learn how to create a timeline.
- Students will paint and draw whales.

HOW PARTNERS WILL BENEFIT:

Students along the Atlantic shore will learn about the life history traits of the humpback whale by pooling their knowledge. All partners will receive the information collected. All partners will be invited to create a timeline and illustrated storybook of their online adventure.

PROJECT TIMELINE:

January 1	Research begins
January 24	Hugh's postcards due to project coordinator
January 28	All partners receive set of Hugh's postcards
February 5	Timelines due
February 12	Storybooks due

REQUIREMENTS:

All participants must:

- Research the life of humpback whales in their area (what time of year are whales in their area? What do they do in their area, etc.? What are their challenges?)
- Submit one postcard from Hugh to the project coordinator outlining what is happening in Hugh's life at a designated time
- Create a timeline of Hugh's life (optional, but recommended)
- Create an illustrated storybook of Hugh's life entitled "A Whale's Tale" (optional, but recommended)

PROJECT COORDINATOR: Earl R. Parker, 4th grade teacher, Rockmeadow Elementary School, *Parker@jo-earl.elementary.k12.us*

FIGURE 3-3   *A Whale's Tale Call for Collaborators*

CREATING A WEB SITE

If you think you would like to create a Web site for either an Internet project or your larger school community, here are some steps you can take to ensure a successful process. Your plan may be simple or complex, depending on the purposes you are intending to meet.

STEP 1: RESEARCH OTHER SCHOOL SITES

Look at other school sites and project sites as a model for your site. What works? What doesn't work? If you find a site you particularly like, ask their Webmaster if they have any advice about building a similar site. You can find a directory of other schools with Web sites at Web66 (*http://web66.coled.umn.edu/schools.html*) and at Classroom Connect's ClassroomWeb (*http://www.classroom.net/classweb/*).

TIP

Turn this task into a classroom project. Have students research and save (or print) a wide variety of school sites as a beginning Web Research task. Require students to include an outline of each site, the purpose of the site, and any other interesting details in a written school site profile. Then create criteria and evaluate each site as a class.

STEP 2: INVOLVE OTHERS

Even if you are only planning to post a simple page for a classroom project, it goes without saying that it is always wise to involve your school's administration. Web sites are public venues and therefore need the consideration of those individuals invested with the responsibility for your school's public image. Create a small task force of key administrators, faculty, and students that meets at least once to address any larger implications and to review your site's content and message. Outline with the group what their involvment will be.

TIP

Involve a small group of students early in the process of developing your site. Start a Web site club! You'll have an informed and committed group of students to support your ongoing efforts.

STEP 3: CLARIFY YOUR PURPOSE

With your task force, clarify the purpose of your site. Will your site serve the needs of this project only? Are there larger school or community needs that might also be addressed by this site?

Keep it simple! Your first site probably won't be able to meet all of the purposes you would like it to. Remember that you can always add to your site as time goes on. Do a thorough needs assessment and then prioritize those needs. Start by serving the most important goal first.

STEP 4: IDENTIFY NECESSARY RESOURCES

With your task force, identify any necessary resources that you might need to achieve your goals. What key support will you need? What software or hardware do you need? Is a financial investment necessary? If so, where will the money come from? How will time resources be allocated for a) creating the site, b) maintaining the site, and c) troubleshooting and responding to problems?

A local business may be willing to sponsor your Web site, either through a financial gift or by providing help in actually developing the site. Look for businesses that already have Web sites. They may have the internal resources to create and maintain your site.

STEP 5: PLAN YOUR SITE IN STAGES

Outline the content of your site. Create what's called a hierarchical Web, outlining the pages that will be included and how they will be linked. Create a multistaged plan for building your site.

Since you can add to your site as you go, it's important to start building your site with the most important information first. Focus your attention on text only, adding graphics after you have served your original objective.

TIP

Unless you have great resources for maintaining your site, you'll want to stay away from including time-sensitive information that would require constant updating. Start with broader missions, descriptions of programs, etc., and add more time-sensitive information once it is clear that you will have some support.

STEP 6: KEEP THE DESIGN SIMPLE AND CONSISTENT

Unless you are a graphic designer, the rule of thumb for your Web site is: the simpler, the better. While you might be tempted to create an elaborate home page, it's best to think of your home page as a table of contents, rather than the cover to a book. Unlike a book cover, your home page's purpose is not to catch attention as much as to help viewers ascertain whether or not this site will include something they are interested in. Outline the contents of your site as clearly as possible. Then add a few simple graphical elements to make your home page interesting.

You'll also want to include the same features on each page that show how to use your site: include a way to navigate home and to mail a message to the Webmaster. Memory-hogging audio and video files should be used sparingly, if at all.

STEP 7: TEST YOUR SITE

It's okay to make your site public before it is ready. It's preferred, in fact. Keep a prototype of your Web site on another computer, moving pages as they become finished. Give your site's address to a small cadre of people whose opinions you trust your address and ask for feedback. Then modify as necessary. Chances are you'll want to make changes to the site after a few months of use.

TIP

Include a feedback mechanism for users to give you their reactions right on your Web site. Keep a file of the feedback to peruse on your next scheduled update of the site.

STEP 8: ADVERTISE YOUR SITE

Have students create a poster campaign for your site around your school and community. Then register your site through Web66 (*http://web66.coled.umn.edu/schools.html*), The PostMaster (*http://www.netcreations.com/postmaster/registration/try.html*), and Submit It! (*http://www.submit-it.com/*).

A WORD ABOUT COPYRIGHT LAW AND FAIR USE

Keeping It Legal: Questions Arising Out of Web Management
http://www.pacificrim.net/~mckenzie/jun96/legal.html

This article appears in From Now On, an online publication by educator Jamie McKenzie.

Whether you and your students are publishing a Web site or using information you found online, you'll want to read Jamie McKenzie's article to know your school's legal responsibilities and to teach your students good habits.

PULLING IT ALL TOGETHER: SOME TIMELY TIPS FROM THE FIELD

These tips were adapted with permission from a list provided by Sharon Hayes, a teacher at Capay Joint Union Elementary School in Orland, California.

Before the project:

- Bounce ideas off a friend or colleague. Then test-run a modified mini-version of your project with your colleague.
- Plan your project with ample time. Don't make it hard on yourself and others by setting unrealistic deadlines.
- Avoid planning a project for the beginning or end of the year or the end of semesters when everyone is too busy with other demands.
- Send out reminder notices to all participants one month prior, and then again two weeks prior, to your project launch. In your last reminder, ask for confirmation of participation. Some teachers may no longer be able to join your project.
- Decide in advance how you will compile information, using forms or databases, for example. Consider your options.
- Be prepared to answer lots of mail. It is best to prepare form letters for various purposes (to respond to registrants, to turn down registrants, to post responses, to remind registrants of upcoming

deadlines, etc.). Set up a schema for how you will sort and retrieve email quickly. Involve students in this task, if possible.

During the project:

- Put up and mark a map to show students the places that have responded to your project.
- Have students introduce themselves to each other via a short email message in the early stages of the project. This will help generate enthusiasm.
- Check your mail daily and post responses immediately.

After the project:

- Have students formally thank all the participants.
- Assess the project: What went right? What needs improvement? Keep notes for the next time.
- Be willing to share what you have learned—both with your colleagues and others participating in the project.

For additional advice from the field, see *NetLearning: Why Teachers Use the Internet*, by Ferdi Serim and Melissa Koch, published by Songline Studios and O'Reilly & Associates, 1996.

WHEN YOU HAVE ONLY ONE COMPUTER

Many of the projects outlined in Part II of this book can be done in classrooms that have access to only one computer. There are a few tricks, however, that can really maximize your use of this precious resource:

- Schedule students to work in pairs at the computer in 20-minute intervals. While one pair is working at the computer, have other students research using other resources, such as books, periodicals, etc.
- Create a folder on your computer's desktop for the daily email related to the project. Schedule a student each day to read and respond to your project's email.
- Download important Web pages for later use when the site you are calling is busy or your server is slow. You can open them in Netscape (or most any browser) and continue to work.

- Use a projector compatible with your computer so you can demonstrate Web navigation and searches to your entire class at once.

TIPS FOR TEACHING STUDENTS TO WORK WELL TOGETHER

Most well-designed Web projects require students to work together collaboratively. But successful cooperative learning does not come from simply combining students in a group to work on a task. Help students learn to work more effectively together—in the classroom and online.[2]

- Establish specific criteria for group success and outline clearly.

- Assign group tasks so that everyone has a role. This will help distribute the responsibilities in the group.

- Promote interdependence in your project by structuring it to depend on each part of the group's resources.

- Give each member of the group two grades: one for the group's work and one for individual work. It is critical that students have both individual and group accountability to be fully invested in cooperation.

- Help students learn active listening and other social skills. Design activities that require students to listen to one another without interruption and then practice paraphrasing back what was heard.

- Facilitate groups by circulating and intervening with suggestions or questions that correct unproductive group processes.

- Have students establish their own ground rules for group work. How do they think they would most effectively work together?

- When younger students have difficulty waiting their turn to speak, employ a talking stick. Have students pass a stick around their group. It is a student's turn to talk when he or she has the talking stick. (Online, you can create a virtual talking stick. Establish an order for how students will communicate. Make sure that everyone gets a turn to respond.)

- Get input from the entire group on an issue before making a decision or discussing a topic. Go around the group and let each

---

[2] For more excellent ideas on helping students to work together, see *Designing Group Work: Strategies for the Heterogeneous Classroom*, by Elizabeth G. Cohen. Available from ESR at 800-370-2515.

person voice his or her thoughts. Group members must listen carefully and not respond. Repeat until the group is ready to put the issue to an open discussion or vote.

- When planning for a group presentation, divide students into groups addressing one topic or question. Then form new groups consisting of a representative from each original group. Each person in this new group must now do a presentation for the other group members (who can peer-evaluate the performance based on established criteria). This will help to minimize one student doing most of the work for a group presentation.

- When one student is dominating a group, give each student a certain number of chits to "spend." For each time they contribute to the group, each student must put a chit in a hat in the center of the group's circle. Each student must use all of their chits.

- Be sure to have groups self-evaluate. What has worked well in achieving their goals? What has not?

A NOTE BEFORE YOU GO

Take what is offered here and make it your own. Only you can know what will work best for *your* students. When it comes to the Web, the only limitation is your imagination (and, perhaps, the speed of your connection!).

A quick message flies from a server in Japan, bounces off a satellite, and seconds later pops onto a screen in your school. The world for just a moment is a bit smaller, its resources more precious. Our commonality as humans begins to sharpen. And the call for a student's participation is a hint more palpable.

All the great thinkers who have shaped our common wisdom about education point to the importance of community in preparing students to enter the world. Nowhere is this community-building more important than in your classroom. Whatever the potentials of the Web, it all comes back to good old basics. Knit the fabric of your classroom first. Create a sense of connection and respect at home. The old maxim holds: Think globally. But act locally.

Best of luck on your adventure![3]

---

[3] Let us know how it goes! If you have lesson plans you created that you'd like to share with others or changes to make to those contained here, drop in to see us at the Net Lessons page on *http://www.bedrockbarn.com*.

Part II

From Theory

to

Practice

Art and Music

ORIGAMI OUTING

Students collaborate with Japanese students to learn the art of origami.

OBJECTIVES

- U.S. students learn the art of origami.
- Japanese students practice English.
- Students practice cooperation and communication skills across cultures.

PREREQUISITES

None

PROCEDURE

1. Solicit one class of ESL Japanese students (secondary school age) by posting a Call for Collaborators on an international project center such as I*EARN at *http://www.iearn.org/iearn/*. (Note: Japanese partners will benefit by practicing English with a native speaker.)

2. Pair students or groups of students with Japanese student mentors.

3. Introduce students to the art of origami by showing a few pictures or bringing in a sample.

4. Have students in small groups brainstorm questions about origami for their Japanese mentors. Give examples of possible questions: When did people begin practicing origami in Japan? How has origami evolved? How do people in Japan learn origami?

5. Schedule computer time for students to research the significance of origami in the Japanese culture with their mentors via email.

6. Ask Japanese partners to develop and send via email or postal service written instructions on the art of origami, including diagrams developed in a graphics/paint program or hand-drawn. (If sending via electronic mail, partners will need to save or convert their graphic files to GIF or JPEG and email files to project coordinator. See the graphics format page at *http://VTGinc.com/ebennett/xplat.graph.htm/* for conversion tools.)

7. Children create origami. (Younger children will need your assistance.)

8. Photograph the children and their work. Have students create a collage with the photos, including their names. Via mail, exchange collages with partner classrooms.

Subject:
Art, Language Arts, Social Studies, Conflict Resolution

Grade level:
Grades 4-8

Activity type:
Web Mentor

Activity level:
Beginner

Time frame:
4 weeks

Partners:
1 Japanese student per student in your class.

Materials Needed

- One computer with email access
- Graphics/paint program (Japanese partners only)
- Construction or origami paper
- Scissors

ORIGAMI OUTING

9. Discuss with students: Was it difficult to communicate with your partner? Why? What differences came up between you and your partner? How did you handle those differences? What would you do differently next time?

10. Optional: Create a class mobile featuring the students' origami. Send the mobile to the Japanese partner classroom as a thank-you present.

TIMELINE

Week 1   Post Call for Collaborators soliciting participants.

Weeks 2-3   Partners email background and instructions on the art of origami.

Week 4   Classrooms photograph projects and mail to partner classroom.

LANGUAGE ARTS EXTENSION

Have students create booklets on the art of origami, complete with diagrams and illustrations. Have students solicit quotes and photos of their origami from Japanese students to include.

TIP   Joseph Wu's Origami Page (*http://www.datt.co.jp/origami/*) is an award-winning site featuring everything you'd ever want to know about origami. Creator Joseph Wu gives great background on the art, folding instructions, and links to other origami sites, and features photographs of awe-inspiring examples of this art form.

THE PAPER CHASE

Students research how paper is made, communicate with a classroom from a logging community to learn more about the industry, and then make paper!

OBJECTIVES

- Students learn about the process of paper manufacturing.
- Students practice communication skills.
- Students develop Web research skills.
- Students learn about logging.

PREREQUISITES

None

PROCEDURE

1. Ask: Where does paper come from? How is it made? Help students research this question using the Web and other library resources. The Forest Products Page (*http://www.athenet.net/%7Ejlindsay/Paper.shtml*) is a good beginning source for researching paper and papermaking.

2. Post a Call for Collaborators on the Web looking for a partner classroom from a paper mill and logging community. (This may be two different communities.)

3. Have students in pairs generate a list of questions for the partner class-room about the paper milling process and the industry in general. What challenges does the paper industry face? What are the issues? What seems to be working and not working?

4. Email questions to your partner class for response. Allow two weeks for their response. (They can research the answers by interviewing local loggers or local people who work in paper mills.)

5. Facilitate a discussion: Who other than the paper industry is affected by the paper industry's actions? How? What do you think should be done? Remind students that there are always at least two sides to an issue. Post any remaining questions/thoughts to the partner classroom for a response. Continue to facilitate the process as the questions deepen and the issue becomes more complex.

6. Have students make paper!

Subject:
Art, Science, Social Studies, Mathematics

Grade level:
Grades 3-8

Activity type:
Simulation

Activity level:
Intermediate

Time frame:
6 weeks

Partners:
1-2 classrooms

Materials Needed

- One computer with email/Web access

For papermaking (may vary depending on paper recipe):

- Waste paper (non-waxed or non-plasticized paper)
- 5-gallon pail with lid
- Screen and deckle (from craft shops and suppliers)
- Blender
- Shallow oblong container
- Smooth, reusable kitchen cloths (J-cloths)
- 2 pressing boards
- Old reusable towels
- Couching board (from craft shops and suppliers)

THE PAPER CHASE

TIMELINE

Weeks 1-2   Research paper origin and post Call for Collaborators.

Weeks 3-4   Prepare questions for partners and post.

Weeks 5-6   Partners respond.

MATH EXTENSION

Have your students research and calculate the effect of the Web on the paper industry. Has the Internet cut down on printing? If so, by what percentage? What are the expectations for its effect over time? How many trees will this save? What other effects of the Web can you calculate? (A related matter to also research involves the effects of recycling on the paper industry.)

TIP   What local industry can your students offer to research for your partner classroom in exchange for their help? Be creative!

PASSPORT TO ART

Students travel virtually to the Louvre in Paris and the Sistine Chapel in Rome, comparing high and low Renaissance periods in Italian art.

OBJECTIVES

- Students develop art criticism skills.
- Students learn what characterizes the high and low Renaissance art periods.
- Students write and edit papers.

PREREQUISITES

None

PROCEDURE

1. Pair students as "traveling buddies" for their virtual art tour.
2. Schedule students at the computer in 20-minute intervals for their art tours.
3. Assign students to visit both the Louvre in Paris (*http://mistral.culture.fr/louvre/*) and the Sistine Chapel in Rome (*http://sgwww.epfl.ch/BERGER/Sandro/33sixtine_english.html*). Have student pairs search the Louvre for an Italian high Renaissance painting of their choice to compare and contrast to a low Renaissance painting from the Sistine Chapel. What differences, if any, do they see in style? In content? What characteristics do the paintings have in common? Have each student take his or her own notes on the paintings visited.
4. Using the Web and other library sources, have students research background information about their selected paintings, artists, and Renaissance history.
5. Assign students to write a critical analysis comparing/contrasting the two periods.
6. Have students submit and peer-edit critical papers.
7. Schedule 5-minute conferences with each student to give feedback on their papers. Assign second draft.
8. Optional: Using a projector compatible with your computer, have student pairs present their paintings to the class. Have students compare/contrast the paintings presented. Discuss.

FOR YOUNGER STUDENTS

Adapt this project for elementary students by providing students with an "itinerary," listing paintings and sculptures they will visit, with space for students to write something they liked about each painting. Have students

Subject:
Art, Language Arts, Foreign Languages

Grade level:
Grades 7-12

Activity type:
Web Simulation

Activity level:
Intermediate

Time frame:
2 weeks

Partners:
None

Materials Needed

- One computer with email/Web access (one computer per several students is preferable)

WebMuseum
http://sunsite.nus.edu.wm/

An excellent Web site organized by museum and including hundreds of slides and links to other online museums.

PASSPORT TO ART

Jacques-Edouard Berger's Sandro Botticelli Page
http://sgwww.epfl.ch/ BERGER/Sandro/ 1frontispice_english.html

This is an excellent site for background information on Botticelli.

make a passport out of construction paper that you stamp as they visit each piece of artwork.

TIMELINE

Week 1   Take the virtual art tour and research periods.

Week 2   Write critical papers.

TAKE YOUR TRIP WITH THE FRENCH CLASS

Don't leave anyone behind on this virtual field trip. Plan a trip to Paris and explore cafes, monuments, shops, etc.—all while practicing French. See WebMuseum, Paris (*http://sunsite.unc.edu/wm/paris*) for virtual tours.

Graphic idea: Have a passport stamped with "Louvre" and "Sistine Chapel."

THINGS THAT ARE RED:
THE WORLD WIDE WEB COLORS BOOK

Kindergarten and 1st grade students partner with older students using computer technology to create a Web-published picture about their home town.

OBJECTIVES

- Students learn colors and color names.

- Students are introduced to computer technology as a tool to create, compose, communicate, and publish.

- Students practice writing.

PREREQUISITES

None

PROCEDURE

1. Post a Call for Collaborators soliciting partnership with other schools that have cross-age tutors available.

2. Pair kindergarten/1st grade students with older cross-age tutors from your school or district.

3. With tutors' help, have students draw pictures on the computer representing their home town. Ask: What are the features of your area that are unique? What time of year does your picture show?

Subject:
Art, Language Arts, Computer Technology

Grade level:
Grades K-6

Activity type:
Web Publishing

Activity level:
Advanced

Time frame:
10 weeks

Partners:
Unlimited

Materials Needed

- One computer with email/Web access

- Graphics/paint software program

- Internet Service Provider that offers space on their Web server

John Patten

From an activity by John Patten, teacher, Abraham Lincoln Elementary School, San Bernardino, California.

THINGS THAT ARE RED: THE WORLD WIDE WEB COLORS BOOK

The Macintosh Internet Server Cookbook
http://web66.coled.umn.edu/ Cookbook/MacContents. html

This site contains tools and complete instructions for creating your own Web site.

Tutors help students:

   a) Use graphic/paint program to draw a picture

   b) Write a one-line description of their picture and the colors included

4. Participating classrooms then save or convert their graphic files to GIF or JPEG and email files to project coordinator. (See the graphics format page at *http://VTGinc.com/ebennett/xplat.graph.html* for conversion tools.) Be aware: Depending on your Internet Service Provider, you might need to BinHex your file before attaching it to your email. Tools to BinHex your file are available at *http://helpdesk.uvic.ca/how-to/support/mac/ hqx.html*.

5. The project coordinator's classroom then creates and publishes the drawings to a Web site. (Don't be intimidated. Creating a simple Web site has become very easy to do—even for the beginner.)

TIMELINE

Week 1   Post Call for Collaborators soliciting participants.

Weeks 2-3 Email procedures to all registered schools.

Weeks 4-8 Schools respond.

Week 9-10 Create Web site and publish your World Wide Web Colors Book.

TIP   Choose student tutors who could benefit from additional practice in communicating and writing for this project. While they may be intimidated at first by the project, you'll find that with some group training and experience helping the 1st graders, the older students will become pros.

A THUMBNAIL QUILT

Students create a digital quilt with squares representing all fifty states and publish on a Web site.

OBJECTIVES

- Students learn how to draw or paint using paint software.
- Students research the history of their home state.
- Students learn about the history of all 50 states.

PREREQUISITES

Ability to digitize artwork

PROCEDURE

1. Post a Call for Collaborators soliciting partner classrooms (one from every state in the U.S.).
2. Have students in small groups research their state's history using library and Web resources. (Schedule students in 15-minute intervals at the computer for researching.)
3. Have each small group write a report and present their findings to the group. Discuss the unique aspects of your state. What is most interesting about your state? What are some possible symbols for your state?
4. Have each student draw or paint their own quilt square on paper (if you have a scanner) or onscreen using a paint software program (scheduling students in 20-minute intervals). See the following math extension for some helpful size parameters for the students' squares. Digitize any artwork created on paper by scanning it.
5. Have student pairs share and discuss their square and report.
6. As a class, create criteria for selecting a square to represent your state. Using the developed criteria, vote on the square and written history report that students would like to represent their state. (Or simply randomly choose one square.)
7. Partners then submit their graphic files to the originating classroom. (Note: Everyone will need to convert graphic files to GIF or JPEG.)
8. Publish all 50 quilt squares to the Web as thumbnails. (See "Creating a Web Site," Chapter 3, for more information.) Hyperlink the thumbnails to the larger original and to the text files of the state's history.

TIMELINE

Week 1	Post message for partners.
Week 2	Have students research their state.
Week 3	Students write reports and present to class.

Subject:
Art, History, Mathematics

Grade level:
Grades 5-12

Activity type:
Multimedia

Activity level:
Advanced

Time frame:
7 weeks

Partners:
50 classrooms (1 each for all 50 states)

Materials Needed

- One computer with email/Web access
- Scanner (optional)
- Graphics/paint software

A THUMBNAIL QUILT

Week 4   Students create their quilting squares.

Week 5   Students develop criteria and select a representative square.

Weeks 6-7 Publish to Web site.

MATH EXTENSION

Involve students in a "real world" math problem that graphic designers and Webmasters face daily. Post the challenge this way: You'll want the image to be no larger than 460 width by 345 height in pixels, with an aspect ratio of 4:3. In order to accommodate all 50 states at the same size, what size would the individual thumbnails of the states be?

TIP   Before you hyperlink the squares to the text, hold a contest and have students try to guess the state from nothing more than its quilt square. The school that accurately guesses the most states wins!

A HISTORY RAP

Using MIDI files available on the Web, students write and produce a rap tune outlining major events in U.S. history.

OBJECTIVES

- Students review U.S. history.
- Students manipulate MIDI files to create an original musical composition.
- Students write a history rap.

PREREQUISITES

Some familiarity with QuickTime and MoviePlayer. See "Multimedia Tools," Chapter 2.

PROCEDURE

1. Introduce the tools of QuickTime 2.5 and MoviePlayer to students through the tutorials. Explain the assignment.

2. Schedule students in 25-minute intervals to find and download a MIDI file from the Web that can be adapted to a rap tune.

3. Have students schedule their own time at the computer for customizing the MIDI file using MoviePlayer as their rap's rhythm track (i.e., masking the melody track, etc.).

4. Students each write an original rap tune outlining major events in U.S. history from the pilgrims' landing through World War II. They must include dates of major events and names of important historical figures.

5. Students schedule time to use the microphone to record their rap as a new track in the MoviePlayer file.

6. Optional: Publish as a QuickTime file on a Web site. (See "Creating a Web Site," Chapter 3, for more information.)

A WORD ABOUT COPYRIGHT

It is important to stress with students that most published material on the Web is copyright protected. Teach students the importance of not infringing on copyright. Once they have located a desirable sound clip, have students formally request permission to use it for educational purposes. Be sure to specify if you intend to use the final results in your own Web site.

TIMELINE

Week 1	Introduce or review tools.
Week 2	Find MIDI files on Web.
Weeks 3-4	Manipulate MIDI files to customize as a rhythm track.

Subject:
Music, History, Computer Technology

Grade level:
Grades 7-12

Activity type:
Multimedia

Activity level:
Advanced

Time frame:
8 weeks

Partners:
None

Materials Needed

- One computer per three students with email/Web access and built-in microphone
- QuickTime 2.5 and MoviePlayer

A HISTORY RAP

Weeks 5-6 Write history rap.

Weeks 7-8 Record rap.

TIP For a different twist or to link with your curriculum, plan a special focus for a history rap. Create a rap around women's or African-American history, or choose one event to write different raps from different perspectives (for example: a northerner's and southerner's view of the Civil War). Involve students in choosing the focus.

LISTEN TO THESE PICTURES

Using audio or MIDI files available on the Web, students put a soundtrack to still pictures.

OBJECTIVES

- Students are introduced to the tools of multimedia.
- Students manipulate audio and graphics files to create an original expression.
- Students "score" a series of pictures.

PREREQUISITES

Some familiarity with QuickTime, MoviePlayer, and Apple Interactive Music Toolkit. (For a tutorial and tools, see Bedrock Barn's homepage at *http://www.bedrockbarn.com/pages/tools.htm* and following sites: *http://www.quicktime.apple.com/* and *http://www.amp.apple.com/imt/*.)

PROCEDURE

Note: Integrate this lesson plan by pairing your music class with another discipline.

1. Pair students for this project across disciplines. For younger children, arrange for cross-age tutors to serve as technical assistants. (See "Multimedia Tools," Chapter 2, for more information about using multimedia in the classroom.)

2. Explain the assignment: Student pairs will create a scored movie montage that links to a topic they have been studying in class this year. It can be any topic, provided that the movie montage is an artistic expression of the topic.

3. Introduce the tools of QuickTime, MoviePlayer, and Apple Interactive Music Toolkit to students, using the tutorial found at *http://www.bedrockbarn.com/pages/tutorial.htm*.

4. Schedule students in 25-minute intervals to find and download a MIDI or audio file and pictures from the Web. (Some interesting sites that students can start with include *http://www.bedrockbarn.com/pages/samples.htm* and *http://www.quicktime.apple.com/sam/*). Have students convert any MIDI files to QuickTime movies using MoviePlayer.

5. Have students schedule their own time at the computer for integrating music and pictures using Apple Interactive Music Toolkit (i.e., reordering pictures, trying different music files, etc.).

Subject:
Music, (All)

Grade level:
Grades 3-12

Activity type:
Multimedia, Web Resource

Time frame:
8 weeks

Partners:
None

Materials Needed

- At least one computer with email/Web access (more is preferred)
- QuickTime, MoviePlayer, and Apple Interactive Music Toolkit

From Douglas Parker Roerden, multimedia producer, Bedrock Barn Productions, Boston, Massachusetts.

LISTEN TO THESE PICTURES

6. Hold a film festival in class! Have student pairs present their movies 3. Then have the class respond in journals, completing the statement: "The movie montage contributed to my understanding of [*topic*] by . . ."

7. Optional: Publish as a QuickTime file to a Web site. (See *http://www.bedrockbarn.com/pages/web.htm*, *http://www.quicktime.apple.com/dev/devweb.html*, and "Creating a Web Site" in Chapter 3 for more information.)

TIMELINE

Weeks 1–2 Introduce or review tools.

Weeks 3–4 Find audio and graphics files on the Web.

Weeks 5–6 Order the graphics in a series.

Weeks 7–8 Add the music track.

AND THE WINNER IS. . .

Students around the world select and score films downloaded from the Web, which are then published to a Web site and judged in an international virtual Academy Awards.

OBJECTIVES

Students explore the role of music in film.

Students learn about other cultures.

PREREQUISITES

What You Should Also Know (Chapter 5)

Listen to These Pictures (Chapter 4)

Some familiarity with QuickTime, MoviePlayer, and Apple Interactive Music Toolkit. (For a tutorial and tools, see Bedrock Barn's homepage at *http://www.bedrockbarn.com/pages/tools.htm* and the following sites: *http://www.quicktime.apple.com/* and *http://www.amp.apple.com/imt/*.)

PROCEDURE

1. Post a Call for Collaborators soliciting partner classrooms around the world.

2. Pair students for this project. For younger children, arrange for cross-age tutors to serve as technical assistants. (See "Multimedia Tools," Chapter 3, for more information about using multimedia in the classroom.)

3. Review the tools of QuickTime, MoviePlayer, and Apple Interactive Music Toolkit to students, using the tutorial found at *http://www.bedrockbarn.com/pages/tutorial.htm*. Explain the assignment.

4. Schedule students in 25-minute intervals to find and download QuickTime movies from the Web that they will later score. (Some interesting sites students can start with include *http://www.bedrockbarn.com/pages/samples.htm* and *http://www.quicktime.apple.com/sam/*.)

5. Schedule students in 25-minute intervals at the computer to find appropriate music to score the movie.

6. Have students sign up for computer time to score their film using Apple Interactive Music Toolkit.

7. Partner classrooms submit their films to the originating classroom.

8. Publish as QuickTime files to an "Academy Award" Web site. (See "Creating a Web Site," Chapter 3, for more information.)

9. Have students as a class create criteria for judging the films and their scores. What categories do they want to give "Best" awards for? Create

Subject:
Music, Language Arts

Grade level:
Grades 3-12

Activity type:
Multimedia

Activity level:
Advanced

Time frame:
8 weeks

Partners:
Unlimited

Materials Needed

- One computer with Web access (more is preferred)
- QuickTime, MoviePlayer, and Apple Interactive Music Toolkit

AND THE WINNER IS. . .

an online ballot for students to fill out. Each student (including partners) receives one vote for each category.

10. Have partner classrooms submit their ballots to the originating classroom.

11. Have students tabulate the results.

12. Hold a virtual Academy Award ceremony and announce the winners!

FOR YOUNGER STUDENTS

MoviePlayer is so easy to use, even elementary students can enjoy this assignment. Supply younger students with 3-5 video clips (animated cartoons work well) and 3-5 soundtracks from which to choose. Allow them to try a few different combinations for scores. Which do they like best? How are they different? Which one is most serious? Which one is silliest?

TIMELINE

Week 1	Introduce or review tools.
Week 2	Find video files on Web.
Week 3	Choose music for score.
Weeks 4-5	Score film.
Weeks 6-7	Hold Academy Award judging.
Week 8	Announce winners.

ENGLISH EXTENSION

Have middle and high school students film their own movies to score. Tie the assignment to a text you are reading. Have students create a film adaptation of a scene from the book. With partners, collect all the clips in a Web "video library." As students read texts they can peruse the library for other students' film interpretations.

Language Arts

5

ONCE UPON A TIME. . .

Students from different locations create a story together highlighting local characteristics such as animals, historical characters, or weather.

OBJECTIVES

- Students learn about some aspect of life in another location.
- Students work on reading and writing skills and learn the elements of creating a story.
- Students work cooperatively with students in other locations and with students of other ages.

PREREQUISITES

None

PROCEDURE

1. Post a Call for Collaborators soliciting partners for the project. Indicate any differences in regional characteristics, such as urban/rural, plains/mountain/desert, or warm/cold climate, that you would like to highlight. Ask the responding teacher(s) to describe some of the characteristics of their region.

Subject:
English, Art

Grade level:
Grades K-12

Activity type:
Cooperative Challenge

Activity level:
Beginner

Time frame:
Ongoing

Partners:
2 classrooms

Materials Needed

- One computer with email access

Sue and William Miller

From an activity by Sue Miller, technology specialist, Lexington High School., Lexington, Massachusetts.

ONCE UPON A TIME...

2. Match each student with a "writing buddy" from another location who will collaborate on the story.

3. Each student writes the beginning of a story. Younger students can work with older helpers on storywriting and keyboarding.

4. Save the results in one file and mail to the collaborating teacher(s). That teacher should pass on each story introduction to a student.

5. Each student in the partner school writes the next part of the story, adding in local characteristics.

6. The teacher emails back these parts of the story.

7. Students take this part of the story and add another section to it.

8. This exchange continues until the story is completed. Younger students might write 2-3 parts with 2-3 sentences for each part. Older students might write several pages.

9. When the stories are completed, print them and have each student read aloud the story he or she wrote with the "writing buddy."

TIMELINE

Week 1   Post Call for Collaborators soliciting partner schools.

Week 2   Email procedures to all registered schools.
Have students begin writing story introductions.

Weeks 3-5   Exchange story parts with participating classes.

Week 6   Prepare final stories and have students read them aloud.

ART EXTENSION

Students can use the computer to draw or copy pictures to add to their stories.

TIP   Stage a play featuring highlights from cooperatively written stories and invite parents. Take photos at the play, then make double prints. Create an album for your classroom featuring both the stories and the photos. Share the extra prints with your partner classroom.

THE KID'S KORNER

Students partner with other students around the world to write reviews of children's Web sites.

OBJECTIVES

- Students write and edit.
- Students are introduced to computer technology as a tool to create, compose, communicate, and publish.
- Students learn about the resources available on the Web.

PREREQUISITES

None

PROCEDURE

1. In small groups at the computer, work with students to teach the basics of navigating the Web. As an example, do a basic search on children's Web sites. Or if you have a computer-compatible projector, review Web navigation with the entire class.

2. Together with small groups, visit a few sites you have preselected. Explain the basics of using your browser to navigate the Web. Answer children's questions.

3. Post a Call for Collaborators soliciting partner classrooms and students to review Web sites.

4. Hold a brief discussion: What makes a Web site good or bad? As a class, develop a list of criteria to use in judging the Web sites. (This will vary in sophistication with the age of the children.)

5. Schedule children in 15-minute intervals at the computer with your supervision to visit sites for review. Discuss the contents of the sites with the children as they navigate. Ask: Is the site easy to use? Is it interesting? If yes, why? How could it be improved? Have children make notes addressing the criteria they have previously listed.

6. Assign children to write reviews of 3 selected sites each. The reviews must include:

   - A brief description of the contents of the site
   - An evaluation of the site (based on the criteria)

7. Exchange reviews with partner classrooms.

8. With your supervision, have the children visit interesting-sounding sites from the partner classrooms' reviews. Do they agree with the reviews?

From an activity by Sue Miller, technology specialist, Lexington High School, Lexington, Massachusetts.

Subject:
Language Arts, Computer Technology

Grade level:
Grades 3-6

Activity type:
Web Collaboration

Activity level:
Beginner

Time frame:
Ongoing

Partners:
Unlimited

Materials Needed

- One computer with email/Web access
- An Internet Service Provider that offers space on their Web server

Children's Resources

http://www.acpl.lib.in.us/ information_resources/ childrens_resources.html

This site is a good place to start your Web search, offering links to interesting children's resources.

THE KID'S KORNER

9. Collect all of the reviews created by partner classrooms and create a directory for your school of interesting Web sites. Distribute your directory to all teachers.

10. Optional: Publish the reviews to a Web site. (See "Creating a Web Site," Chapter 3.)

FOR OLDER STUDENTS

Adapt this lesson for middle and secondary students. Have students create an assessment tool for reviewing the sites. Provide parameters for the review that link with your curriculum, such as having students review educational sites regarding history, or sites related to Victorian literature, Shakespeare, etc.

TIMELINE

Week 1   Teach basics about the Web.

Week 2   Post Call for Collaborators soliciting participants.

Weeks 3-4 Research sites and write reviews.

Weeks 5-6 Create directory and Web site.

TIP   This is an excellent activity to do before teaching students to use the Web for research. Try it without partners for your first time out.

REFLECTIVE WRITING

Students are introduced to the tools and etiquette of email by corresponding with keypals and maintaining a personal journal about their observations.

OBJECTIVES

- Students learn to conduct correspondence via email.
- Students learn email etiquette.
- Students develop reflective writing skills.

PREREQUISITES

None

PROCEDURE

1. Post a Call for Collaborators soliciting keypals partners for the project.
2. Based on responses, match each student with a keypal from another location.
3. Each student writes an initial brief biography about name, age, pets, school interests, and hobbies. Teacher consolidates information into one message and emails information to participating school. Note: Call the participating school to verify the information you receive.
4. Students begin journals in which they will describe their experiences with email correspondence. Provide suggestions for different stages of the students' journal writings:

At the beginning of the project:

- What would you like to learn about your keypal?
- What would you like to learn about the area in which your keypal lives?
- What would you like your keypal to know about you and about where you live?
- What do you think it is like where your keypal lives?

After writing the first entry:

- What is it like to describe yourself to someone you do not know? What is the hardest part of it? What is the easiest or most fun part of it?
- After receiving the first keypal message:
- What was your reaction to the first message from your keypal? Do you want to find out more? Are you surprised by the information?

Subject:
Language Arts

Grade level:
Grades 3-12

Activity type:
Keypals

Activity level:
Beginner

Time frame:
Ongoing

Partners:
Up to 6 schools

Materials Needed

- One computer with email access

From an activity by Sue Miller, technology specialist, Lexington High School, Lexington, Massachusetts.

REFLECTIVE WRITING

Ongoing:

- How is it different to know someone just from email rather than knowing him or her in person? Has your impression of your keypal's area changed? If so, in what ways?

End of project:

- What are the important parts of saying good-bye to someone? How do you feel about it? What have you learned about yourself, your key-pal, and where your keypal lives from this activity?

- What was the hardest part of this activity? What was the easiest or most fun part?

5. Organize students into groups of 3-4 students each. Once a week, students read their journals to each other and discuss what they are learning.

6. Continue the exchange of messages and journal writing for at least 4 weeks (or longer if desired).

7. To conclude project, students write a goodbye message and a final journal entry about the project. Provide suggestions about the contents of a goodbye message, for example:

- Say goodbye.

- Say thank you for the opportunity to do this project.

- State briefly what you have learned from this project.

TIMELINE

Week 1   Post Call for Collaborators soliciting up to 6 partner schools.

Week 2   Email procedures to all registered schools.

Weeks 3-6 Exchange keypal messages. (Note: this project could continue much longer.)
Write journal entries.
Discuss journal entries in small groups.

Week 7   Write goodbye message and final journal entry.
Discuss final journal entry.

TIP   Students can practice using email while meeting your curricular goals. Partner with other classrooms studying the same topic or book. Pair students across schools (and cross-age!) to research and answer directed questions or debrief on the topic you are studying. Direct the communication to address difficult issues related to your curriculum.

PASS THE TORCH

Students create an email chain letter around the world where they write about their good deeds or kindnesses.

OBJECTIVES

- Students are recognized for their acts of kindness.
- Students learn about other cultures.

PREREQUISITES

Kisses for Everyone? (Chapter 2)

PROCEDURE

1. Post a Call for Collaborators looking for 10 participant classrooms around the world.

2. Begin by asking one student to write about a time when he or she did a good deed or was kind to someone. Create an order for each student in your classroom to respond (similar to a chain letter).

3. Have the next student in order respond to the first's essay with his or her own essay. They must begin their essay building on the previous person's essay (a single word, topic, theme, etc.). For example, they might begin with "I, too, helped a stranger. . ."

4. Email your class's essays to the list of participants with instructions on how to continue the chain to 10 more classrooms (with a deadline), keeping your classroom's email address at the bottom of the list.

5. Watch as the essays flood in! Are there similarities between the essays? Are there differences? What have you learned from other students' acts of kindness?

6. Pose a challenge: once a week, practice anonymous acts of kindness for someone who might not expect it.

7. Mark on a wall map where the essays come from.

8. Create a scrapbook from the collection of essays and illustrate.

9. Have students read selected essays from the chain and discuss. How do these acts affect the world?

TIMELINE

Week 1   Post Call for Collaborators soliciting 10 partner schools.

Week 2   Have students write essays and email to participants.

Ongoing Discuss essays.

This project was inspired by Kids' Conscious Acts of Peace, a joint project of Ben & Jerry's, Educators for Social Responsibility (ESR), and the Corporation for Public Broadcasting.

Subject:
Language Arts, Social Studies, Character Education

Grade level:
Grades K-12

Activity type:
Cooperative Challenge

Activity level:
Beginner

Time frame:
Ongoing

Partners:
10 classrooms

Materials Needed

- One computer with email access

Educators for Social Responsibility
For more information on Kids' Conscious Acts of Peace, call ESR at (800) 370-2515.

WORDSMITH

Subject:
Language Arts, Art

Grade level:
Grades 3-12

Activity type:
Cooperative Challenge,
Web Publishing (optional)

Activity level:
Beginner

Time frame:
6 weeks

Partners:
1 classroom

Materials Needed

- One computer with email access
- 3x5 index cards (optional)

Kids' Web: A Child's Garden of Verses
http://www.primenet.com/~sburr/verses.html

This site features specially selected poems for kids by Robert Louis Stevenson, Robert Frost, Lewis Carroll, and William Wordsworth.

Students partner with another classroom from a different culture to cooperatively write poetry.

OBJECTIVES

- Students develop language skills.
- Student work cooperatively.
- Students are introduced to computer technology as a tool to create, compose, and communicate.
- Students problem solve and resolve conflicts.

PREREQUISITES

Kisses for Everyone? (Chapter 2)

PROCEDURE

1. Post a Call for Collaborators soliciting a partner classroom with a different profile than your own.

2. Pair each student with a student from the participating classroom. Have students exchange introductory email describing themselves, their school, and their community.

3. Provide some poetry examples and discuss. Students can look for inspiration on the Web.

4. Have each student in the originating classroom write the first line of a poem and give it to you on a 3x5 index card with his or her name. (Or schedule students in 5-minute intervals at the computer.)

5. Email the children's lead line of poetry to the participating classroom. The children's partners then add another line and email them back. Allow a week for response.

6. Continue the cycle 3 more times (until each student has written 4 lines), allowing students access to the computer in 5-minute intervals. (Students at this stage may want to discuss the direction of the poem or suggest changes to their partners. This may cause conflict. Allow the children to work it out among themselves, helping only if the children get stuck.)

7. Have the students compile the poetry and email to participating classroom.

8. Have students illustrate the poetry.

9. Facilitate a discussion (or have students address in their journals): What was it like working together on this? What different perspectives or experiences did your partner bring to the collaboration? How did this contribute to the collaboration? What problems arose for you? How did you

solve them? How do you feel about the end result? What did you learn about working together?

WORDSMITH

10. Optional: If you have access to a Web server, consider publishing the poetry to a Web site. (See "Creating a Web Site," Chapter 3, for more information.)

TIMELINE

Week 1   Post Call for Collaborators soliciting participants.

Weeks 2-6 Cooperatively write poetry.

TIP

Try out this project first among students in your own classroom. Then move to the online partnership. Have students explore the differences between the two interactions. Was it more or less difficult to work with the online partners? When you had a conflict, was it more or less difficult to work it out online? Why?

EMAIL EPILOGUE

Subject:
Language Arts

Grade level:
Grades 3-12

Activity type:
Web Collaboration

Activity level:
Beginner

Time frame:
Ongoing

Partners:
Unlimited

Materials Needed

- One computer with email access

Students write and share epilogues on a book(s) they have all read.

OBJECTIVES

- Students critically respond to literature.
- Students see how students from other places and cultures respond to literature.

PREREQUISITES

None

PROCEDURE

1. Post a Call for Collaborators soliciting partner classrooms who have read (or will read) a specific list of literature and respond with epilogues by a scheduled date.

2. Have students read the book(s) if they have not already done so.

3. Review epilogues to other books as an example. In small groups discuss: What is an epilogue? What should be in one?

4. Have each student write an epilogue by the scheduled deadline.

5. Partner classrooms submit their epilogues to the originating classroom.

6. Share all epilogues with participating classrooms. Have students mark on a wall map the location of the participating classrooms.

7. Distribute epilogues between small groups to read and discuss: How are the epilogues similar? How are they different? Were there trends within a classroom in terms of their perspectives? What were some of the more unusual perspectives? Have each student pick one essay that is most like theirs and one that is least like theirs.

8. Have each small group present their findings to the class. Discuss as a group. In journals, have students answer the question: How have your ideas about the book changed because of the epilogues?

9. Optional: Have each student write a book review and exchange with other classrooms through WCU BookRead (*http://micronet.wcu.edu/ projects/bookread/index.html*) or Houghton Mifflin's Education Place (*http://www.eduplace.com*).

From an activity by Phil Cliffe, teacher, Badillo Elementary School, Covina, California.

TIMELINE

Schedule to parallel reading of book.

This project works best if organized around a book you are about to read. Post your call for participants who have read or would like to read that title, then read the book together. Establish a schedule for when the epilogues are due, giving everyone plenty of time to both read the book and write the epilogues.

TIP

THE CRITIC'S CORNER

Subject:
Language Arts, Music

Grade level:
Grades 7-12

Activity type:
Web Publishing

Activity level:
Beginner

Time frame:
1 week

Partners:
None

Materials Needed

- One computer with email/Web access
- A few issues of *Rolling Stone*

Students write music reviews and publish to *Firefly*, an online magazine.

OBJECTIVES

- Students develop critical listening skills.
- Student learn about the music review genre.
- Students write and edit.

PREREQUISITES

None

PROCEDURE

1. Have students read and analyze music reviews from *Rolling Stone*. What features do music reviews contain? Create an outline from a review.

2. Have students practice writing lead lines for a music review of their favorite recording. Pair students cooperatively for peer-editing and review.

3. Assign students to write a full-length music review on a recording of choice.

4. Pair students again for peer-editing and review.

5. Have students submit edited draft. Schedule 5-minute conferences with each student to give feedback. Assign second draft to incorporate your suggestions.

6. Submit the music reviews to *Firefly*, an online magazine (*http://www.ffly.com*).

TIMELINE

Week 1 Write and publish your music reviews.

TIP   Extend this project by having students respond to the reviews posted on *Firefly*. Have them choose and rewrite a review they download from the site.

THE DAILY NEWS

Students publish a daily newspaper using Web resources.

OBJECTIVES

- Students develop editorial skills such as editing, proofreading, and headline writing.
- Students read daily news.

PREREQUISITES

Navigating News (Chapter 5)

PROCEDURE

1. Bring in several copies of different newspapers as examples, or, if students have more advanced Web research skills, have students in small groups search online for different newspapers.

2. Break students into small groups to review a newspaper. What are the various elements of your newspaper? What types of stories are featured?

3. Have students develop editorial guidelines for their very own newspaper. Who is their audience? What type of news do they want to feature (national, international, hard, soft)?

4. Using the CRAYON site (CRe-Ate Your Own Newspaper at *http://crayon-net*), students in pairs create their own newspaper. They first choose a name for their newspaper and pick through a list of Web addresses with news items of interest. When they are done, they get a page with a collection of links that can be saved and loaded each day for news.

5. Students download their news, edit, and write new headlines daily.

TIMELINE

Ongoing

Subject:
Language Arts

Grade level:
Grades 7-12

Activity type:
Web Publishing

Activity level:
Beginner

Time frame:
Ongoing

Partners:
None

Materials Needed

- One computer with Web access (one per pair of students is preferred)
- Various newspapers (optional)

Online Newspapers
http://www.intercom.com.au/intercom/newsprs/index.htm

This site provides a listing of international newspapers available online.

The best way for children to learn to write news is to have them read it. Require that students read the daily newspaper. Begin each class with a brief discussion of the news (and a pop quiz!). Or have a current events game. The team that wins has editorial control over the newspaper that week.

TIP

NAVIGATING NEWS

Subject:
Language Arts, Social
Studies, Media Literacy

Grade level:
Grades 7-12

Activity type:
Web Resource

Activity level:
Beginner

Time frame:
2 class periods

Partners:
None

Materials Needed

- One computer with
  Web access (one
  workstation per
  student pair is ideal)

Online Newspapers

*http://www.intercom.com.au/
intercom/newsprs/
index.htm*

This site provides a listing of
international newspapers
available online.

Students critically evaluate the news media by comparing the top news stories in one day from several news sources.

OBJECTIVES

- Students develop critical reading abilities and analytical skills.
- Students explore the role of the news media in our society.

PREREQUISITES

None

PROCEDURE

1. Students working in pairs choose 3 major sources of news to compare. Featured national and international daily news stories from print media are available through the CRAYON Web site (*http://crayon.net*) and other Web sites. (Have students research additional sources for extra credit.)

2. Have students download and print the top news stories on a designated day from their 3 news sources. (Students should have at least 2 stories about the same topic to make this exercise meaningful.)

3. Explain to the students that there are several national news sources, such as the AP and UPI wires, that supply all papers with the same information. Most major newspapers rely on these sources primarily for national and international news, using their in-house writers to cover local news. However, news editors decide what stories to feature when and where, and through their editing and headline writing give the story their own unique "spin." Therefore, the top news story (the story featured on the front page, right-hand column) in major newspapers can vary widely.

   Most papers strive to present an unbiased account of the news. Ask: What constitutes an unbiased account? What would make a news story biased?

4. After a brief discussion about bias, ask the student pairs to develop their own criteria for assessing whether an article is unbiased. This will become the criteria against which they will judge the 3 articles they have printed.

5. For homework, have students read their articles, noting similarities and differences between the featured articles.

6. Again, in the same pairs as before, ask students to address the following about their articles:

   - Of the different stories featured, what can you infer about the newspapers' priorities?

- Of the stories covering the same topics, are they biased or unbiased? (Have students use the criteria developed the previous day.)

- How might each story affect the reader's opinion about the topic?

- How does the headline affect the reader's opinion about the topic? Is it biased or unbiased?

Have high school students place the story on the political spectrum:

- Does one story present more liberal views? Is one more conservative? Why?

7. Have student pairs report on their findings to the group.

8. Facilitate a group discussion about the role of the media in our society. Ask: How does the media affect our view of the world? How might this affect our actions in the world? Why might a newspaper be biased? What other examples of bias have you noticed in the media? (How are people of color and other minorities represented? What about women?)

Note: The prevalence of violence in the media might be an important issue to address here. Research shows that most Americans assume a greater incidence of violence in their neighborhoods than actually is the case. Most Americans also falsely assume a greater incidence of random violence, when research shows that the majority of violent acts and murders occur between two people who know one another. Why might that be so?

TIMELINE

Class 1   Students choose and download news sources and develop criteria for assessing an article's bias.

Class 2   Students critically examine the articles and discuss the larger impact of the news on society.

MEDIA LITERACY EXTENSION

Continue your investigation in the media by asking 3 volunteers to tape different television network news for the same evening. Critically examine the tapes during class and discuss differences in coverage and their impact on society.

NAVIGATING NEWS

TIP

BRING IT HOME

Have students write a 2-3 paragraph article about a recent controversial happening in your school or community. Have students read their accounts aloud. What differences in perspective do you notice? Pair students together to peer-edit and "neutralize" one anothers' stories. Or invite a reporter from a local paper to visit the classroom. Students can prepare to interview him or her and get a first-hand account on bias in reporting.

CAMERAS AND COURTROOMS

Students learn more about this controversial topic by taking both sides of the issue and polling news media professionals and trial lawyers and justices.

OBJECTIVES

- Students learn more about a controversial topic.
- Students learn about differing perspectives in a conflict.
- Students explore the benefits and limitations of media coverage in the courtroom.

PREREQUISITES

None

PROCEDURE

1. Have students in small cooperative groups research the issue (using library and Web resources):
   - What is the history of the use of TV cameras in courtrooms?
   - What are its benefits?
   - What are its disadvantages?
   - Who are the different stakeholders in the issue?
   - What is each stakeholder's perspective on the issue?
   - What are each stakeholder's positions and interests? (Positions are what each stakeholder is demanding. Interests are *why* they need them—the underlying need being addressed by the demand.)

2. Using the facts learned in their research, have students in small groups brainstorm questions for a survey to poll trial lawyers, justices, and media professionals on the issue.

3. Bring the class together. Have each small group report on their questions. As a class, construct a poll about the issue.

4. Have students research mailing lists for media and legal professionals and post their results. Be sure to include a deadline for response and information about your class and how the survey will be used. Media and legal professionals will be more inclined to help if they know that the survey will be used for educational purposes only.

5. Again in small groups, have students frame the debate question. Assign each group a side on the issue (evenly dividing the class). Have small groups prepare for the debate.

Subject:
English, Social Studies, Media Literacy

Grade level:
Grades 6-12

Activity type:
Web Survey

Activity level:
Intermediate

Time frame:
6 weeks

Partners:
None

Materials Needed

- One computer with email/Web access

CAMERAS AND COURTROOMS

Suggested small group process for preparing for the debate:

- Prepare a list of the relevant issues on both sides of the argument.
- For each issue, identify both the positions and interests.
- Prepare rebuttals for the other side's arguments.
- Decide on the most persuasive arguments to use in an opening argument.
- Prepare opening argument and review key issues.

6. Begin the debate by exchanging opening arguments, followed by:
   a. rebuttal
   b. cross-examination
   c. rebuttal
   d. cross-examination
   e. rebuttal
   f. cross-examination (repeat until each student has had a turn)

7. Anonymously poll all students on their individual positions on the debate.

8. Reverse positions on the issue and hold another debate. Repeat steps 4 through 6.

9. Facilitate a discussion: How have your views been affected by the debate? Did anyone change his or her mind? Why? How did it feel to argue the other point of view? What did you learn? What is the role of media in our society?

10. Assessment (Optional): Students can peer-evaluate the debate using speaker points. Each student is given a score from 1 to 30 (with 30 being the highest). The scores are then added up and the team with the highest score wins. Explain that the assignment will be judged on the following criteria:
    - Effectiveness of persuasive arguments
    - Use of supporting facts

Have students write an unbiased magazine-length article about the issue, presenting both sides of the story. Clip other articles of this nature to serve as models.

TIMELINE

Weeks 1-2 Research the issue and prepare arguments.

Weeks 3-4 Hold first debate.

Weeks 5-6 Hold second debate.

MEDIA LITERACY EXTENSION (FOR OLDER STUDENTS)

Have students explore this controversial topic further. Much has been written on the effect of TV cameras on the O.J. Simpson criminal trial. Have students research the issue. How might the trial have been different if TV cameras were not allowed in the courtroom? How might it have affected the verdict?

For more practice for your students with conflict resolution techniques, use *Elementary Perspectives: Teaching Concepts of Peace and Conflict* (for elementary students), *Conflict Resolution in the Middle School* (for middle school students), and *Making Choices, Part I* and *Part II* (for high school students). These resources are all available through Educators for Social Responsibility, 23 Garden Street, Cambridge, MA 02138 (800) 370-2515.

TIP

GREAT EXPECTATIONS

Subject:
English, History

Grade level:
Grades 9-12

Activity type:
Web Resource

Activity level:
Intermediate

Time frame:
6 class periods scheduled throughout the reading of the novel

Partners:
None

Materials Needed

- One computer with Web access per three students
- Chart paper

Brown University's Victorian Web
http://twine.stg.brown.edu/ projects/hypertext/landow/ victorian/victov.html

This site contains links and resources to help students research the Victorian era.

Students deepen their understanding of *Great Expectations*, by Charles Dickens, by using Web resources, including a walking tour of Dickens' England, a site about the Victorian era, and a 100-year-old review of the book.

OBJECTIVES

- Students research the Victorian era.
- Students analyze the text of *Great Expections*.
- Students improve their research skills.

PREREQUISITES

Students read Charles Dickens' *Great Expectations*.

PROCEDURE

(Note: Each of these three focused research topics can be scheduled as modules for appropriate time periods throughout the reading of the novel, depending on your goals and focus.)

The Setting

1. Break students into small groups to review the text of *Great Expectations*. How does the setting impact the novel? Assign each student to find one citation from the text to contribute to the group's ideas.

2. Bring the group together. Have each group report on their findings and record on chart paper. Facilitate a discussion.

3. For homework, schedule students to research the novel's setting using the Web (or use class time if you have sufficient computers available for everyone to use). Applicable information can be found at Dickens' Kent (*http://lang.nagoya-u.ac.jp/~matsuoka/Dickens.html*).

4. Break students again into small groups to share what they have learned. How does this information deepen their understanding of the novel? (Refer back to group's earlier ideas recorded on chart paper.)

The Victorian Era

1. Schedule students to individually research the Victorian era using the Web. Have them address the following questions in writing:

   - What are the characteristics of the Victorian age? Where do we see these elements in the novel?

   - What does it mean to be Victorian in your attitudes? Which characters were the most Victorian?

   - How did his change in circumstance (from a life of gentlemanly leisure to that of a working man) affect Pip?

   - How did Dickens' childhood influence *Great Expectations*?

From an activity by Nancy Skomars Davis, teacher, Advanced Technologies Academy, Las Vegas, Nevada.

GREAT EXPECTATIONS

2. Bring students together in small groups to share what they have learned. Have each group report to the class on their combined knowledge.

3. Have students address the following question in journals (or in essay form if your class does not use journals): What kind of expectations do you live with? How are these expectations related to the time in which you are living?

4. Facilitate a discussion about cultural expectations:

   - What kind of expectations were put on Pip?
   - How do these expectations relate to the times he was living in?
   - Was Pip able to meet those expectations?
   - What kind of expectations are put on young people today?
   - Are you able to meet the expectations placed on you?
   - What do you do if you cannot meet others' expectations?

A Style Analysis

1. Have students read a review of *Great Expectations* written 100 years ago (see Atlantic Unbound's Classic Reviews, *http://www.theatlantic.com/ atlantic/atlweb/classrev/greatexp.htm*). You can print the review or have students review it online.

2. Have students address the following questions in their journals:

   - What does the reviewer specifically point to that makes *Great Expectations* a great novel?
   - What does the reviewer say about Dickens' abilities as a writer?
   - Which points do you agree or disagree with?
   - Which words or phrases did you have difficulty with? Discuss for meaning.
   - How does the style of the review compare to the style of the novel? Cite examples from both.

3. Facilitate a discussion in class: In general, what makes a work of art a classic? Why is *Great Expectations* considered a classic?

4. For homework, have students write their own review of Dickens' novel.

TIMELINE

Week 1   Research the setting of the novel and the Victorian era.

Week 2   Critically analyze issues of style.

CREATIVE WRITING EXTENSION

Dickens' novels first appeared serialized in periodicals. Have students practice creative writing mimicking Dickens' style in serial as they read, adding their own plot twists and turns. Begin with the very first chapter so that students can create a different but parallel story of their own.

PRIDE AND PREJUDICE

Students explore the relationship of nature and art in late 18th century literature through the lens of Jane Austen's *Pride and Prejudice* and a Web resource.

Subject:
English, Writing, History, Political Science

Grade level:
Grades 9-12

Activity type:
Web Resource/Keypals

Activity level:
Intermediate

Time frame:
4 class periods

Partners:
Unlimited

Materials Needed

- One computer with email/Web access per three students

The Jane Austen Information Page
http://uts.cc.utexas.edu/ ~churchh/janeinfo.html

This site contains the entire text of *Pride and Prejudice,* background information on the late 18th century, and Austen's personal letters.

OBJECTIVES

- Students research late 18th century thinking.
- Students analyze the text and Jane Austen's personal letters.

PREREQUISITES

Students need to have read Jane Austen's *Pride and Prejudice.*

PROCEDURE

1. Break students into small groups to review the text of *Pride and Prejudice* and explore the role of nature. How is nature or "the natural" portrayed in the text? Positively? Negatively? How does the natural relate to the artificial? Assign each student to find one citation from the text to contribute to the group's ideas.

    (Note: If students have trouble getting started, ask them to consider the role of gardening in the novel.)

2. Bring the group together. Have each group report on their findings. Facilitate a discussion. (Note:.Austen sets up a dichotomy between the natural and the artificial, between nature and society, between what is "God-made" and human-made, elevating the natural. This is expressed thematically throughout the novel.)

3. Schedule individual students for two 15-minute blocks of time at the computer to research how Austen's sentiment about nature reflects her own feelings and late 18th century thinking. (Hint: Her personal letters reveal her feelings on the topic.)

4. Break students again into small groups to share what they have learned.

5. Facilitate a group discussion on the topic.

TIMELINE

Class 1   Research the role of nature in the text and discuss.

Classes 2-3 Research Austen and late 18th century thinking online.

Class 4   Share what students learn and discuss.

CREATIVE WRITING EXTENSION

Pride and Prejudice was likely first written as a collection of letters between characters, as was fashionable at the time. Using email, partner students from classrooms around the world to write letters as Austen herself may have originally written them. Assign each student a role for which they will write a letter. Their partner will play another role and respond. Assign a different scene from one chapter to each student pair. Then compile all the letters together as a chapter.

PRIDE AND PREJUDICE

POLITICAL SCIENCE EXTENSION

Have students read Burke, Rousseau, Priestley, and Paine for more foundation on the late 18th century role of nature as it grew out of the rationalistic spirit of the age.

MIDDLEZINE MAGAZINE

Subject:
English, Reading, Art,
Computer Technology

Grade level:
Grades 3-12

Activity type:
Web Publishing

Activity level:
Advanced

Time frame:
Ongoing

Partners:
Unlimited

Materials Needed

- One computer with email/Web access
- An Internet Service Provider that offers space on their Web server
- GIF converter (shareware)
- Photoshop (optional)

Middle school students partner with other students around the world to create an online creative writing magazine published biannually to the Web.

OBJECTIVES

- Students write and edit.
- Students are introduced to computer technology as a tool to create, compose, communicate, and publish.
- Students are provided a global audience for their writing.

PREREQUISITES

None

PROCEDURE

1. Work with a small group of interested students and together learn how to create a Web site. (See The Macintosh Internet Server Cookbook at *http://web66.coled.umn.edu/Cookbook/MacContents.html* for tools and complete instructions, and "Creating a Web Site," Chapter 3.)

2. Develop an editorial board to design the general format and editorial guidelines for the magazine. The editorial guidelines should include the information authors will need in order to submit their work, including focus/goal for the publication, special requirements for format or size, deadlines for submission (allow 2 months for submissions), and legal rights and obligations. (See the following "General Guidelines for Middlezine Magazine" from Hudson Middle School in Hudson, Ohio, for an example.)

   You may wish to assign students different roles. One group of students can be editors (or editorial board), another the design and production team. Or you can choose to have all students fulfill all functions.

3. Post a Call for Collaborators soliciting partner classrooms and students to submit their writing and artwork. Include editorial guidelines.

4. Participating classrooms submit their original writing and/or artwork via email (or mail if necessary). Inform classrooms submitting artwork via email to save or convert their graphic files to GIF or JPEG. (See the graphics format page at *http://VTGinc.com/ebennett/xplat.graph.html* for conversion tools). Be aware: Depending on the Internet Service Provider, you might need to BinHex your file before attaching it to your email. Tools to BinHex your file are available at *http://helpdesk.uvic.ca/how-to/support/mac/hqx.html*.

From an activity by Harry R. Noden, language arts teacher, Hudson Middle School, Hudson, Ohio.

5. The editorial board selects the best pieces to be included in the magazine. Students then edit the pieces. (Note: Younger students can be paired with older students for help in editing.)

6. Students publish the magazine on a Web site. For an excellent example of a student-created publication, see Hudson Middle School's Middlezine Magazine at *http://www.salamander.net/people/hnoden/*.

MIDDLEZINE MAGAZINE

TIMELINE (ONE ISSUE)

Weeks 1-2   Create editorial guidelines.

Week 3   Post Call for Collaborators soliciting participants.

Weeks 4-11   Allow 2 months for schools to submit samples.

Weeks 12-16 Create Web site and publish your magazine.

EXTRA-CURRICULAR ADAPTATION

Publishing a magazine is an excellent extra-curricular project. Find a few students who have experience on the Internet and who have at least an elementary knowledge of HTML. Combine them with a talented and motivated group of editors.

Publishing a magazine is very time consuming. In general, delegate as many tasks as possible to the students. But be prepared to spend some of your own time double-checking layouts, reviewing email, and monitoring progress.

TIP

General Guidelines for Middlezine Magazine from Hudson Middle School in Hudson, Ohio

Acceptance/Rejection

Our goal is to make Middlezine one of the highest quality middle school magazines in existence. We want acceptance in this magazine to be viewed as an honor. Consequently, we try to publish only outstanding works. Generally, approximately 60 to 70 percent of those items submitted are rejected.

With international submissions, we take a higher percentage of works because we value cross-cultural representation, and teachers in other countries often screen works, sending only what they consider to be the best representative writing from their school.

All works are evaluated by a team of 10 students and 2 teachers, known as the "Zine Team." Once a decision is made, we will email you an announcement. Generally, it takes 1 to 2 weeks to decide on whether to publish a writing.

Parental Permissions

We ask those teachers submitting works from their students to secure parental permission for publication and for the use of photographs. Teachers must send an email indicating this permission has been given.

Legal Rights

Middlezine asks for one-time rights for any submitted piece. This means that after publication in our zine, the author may publish the piece in any other electronic or hard copy magazine he or she wishes. All rights remain the property of the writer.

Plagiarism

All written work and art work must be original, that is, created by the author or artist. Do not submit copies of anything not totally created by the writer or artist. Computer-generated art is welcomed as long as it is not a "paint by numbers" template.

References

We welcome illustrations—photos and drawings to accompany writing. However, be sure to secure permission from the artist or photographer before submitting the work. Send us a copy of your email permission with your illustration. With research papers, the same guidelines apply. All summarized paragraphs and direct quotes should be referenced using APA or any acceptable style.

Reprinted with permission from Hudson Middle School's Middlezine Magazine at *http://www.Salamander.net/people/hnoden/*

THE HOMEWORK HOME PAGE

Students create on the school's Web site a Homework Home Page, a Web page where parents (and students) can find details about that night's homework assignment.

OBJECTIVES

- Parents are encouraged to support children in their homework.
- Parents are shown they are valued and important members of the school community.
- Students become more fully invested in their homework assignments as they share responsibility for updating the homework center.

PREREQUISITES

None

PROCEDURE

1. Explain the project: Students and teachers together will create a place on the school's Web site where families can find out the night's homework assignment. The center will be updated by students on a daily basis.

2. Teach students the basics of HTML. (See The Macintosh Internet Server Cookbook at *http://web66.coled.umn.edu/Cookbook/MacContents.html* for tools and complete instructions for creating your site. Also see "Creating a Web Site," Chapter 3, for additional advice.)

3. Create a schedule and process for a different student to update the homework center daily with the class assignment. Ask at the end of each class for homework completion tips to include on the site. Include some of your own tips!

4. Optional: If your school does not have a Web site, help students create a Homework Home Page. (See "Creating a Web Site" in Chapter 3 for additional information.)

5. Supervise students updating the Homework Home Page site.

TIMELINE

Ongoing

Subject:
Computer Technology

Grade level:
Grades 4-12

Activity type:
Web Publishing/Community Connection

Activity level:
Advanced

Time frame:
Ongoing

Partners:
Every classroom in your school

Materials Needed

- One computer with email/Web access
- An Internet Service Provider that offers space on their Web server

TIP   Include in your Homework Home Page some basic tips and guidelines for parents for helping their children succeed with homework. Suggest that an adult or older sibling be assigned each evening as the Homework Helper, available for questions or to offer help. Offer specific suggestions for completing the night's assignment. Other tips to parents might include:

- Create a consistent and quiet place for children to do their homework.
- If possible establish and stick to a regular nightly schedule.
- Create an enjoyable ritual around a child's completion of homework.

WHAT YOU SHOULD ALSO KNOW

Using QuickTime movies available on the Web, students add text to describe each scene and shed more light on a topic you are studying.

OBJECTIVES

- Students are introduced to multimedia tools.
- Students react to and write about what they see.
- Students "virtually collaborate" with Apple Interactive Music Toolkit to create an original film.
- Other curricular objectives as determined (see step 2)

PREREQUISITES

Some familiarity with QuickTime, MoviePlayer, and Apple Interactive Music Toolkit. For a tutorial and tools see Bedrock Barn's homepage (*http://www.bedrockbarn.com/pages/tools.htm*) and the following sites: *http://www.quicktime.apple.com/* and *http://www.amp.apple.com/imt/*.

PROCEDURE

1. Pair students for this project. For younger children, arrange for cross-age tutors to serve as technical assistants. (See "Multimedia Tools" Chapter 2, for more information about using multimedia in the classroom.)

2. Explain the assignment: Student pairs will create a movie production annotated with text that links to a topic you have been studying in class this year. It can be any topic, provided that the movie and text have something to add to your class's understanding of the topic.

3. Using the tutorial found at *http://www.bedrockbarn.com/pages/tutorial.htm.* introduce the tools of QuickTime, MoviePlayer, and Apple Interactive Music Toolkit to students,

4. Schedule student pairs in 25-minute intervals to find and download a QuickTime movie from the Web that can be adequately annotated with text. Some interesting sites that students can start with include *http://www.bedrockbarn.com/pages/samples.htm* and *http://www.quicktime.apple.com/sam/*.

5. Have students schedule their own time at the computer for writing text and incorporating it with the QuickTime movie using Apple Interactive Music Toolkit (i.e., perhaps deleting music, reordering scenes, etc.).

6. Hold a film festival in class! Have student pairs present their movies. Then have the class respond in journals, completing the statement: "Something I didn't know about [topic] until this film is . . ."

From Douglas Parker Roerden, multimedia producer, Bedrock Barn Productions, Boston, Massachusetts.

Subject:
English, (All)

Grade level:
Grades 3-12

Activity type:
Multimedia, Web Resource

Time frame:
8 weeks

Partners:
None

Materials Needed

- At least one computer with Web access (more is preferred)
- Word processor
- QuickTime, MoviePlayer, and Apple Interactive Music Toolkit
- Construction or origami paper

WHAT YOU SHOULD ALSO KNOW

7. Optional: Publish as a QuickTime file to a Web site. (See *http://www.bedrockbarn.com/pages/web.htm*, *http://www.quicktime.apple.com/dev/devweb.html*, and "Creating a Web Site," Chapter 3, for more information.)

TIMELINE

Weeks 1-2   Introduce or review tools.

Week 3   Find QuickTime movie files on Web.

Weeks 4-6   Customize QuickTime files.

Weeks 7-8   Write and incorporate text.

Mathematics

6

- The Animal Project
- Solve It!
- Record Recycling
- Mighty M&M Math
- A Taste of Trig
- The Cost of Living
- A Kids' Consumer Price Index
- PrimeTime
- Fantasy Hoops: Mathematics and the NBA
- Taking Stock
- Crime at School
- Social Security or Bust?

THE ANIMAL PROJECT

Students around the world record and compare the animals seen during a given week.

OBJECTIVES

- Students learn about animals and their habitats.
- Students learn about the location of different states and countries, and develop basic map-reading skills.
- Younger students acquire basic math skills such as adding and interpreting. Older students predict, graph, and analyze data.
- Students draw animals.

PREREQUISITES

None

PROCEDURE

1. Post Call for Collaborators soliciting partner schools around the world.
2. Students from participating classrooms around the world record animals sighted every day during a given week on a "Seen Daily" list.
3. Classrooms compile and post their data to the project coordinator via email. The project coordinator shares all data with participating classrooms via email.
4. Have students:
   - Collect and organize the data. (For younger students, design and post a chart on which students can write their findings daily. Older students can work in small groups to design their own charts to present the information.)
   - Locate and mark partner schools on a map.
5. Working in pairs, have students interpret the data through a cooperative challenge.

   Have younger students address:
   - How many different animals, birds, insects, etc. were seen
   - Which animal was the most popular (i.e., seen in the most places)
   - Which place saw the most and least animals
   - How many states and countries participated
   - How many states and countries they can find on the map

   Have older students address:

Subject:
Mathematics, Science, Geography, Art, English

Grade level:
Grades K-8

Activity type:
Web Collaboration

Activity level:
Beginner

Time frame:
6 weeks

Partners:
Unlimited

Materials Needed

- One computer with email access
- World wall map

Linda Little and Sharon Hayes

From an activity by Sharon Hayes and Linda Little, teachers, Capay Joint Union Elementary School, Orland, California.

THE ANIMAL PROJECT

- Which state had the least percentage sightings of a given animal
- Compute the average number of sightings per animal
- Compute the median number of sightings per animal
- Identify and group the animals into the following categories: reptiles, mammals, birds, insects, etc.

6. Have students draw pictures of all animals sighted or download pictures from the Web. (See "A Word About Copyright Law and Fair Use," Chapter 3.)

7. With the students, create a bulletin board in a central place in your school featuring the data, interesting observations, and pictures.

TIMELINE

Week 1   Post Call for Collaborators soliciting partners.

Week 2   Email procedures and introductions of students to all registered schools.

Week 3   Record animal sightings daily.

Week 4   Share data with all participants.

Week 5   Analyze results.

Week 6   Create bulletin board.

LITERATURE EXTENSION

Have children choose an animal from the sightings to research its place in literature. Help younger children locate a picture book that features that animal. How does the animal behave in the book? How much is that like the real animal? Older children can be charged with finding and reading a book, poem, essay, etc., that features their animal. (Hint: Searching books on Web sites by keywords may be of help.) Have students write a response to their selections in their journals. What characteristics has the author chosen to highlight? Why?

TIP   This project generates lots of mail. It's best to be prepared with form letters and a database for tracking the project's progress. Remember, if the response is overwhelming, limiting the number of classrooms to a manageable size is an option.

SOLVE IT!

Students work collaboratively to solve word problems and brain teasers, competing as teams with other students around the world.

OBJECTIVES

- Students think critically and problem solve.
- Students work cooperatively.

PREREQUISITES

Kisses for Everyone? (Chapter 2)

PROCEDURE

1. Post a Call for Collaborators soliciting partner classrooms and students to compete in solving word problems and brain teasers.

2. Clarify the rules to all parties: Children will submit one word problem/brain teaser a week to all participants. The word problem/brain teaser must be solved by the submitting classroom before it can be posted to the entire list. The word problem/brain teaser need not be original. A classroom will receive one point for each problem successfully solved.

3. Get creative juices flowing by providing a few time-honored puzzles and word problems to solve (check out the Math Forum at *http:// forum.swarthmore.edu/*). Divide children in small groups to solve problems.

4. As a class, select one solved problem to post to the partners.

5. Group children cooperatively to solve problems submitted by the partners (you should have one problem per group).

6. Exchange answers with partner classrooms for scoring. Tally scores and announce winning classroom to all participants.

7. Optional: Continue steps 4-6 on a weekly basis for as long as you want.

8. Collect all problems/answers and post to all partners.

9. Optional: Publish the collection of problems on a Web site. (See "Creating a Web Site," Chapter 3.)

FOR OLDER STUDENTS

Adapt this lesson for secondary students. Have students create their own word problems/brain teasers. Assign a math principle for the problem to il-

Subject:
Mathematics, Language Arts

Grade level:
Grades K-12

Activity type:
Cooperative Challenge

Activity level:
Beginner

Time frame:
2 weeks to ongoing

Partners:
1 classroom per 2 children in your class

Materials Needed

- One computer with email access/Web access (optional)
- An Internet Service Provider that offers space on their Web server (optional)

The Electric Origami Shop Puzzle Page
http://www.ibm.com/Stretch/ EOS/puzzle.html

This site, from the IBM Corporation, provides frequently updated puzzles for all levels.

This project was inspired by a course of the same name taught and developed by Gary Shrager at the Saturday Course, Milton Academy, Milton, Massachusetts.

SOLVE IT!

lustrate. Students can develop facility with higher math principles while having fun!

TIMELINE (ONE ROUND)

Week 1   Submit problems to be solved.

Week 2   Solve problems and tally scores.

TIP   Have students from all participating classrooms write an introductory email describing who they are and what they like to do. By getting to know their fellow problem-solvers, students will show more interest in the project.

RECORD RECYCLING

Students conduct a national survey of schools' recycling habits, interpret the results, and develop a plan for their school.

OBJECTIVES

- Students explore the recycling habits of schools worldwide.
- Students analyze, interpret, and report on data.
- Students develop problem solving and planning skills.
- Students use basic math skills such as computing percentages and graphing.

PREREQUISITES

None

PROCEDURE

1. As a class, research your school's recycling efforts. Invite an administrator into your classroom to be interviewed about your program. Evaluate the program. What works well? What could be improved? If you don't have a recycling plan, discuss as a class why a recycling plan is important.

2. Have students work in cooperative groups to draft questions for a survey on recycling habits. Ask: What information would be helpful to us as we plan for (or improve) our own recycling program?

3. Bring students back together in a group. Combine questions from the smaller groups on chart paper or on the board. Together, prepare a questionnaire from the questions.

4. Conduct an email survey of other students around the world by posting the questionnaire in a project center. Allow 3 weeks for schools to respond.

5. Have students analyze data in cooperative groups, making comparisons within and across geographic regions on such factors as goods recycled, poundage of recycled matter by school size, income generated by recycling, etc. (Help students decide which interpretations will be most meaningful.)

6. Have students present their findings in class using graphs, bar charts, and pie charts.

7. As a class, devise a recycling plan for your school. Include an implementation plan.

Subject:
Mathematics, Science, Social Studies, Language Arts, Computer Technology

Grade level:
Grades 3-12

Activity type:
Web Survey

Activity level:
Beginner

Time frame:
10 weeks

Partners:
Unlimited

Materials Needed

- One computer with email/Web access

RECORD RECYCLING

TIMELINE

Week 1   Evaluate your school's recycling program.

Week 2   Devise your questionnaire and post publicly.

Weeks 3-6   Gather results.

Weeks 7-8   Analyze data and prepare presentation.

Weeks 9-10 Devise recycling plan.

TIP   Gather support for your recycling plan by publishing the results of your survey in your school newspaper, along with your recommendations for improving your school's recycling record. Then create a task force of interested students and teachers to lead the implementation efforts.

MIGHTY M&M MATH

Students compare the proportion of M&M candies by color to percentages worldwide.

OBJECTIVES

- Students acquire basic skills such as predicting, collecting, averaging, comparing, contrasting, classifying, analyzing, problem solving, graphing, and decision making.
- Students learn geography through locating participants' cities on a map.
- Students use cooperation and communication skills.

PREREQUISITES

None

PROCEDURE

1. Working in pairs, participating classrooms around the world predict:
   - The total number of M&Ms in each bag
   - The most and least common colors

   Be sure that all participants use the same size bag of plain M&Ms.

2. Have students determine and record:
   - The actual total and number of each color in each bag
   - The ratio and percentage of each color

3. Classrooms then compile their class average percentage for each color and post their data to the project coordinator via email.

4. Help students in cooperative pairs enter all data into spreadsheets (scheduling time for them at the computer in 10-minute intervals). Note: Not all countries have the same colors of M&Ms available. How many color sets are there? Why? It may be necessary to keep different spreadsheets to track the different color sets.

5. Student pairs complete a data table, comparing and analyzing their individual results to the international percentages. If you have Web access, have students compare their data to that on the Mars Company home page (*http://www.m-ms.com/bakery/index.html*). There you will find valuable background information such as details about the candy's manufacturing process and their own percentage targets for each color.

6. Have students present their findings by drawing a graph and writing a report on what they learned.

Subject:
Mathematics, Language Arts, Geography

Grade level:
Grades 4 8

Activity type:
Web Survey

Activity level:
Beginner

Time frame:
8 weeks

Partners:
Unlimited

Materials Needed

- One computer with email access (Web access is optional)
- Spreadsheet software program
- One M&Ms package for each pair of students
- Calculator
- Large world map (optional)

From an activity by Judy Conklin, teacher, North Oceano Elementary School, Grover Beach, California.

MIGHTY M&M MATH

7. On the final day, hold a "Celebration of the M." Have students write alliterations with the letter "M," create crossword puzzles with all "M" words, and write an "M" rap. Students can also decorate the room with stuffed paper M&Ms, post a full-wall spreadsheet of their data, and display all of their empty M&Ms packages.

8. Optional: Create a Web site and publish the results. See The Macintosh Internet Server Cookbook (*http://web66.coled.umn.edu/Cookbook/ MacContents.html*) for tools and complete instructions for creating your site.

TIMELINE

Week 1   Post Call for Collaborators soliciting participants.

Weeks 2-3   Email procedures to all registered schools.

Weeks 4-6   Classrooms compute M&M color percentages and post to project coordinator.

Weeks 7-8   Students complete data table, graph, and report.

GEOGRAPHY EXTENSION

Integrate this project with geography by including a map-skills lesson. Have students find and locate all participants on a world map. Tack empty M&M bags on a large wall map marking all the locations.

TIP   Teach averages, percentages, and spreadsheets before beginning this project. Then help students master the concept by duplicating this activity many times. Every day for one week, count, average, and compute percentages using different flavors and bags each time. There is nothing more motivating than edible work!

A TASTE OF TRIG

Students from different latitudes within one time zone compute the angle of the sun using trigonometry.

OBJECTIVES

- Students apply the inverse tangent function to calculate the angle of the sun.

- Students explore the relationship globally between the sun's position in the sky and latitude.

- Students acquire basic skills such as predicting, collecting, graphing, and analyzing data.

PREREQUISITES

Knowledge of the inverse tangent function

PROCEDURE

1. Post a Call for Collaborators soliciting partner schools from your time zone. You'll want a fairly wide distribution of different latitudes.

2. Break students into small groups. Explain that the goal of this project is to compute the angle of the sun in different latitudes of our time zone. Ask students to develop a methodology for the experiment, using concepts learned in trigonometry. Encourage students to draw diagrams of the earth and sun to explore the concept.

   Note: Students from participating classrooms can measure the shadow cast by a 10-foot pole at a designated time and date every day for the course of a week (to allow for bad weather). The angle of elevation from the sun to the earth can be calculated by using the inverse tangent function.

3. Have classrooms compile and post their data to the project coordinator via email. The project coordinator then shares all data with participating classrooms.

4. Assign students in pairs to plot one classroom's data showing the day-by-day angle of elevation. How does it change? Have students compute the average angle of elevation for their assigned school.

5. Have students plot the average angles by latitude. How do they change by latitude? If you have an adequate data set, compute the rate by which the angle changes.

7. Classrooms share their analyses via email.

TIMELINE

Week 1 Post Call for Collaborators soliciting participants and develop methodology.

Week 2 Take measurements and share data with all participants.

Week 3 Analyze and share results.

Subject:
Trigonometry, Geometry, Mathematics, Science

Grade level:
Grades 9-12

Activity type:
Web Collaboration

Activity level:
Beginner

Time frame:
3 weeks

Partners:
Unlimited

Materials Needed

- One computer with email access
- Large laminated world map
- 10-foot pole
- tape measure

Math Forum
http://forum.swarthmore.edu/
Don't miss this excellent resource for math students and teachers. The forum features a problem of the week, an ask-an-expert forum (Ask Dr. Math), an Internet hunt, and has great additional resources. Engage students in this interesting site by offering extra credit to students who successfully solve the problem of the week.

THE COST OF LIVING

Subject:
Mathematics, Life Skills

Grade level:
Grades 7-12

Activity type:
Web Resource

Activity level:
Beginner

Time frame:
2 class periods

Partners:
None

Materials Needed

- One computer with Web access per student

The Homebuyer's Fair
http://www.homefair.com

This realty-oriented site features a salary calculator that allows students to factor in cost of living and moving expenses for a designated city.

Students create a budget for a place they would like to live, given certain parameters and using the Web as a resource.

OBJECTIVES

- Students practice research skills.
- Students apply life skills such as budgeting.
- Students use basic math to construct a budget.
- Students use problem solving and critical thinking skills.

PREREQUISITES

Some experience using the Web for research

Knowledge of budgeting

PROCEDURE

1. Explain that this lesson will challenge students' research skills. Copy and cut one role play per student from the blackline master, "The Cost of Living Role Play Cards," in Appendix B. Randomly assign a role to each student.

2. Explain the assignment: Students will need to find a community in which they can afford to live given the parameters presented in their role play card. Students must research their scenario using traditional research tools and the Web. They must then create a monthly budget based on actual costs for their line of work and intended area of work.

3. Have student pairs brainstorm the information they will need to know in order to construct their budget.

4. Still in pairs, students must then each create a research plan. Where will they likely find the information needed? What should be looked up on the Web? What is best researched in the library?

5. Schedule time in 20-minute intervals for each student to use the Web during the day or after school. (Optional: If you would prefer to do this during class time, you can bring the remaining students to the library for any additional needed research.) Students will then create their budgets as homework.

6. Have students in pairs review and evaluate their completed budgets. Can the student afford the lifestyle as outlined? What changes should they make?

TIMELINE

Class 1   Students design their research plan.

Class 2   Students peer review budgets.

This activity was suggested by Nancy Skomars Davis, computer and English teacher, Advanced Technologies Academy, Las Vegas, Nevada.

A KIDS' CONSUMER PRICE INDEX

Students explore different costs of living by region through constructing and conducting their own consumer price index survey.

OBJECTIVES

- Students explore the concept of cost of living and the consumer price index.
- Students analyze, interpret, and report on data.
- Students learn to calculate mean, median, and mode.

PREREQUISITES

None

PROCEDURE

1. Explain the significance of the consumer price index and how it is calculated (from a set basket of goods). (For good background information and data, see Consumer Price Indexes at *http://stats.bls.gov/cpihome.htm*.) Introduce students to this project by asking: Does this price index represent the cost of living for you? Why not? How could we calculate the consumer price index for kids across the U.S.?

2. Break students into small groups to identify a methodology for their consumer price index. What spending will they track? What other information needs to be included?

3. Have students prepare a questionnaire and conduct an email survey of other students across the U.S. Allow 4 weeks for participants to complete your survey. All participants will be sent the project guidelines and results.

4. Share results with partners.

5. Have students design a database (either manually or online using spreadsheet software) and compile data, calculating the mean, median, and mode.

6. Explain to students: Economists usually use median to calculate cost of living. Why? Then have students analyze the median data, making comparisons within and across geographic regions and age groups.

7. Have students present their findings in class using graphs, bar charts, and pie charts.

8. Ask students: To what do you attribute regional differences? (This is an opportunity to discuss supply and demand. Use the example of heating-

Subject:
Economics, Mathematics, Social Studies, Media Literacy

Grade level:
Grades 4-12

Activity type:
Web Survey

Activity level:
Intermediate

Time frame:
7 weeks

Partners:
Unlimited

Materials Needed

- One computer with email/Web access
- Database or spreadsheet software (optional)

This activity was suggested by Kent Werst, math teacher, Reading High School, Reading, Massachusetts.

A KIDS' CONSUMER PRICE INDEX

oil in the north being more expensive than anywhere else in the U.S. Explain that while oil is drilled and refined in the southern part of the U.S., the demand for oil is in the cold north.)

TIMELINE

Week 1   Prepare questionnaire.

Weeks 2-5 Conduct surveys.

Week 6   Students compile data.

Week 7   Students analyze and present data.

MEDIA LITERACY EXTENSION

Have students research market segmentation and advertising. How much money is spent a year marketing to children? Then survey television for a week, making note of all the commercials aimed at children, the length of the commercial, and the category of product (sneakers, candy, toys, etc.) advertised. What products are given the most air time? How does this compare to the products you chose for your CPI? Have students also track their spending habits over a period of time. How does the amount of advertising a product receives relate to what you spend your money on? Any correlation? What do you think about companies advertising to children?

TIP   Make this project more complex by conducting a longitudinal study. What is your inflation rate? (How does your Kids' Consumer Price Index change over time?) How does this compare to the national CPI's changes over that same time period? Any thoughts about why?

PRIMETIME

Students explore interdependent relationships between food, health, and the environment by conducting a national survey on the production, packaging, distribution, consumption, and environmental impact associated with their food.

OBJECTIVES

- Students explore the interdependent relationships between food, health, and the environment.

- Students analyze, interpret, and report on data.

- Students enhance their information processing skills through the use of variety of technology tools.

PREREQUISITES

None

PROCEDURE

1. Post a Call for Collaborators soliciting partner classrooms around the U.S. for a survey. Inform all survey participants that they will receive project guidelines and survey results so that they may execute the project as well.

2. Have students work in small groups to identify a favorite food from a major food group to research.

3. Using Web and library resources, student groups research:

    - Areas where the food is grown

    - Farming methods used to produce it

    - Product yield per acre

    - Environmental impacts due to production

    - Methods of shipment to market

    - Product packaging

    - Waste byproducts

    Assign each student in the group to research a different area.

4. Have students prepare a questionnaire and conduct an email survey of other students across the U.S. to determine how often during a 1-week period respondees eat the selected food; the cost of that food in the respondee's area; and the extent to which food packaging and waste byproducts are recycled. (See the sample questionnaire in Appendix B.)

Subject:
Mathematics, Health Science, Language Arts

Grade level:
Grades 5-12

Activity type:
Web Survey

Activity level:
Intermediate

Time frame:
10 weeks

Partners:
Unlimited

Materials Needed

- One computer with email/Web access

- Database or spreadsheet software (optional)

- Multimedia authoring software (optional)

From an activity by Donald Bourdon, computer teacher, St. Bernards School, Saranac Lake, New York.

PRIMETIME

5. Once the results are in, help students design a database (either manually or online using spreadsheet software) and compile data. Share results with all project partners.

6. Have students analyze data, making comparisons within and across geographic regions on such factors as consumption, availability, cost, and recycling habits.

7. Students present their findings in class using graphs, bar charts, and pie charts. (Optional: Use multimedia authoring software to include photos, videos, audio, and original art in the presentation.)

8. Have students in small groups discuss the implications of their findings. Are there health implications to the results? Environmental implications? Economic implications? What are 3 additional questions that students might want addressed in further research given these implications?

9. Optional: Create an additional survey based on the students' questions.

TIMELINE

Week 1   Introduce the project and telecommunications.

Weeks 2-4 Conduct online research.

Weeks 5-6 Obtain and compile telecommunication data.

Weeks 7-9 Analysis of data and multimedia presentation preparation.

Week 10   Presentation of results.

TIP   Invite parent volunteers into the classroom to videotape presentations. Then have students self-evaluate using the video. What would they change? How could they improve their presentation? Do they have any new ideas for their analysis?

Project success will be based on whether or not the following objectives were met/completed:

Assessment Criteria

1. Information Search, Retrieval, and Management
   - The number of sources used to obtain information
   - The number of contacts/responses generated in each geographic region via email
   - The accuracy of the information entered into the database and spreadsheets

2. Information Analysis
   - Comparison of different methods of production; variability of crop yields and availability by season
   - Comparison of food costs within/across geographical areas
   - The number of factors affecting cost differences within and across geographical areas
   - The number of factors impacting nutritional differences within and across geographical areas
   - The environmental factors associated with each food
   - The quality of the charts and graphs used/presented
   - The quality of questions prepared/used in presentation

3. Self-Management Skills
   - Ability of student (or teams) to meet schedules and deadlines

4. Presentation of Information
   - Content
   - Organization
   - Effective use of technology
   - Effectiveness of the presentation

FANTASY HOOPS: MATHEMATICS AND THE NBA

Subject:
Mathematics, Literature, Conflict Resolution

Grade level:
Grades 6-12

Activity type:
Cooperative Challenge

Activity level:
Intermediate

Time frame:
4 weeks

Partners:
3 classrooms per region (up to 6 partner schools)

Materials Needed

- One computer with email/Web access

Students create a regional all-star basketball team and compete, using basic statistics to track their performance.

OBJECTIVES

- Students learn basics of statistics, including the calculation of mean, median, and mode.
- Students perform basic calculations with decimals, fractions, and percents.
- Students work cooperatively with classmates and other schools to choose their team and follow its progress.
- Students explore regional differences and cultural values.

PREREQUISITES

Kisses for Everyone? (Chapter 2)

PROCEDURE

1. Define regions. Post a Call for Collaborators soliciting 3 partners for the project from each of several U.S. regions.

2. Have male and female basketball fans pair to present an overview about the game and the NBA teams in your region to the class for extra credit.

3. Group students in mixed gender pairs. Have each pair research one NBA basketball team in your region. Create cross-school work groups within regions (3 pairs—1 pair from each school—constitutes a work group).

4. Work groups must then collaboratively choose 5 players from NBA teams in their region for their "all-star team" and 2 alternate players in case one of their players gets injured. Whenever possible, each all-star team member must be from a different team in your region. Note: Assign work groups to devise a method for collaborating on this task online. Be prepared to have students sign up for time on the computer to email their team partners. For work groups having difficulty with this task, suggest the following process:

   a. Each school's pair will first explore, discuss, and then agree on their picks for the all-star team. They must be able to justify their picks.

   b. Each of the 3 pairs in the work group will share their picks and justifications via email—in a predetermined order.

   c. Each of the 3 pairs, again in the same order, will respond to the picks and ask any questions for further clarification.

   d. Pairs will answer any clarifying questions.

   e. Everyone votes on the picks.

   f. The top 5 players will constitute that group's all-star team.

From an activity by Beth Flickinger, mathematics teacher, Stephen Decatur High School, Decatur, Illinois.

5. Have work groups follow each member of their team for 5 consecutive games. Work groups will be required to keep records of the following statistics for each one of their chosen players (assign tasks across work groups):

   - Number of points scored
   - Number of rebounds
   - Number of assists
   - Number of steals

   Students may research through several vehicles including TV, newspapers (*USA Today*), or the Web (see SportsLine NBA Statistics at *http://www.sportsline.com/u/basketball/nba/stats.htm*).

6. Have all students calculate:

   - The mean, median, and mode of the number of points scored for each member of the team and the team as a whole
   - The percentage of each individual player's points scored to the all-star team's total

7. Share data via email. The team with the highest average of points scored, rebounds, assists, and steals in the 5-game span (the first 5 games played by each player) will win.

8. Have students proof the math of submitted data. Students who uncover errors will receive extra credit.

TIMELINE

Week 1   Post Call for Collaborators soliciting up to 6 partner schools.

Week 2   Email procedures to all registered schools.

Weeks 3-4 Collect data over 5 consecutive games.

Week 5   Post results to participants and verify math.

Week 6   Announce winner to participants.

LITERATURE EXTENSION

Partner with English classes to integrate this unit. Have students write articles about their all-star team's performance and then publish a sports paper for all participating classrooms (or publish on a Web site).

SURVEY EXTENSION

Have students create a survey for all project participants regarding the importance and role of sports in our lives. Some possible questions for the survey are: What sports are most popular in your area? How much time per week on the average do students spend playing or watching sports? Share results with all participants. Have students analyze and present the data. Facilitate a discussion: What differences (if any) do you see by region? by gender? Why?

TAKING STOCK

Subject:
Mathematics, Economics, Business, History, Literature

Grade level:
Grades 6-12

Activity type:
Web Resource

Activity level:
Intermediate

Time frame:
4 weeks

Partners:
None

Materials Needed

- One computer with email/Web access
- Spreadsheet software program (optional)

Students create and track a mock stock portfolio, competing against an established mutual fund.

OBJECTIVES

- Students acquire basic skills such as predicting, collecting, averaging, comparing, contrasting, classifying, analyzing, problem solving, graphing, and decision making.
- Students learn about the stock market.
- Students use cooperation and communication skills.

PREREQUISITES

None

PROCEDURE

1. Introduce the stock market to students:
   a. Ask students to bring in the business section of the newspaper.
   b. Explain the basic principles of the stock market and define vocabulary.
   c. Have students choose a company to track daily over a week.
   d. Show students how to read the stock market section, going over each column.
   e. Show students how to find the company of their choice on the Web (teach them the usual syntax for corporate addresses, which is *http://www.companyname.com*).

2. Pair students as "business partners" to create a mock diversified stock portfolio, working within an assigned budget (start with $5,000 to $10,000). Schedule students in 20-minute intervals at the computer to research companies whose stock they are interested in purchasing. (Most publicly traded companies will have a Web site with an investor's page outlining important information.)

   Up-to-date stock market information can be found at:
   - Check Free Investment Services (*http://www.secapl.com/cgi-bin/qs*)
   - PCQuote (*http://www.pcquote.com/*)
   - Quote Watch (*http://www.pcquote.com/watch2.html*)

3. As a class, select a mutual fund whose performance students will attempt to surpass with their portfolios. (Scudder Development Fund might be a fun and interesting mutual fund to use as a gauge. It is a top performer, but is extremely volatile because of its reliance on technology stocks.)

   Up-to-date mutual fund information can be found at The Mutual Funds Home Page (*http://www.brill.com*).

4. Have students create a spreadsheet to enter all data related to their portfolio's performance. This spreadsheet should include the day's high and low, the worth of their portfolio at a designated time, the worth of their portfolio at 2 other times throughout the day, and the percentage gained or lost.

5. Using the Web for up-to-date information, students will track their portfolios for a 2-week period. Unlike the newspaper, which tracks only highs and lows for a stock on a given day, the Web sites are virtually live (with a 20-minute to 1-hour lag time), showing just how volatile a single stock's performance is in a given day. For this reason, allow students access to the computer throughout the day, so that they may check their stock's performance as they go. Require at least 3 checks a day (one at a designated time period—preferably your class period).

Students may buy and sell stock as many times as they want during that 2-week period, changing their portfolio as they go. The official worth of their portfolio will be calculated daily at the designated time period.

6. Track the performance of the selected mutual fund at that designated time period.

7. After the 2-week data collection period, have students create a graph, plotting the daily worth of their portfolios. Students calculate the final worth of their portfolios. What percentage gain (or loss) did their portfolios have from start to finish? Compare to the mutual fund's percentage gain or loss. How did everyone do? Did anyone beat the mutual fund's performance?

Were there trends across portfolios? Across types of stocks? How did technology stocks do as compared to manufacturing?

FOR OLDER STUDENTS

Have upper high school students integrate this project with history and literature by comparing John Steinbeck's *Grapes of Wrath* with Tom Wolfe's *Bonfire of the Vanities*. Compare the '30s with the '80s. (Use James Agee's *Now Praise We Famous Men*, an excellent journalistic portrayal of life in the '30s, as a supplemental resource.) Do these novels accurately reflect the times in which they were written? What effect, if any, do extremes of wealth and poverty have on moral character? Are these time periods different than other time periods? Compare/contrast to the times we're living in now.

TIMELINE

Week 1   Choose stock portfolios.

Weeks 2-3   Track stock and mutual fund performance.

Week 4   Access value of portfolios.

TAKING STOCK

INTEGRATED CURRICULUM EXTENSION

Integrate this project with history and literature by pairing it with a study of the stock market crash and Great Depression. Have students read John Steinbeck's *Grapes of Wrath*.

CRIME AT SCHOOL

Students conduct a crime survey in their school and compare it to national statistics on crime.

OBJECTIVES

- Students explore the issue of crime at school.
- Students analyze, interpret, and report on data.

PREREQUISITES

None

PROCEDURE

1. Have students work in cooperative groups to craft questions for a survey on crime in your school. Some possible questions include: Have you ever been the victim of crime? What types of crime do you most expect at your school? What types do you expect least? How many crimes a year would you estimate are perpetrated?

2. Bring students back together. Combine questions from the smaller groups on chart paper or on the board.

3. Look at the national school crime report prepared by the Bureau of Justice (*http://www.ojp.usdoj.gov/bjs/abstract/sc.htm*). Ask: What questions/issues did this survey track? Referring back to your chart paper or the board, what additional questions might we want to include on our survey? As a class prepare a questionnaire.

4. Conduct an *anonymous* survey of students at school. (Depending on the size of your school you may want to limit the survey to one or two grades.)

5. Have students analyze data in cooperative groups. (You can split up the data between groups or have each group present on all data depending on the ages of your students and the breadth of your survey.)

6. Have students present their findings in class using graphs, bar charts, and pie charts.

7. Have students compare their school's results with the national statistics. Have students present their findings regarding the comparison using graphs, bar charts, and pie charts.

8. Facilitate a discussion about the results. Were you surprised by the results? What did this survey tell us about our school? Any thoughts about what should be done as a result?

Subject:
Mathematics, Science, Social Studies, Computer Technology

Grade level:
Grades 9-12

Activity type:
Web Resource

Activity level:
Intermediate

Time frame:
9 weeks

Partners:
None

Materials Needed

- One computer with email/Web access (1 computer per 3 students is preferable)

CRIME AT SCHOOL

TIMELINE

Weeks 1-2   Devise your questionnaire and disseminate.

Weeks 3-4   Gather results.

Weeks 5-6   Analyze school data and prepare presentation.

Weeks 7-8   Compare school's data with national data. Analyze and prepare presentation.

Week 9   Discuss.

WEB COLLABORATION EXTENSION

Plan an online round table discussion by partnering with other schools for this activity. After sharing each classroom's data, students can discuss the findings and troubleshoot solutions using email.

TIP   As you know, any issue with such potential for controversy should be discussed first with your school's administration before going ahead. Solicit its support in addressing the findings in a positive, non-punitive manner. Be sure your administration has a plan of action ready before going ahead with the survey. Have students share with the administration any interesting ideas that arise from their discussion. Work toward creating a plan that involves the entire school in finding a solution.

SOCIAL SECURITY OR BUST?

Students learn more about this controversial topic by polling senior citizens and taking both sides of the issue in a debate.

OBJECTIVES

- Students learn more about a controversial topic.
- Students learn about differing perspectives in a conflict.
- Students learn about the Social Security system.

PREREQUISITES

None

PROCEDURE

1. Have students in small cooperative groups research the issue (using library and Web resources):
   - What is the history of Social Security?
   - What are its benefits?
   - What are its disadvantages?
   - Who are the different stakeholders in the issue?
   - What is each stakeholder's perspective on the issue?
   - What are each stakeholder's positions and interests? (Positions are what each stake holder is demanding. Interests are *why* they need them—the underlying need being addressed by the demand.)

2. Using the facts learned in their research, have students in small groups brainstorm questions for a survey to poll both senior citizens and government officials on the issue.

3. Bring the class together. Have each small group report on their questions. As a class, construct a poll about the issue. How many seniors should you survey for an adequate sample?

4. Have students research mailing lists for senior citizens and government officials and post their survey. (Hint: For elders, post your survey on SeniorNet at *http://www.seniornet.org/cgi-bin/WebX*.) Be sure to include a deadline for response, information about your class, and how the survey will be used. Optional: As a supplement to the survey, students can interview an elder about the topic.

5. Again in small groups, have students frame the debate question. Assign each group a side on the issue (evenly dividing the class). Have small groups prepare for the debate.

Subject:
Mathematics, Social Studies, Conflict Resolution

Grade level:
Grades 9-12

Activity type:
Web Survey

Activity level:
Intermediate

Time frame:
6 weeks

Partners:
None

Materials Needed

- One computer with email/Web access

SOCIAL SECURITY OR BUST?

Suggested small group process for preparing for the debate:

a. Prepare a list of the relevant issues on both sides of the argument.

b. For each issue, identify both the positions and interests.

c. Prepare rebuttals for the other side's arguments.

d. Decide on the most persuasive arguments to use in an opening argument.

e. Prepare opening argument and review key issues.

6. Begin the debate by exchanging opening arguments, followed by:

a. Rebuttal

b. Cross-examination

c. Rebuttal

d. Cross-examination

e. Rebuttal

f. Cross-examination (repeat until each student has had a turn)

7. Anonymously poll all students on their individual positions on the debate.

8. Reverse positions on the issue and hold another debate. Repeat steps 5 through 7.

9. Facilitate a discussion: How have your views been affected by the debate? Did anyone change his or her mind? Why? How did it feel to argue the other point of view? What did you learn? What is the value of Social Security in our society?

10. Assessment (Optional)

a. Students can peer evaluate the debate using speaker points. Each student is given a score from 1 to 30 (with 30 being the highest). The scores are then added up and the team with the highest score wins. Explain that the assignment will be judged on the following criteria:

- Effectiveness of persuasive arguments

- Use of supporting facts

b. Have students research the mathematics and economics related to Social Security. Experts say that at its current pace of income and expense, the Social Security system as we know it will become bankrupt. How would you go about assessing the situation if you were the President's chief advisor on the situation? What would you advise?

TIMELINE

Weeks 1-2 Research the issue and prepare arguments.

Weeks 3-4 Hold first debate.

Weeks 5-6 Hold second debate.

TIP

For more practice for your students with conflict resolution techniques, use *Elementary Perspectives: Teaching Concepts of Peace and Conflict* (for elementary students), *Conflict Resolution in the Middle School* (for middle school students), and *Making Choices, Part I* and *Part II* (for high school students). These resources are all available through Educators for Social Responsibility, 23 Garden Street, Cambridge, MA 02138 (800) 370-2515.

Science

7

THE EXTERMINATOR MYSTERY PROJECT

Students work collaboratively to write mystery essays containing clues to the location and species of an insect to stop the evil ExTerminator.

OBJECTIVES

- Students use science, geography, and map resource materials.
- Students think critically to solve mysteries.
- Students learn about insects.

PREREQUISITES

None

PROCEDURE

1. Post Call for Collaborators soliciting partner classrooms to solve the mystery of the evil ExTerminator. The ExTerminator travels around the U.S. destroying all species of insects with which he comes in contact. Your assignment, if you should choose to take it, is to catch the evil Ex-Terminator by locating the city where he has committed his heinous crimes and to identify the insect he exterminated. Partner classrooms will receive 5 mystery essays to solve on a predetermined schedule. They will have 2 weeks in which to solve the mystery.

2. With students, create a schedule for posting mystery essays to project participants. Allow 2 weeks for participants to solve the mystery. Email to partners.

3. Working cooperatively in small groups and using various resource materials, including road maps, atlases, and insect identification books, have students develop the clues to the mystery. Each group will develop 1 mystery essay containing clues to the location and insect species. Caution groups not to reveal the answers in their essays. Optional: Use the Web to research. City Link (*http://usacitylink.com/*), City Net (*http://www.city.net/*), and Map Quest: the Interactive Atlas (*http://www.mapquest.com/*) all have valuable map resources for students.

4. Test the difficulty of each mystery by circulating finished essays between collaborative groups in your classroom. Have each essay reviewed and solved successfully at least once.

5. Post the first mystery to the participating classrooms as scheduled with a deadline for responding. (Participating classrooms can choose to post in-

Subject:
Science, Social Studies, Conflict Resolution, Art

Grade level:
Grades K-12

Activity type:
Cooperative Challenge

Activity level:
Beginner

Time frame:
3 months

Partners:
Unlimited

Materials Needed

- One computer with email access (Web access is optional)
- Atlas/road maps (or you may use the Web)
- Insect identification books

Marshall Ramme

From an activity by Marshall Ramme, teacher, Broadmeadow Elementary School, Rantoul, Illinois.

THE EXTERMINATOR MYSTERY PROJECT

dividual student answers to the mystery or solve the mystery coopera-tively and post one answer.)

6. Have students correct answers and respond to each participating student or classroom.

7. Repeat steps 5-6 with second through fifth mystery.

8. Optional: Create a Web site for this project! The Broadmeadow School's site for this project can be found at *http://pop.life.uiuc.edu/~meadow/*. (See "Creating A Web Site," Chapter 3, for further information.)

TIMELINE

Week 1   Post Call for Collaborators soliciting partners.

Weeks 2-3   Write mystery essays.

Week 4   Solve first mystery essay in coordinator's classroom.

Week 5   Post first mystery.

Week 7   Correct answers from participants. Post second mystery.

Week 9   Correct answers from participants. Post third mystery.

Week 11   Correct answers from participants. Post fourth mystery.

Week 13   Correct answers from participants. Post fifth mystery.

Week 15   Correct answers from participants.

CONFLICT RESOLUTION EXTENSION

Humanize the evil ExTerminator by sending messages to participating students from him. Show that the ExTerminator is not all bad—perhaps he is hungry and is eating the insects, or he is clumsy and is trying to play with the insects, not hurt them. Involve students in problem-solving about how to nonviolently stop him. What could they say to the ExTerminator? What could they ask? Aim to construct a win-win solution where both the ExTerminator and the insects get what they really need.

TIP   Jim Butsch, an Illinois teacher, uses the first mystery to discuss "keywords" with his class. The students use a variety of resources to follow up on the keywords.

TIP

"My daughter will be eight next week and she's a homeschooled child. It was a true delight to watch her researching the answers to the Gypsy Moth mystery. She went right to the reference books on insects in the adult section of the library... and methodically went through each reference book for all the info on the gypsy moth." — Helene Sue Rock, teacher and homeschooling parent, Los Altos, California.

SPRING FLING

Subject:
Science, Art, English

Grade level:
Grades K-8

Activity type:
Web Collaboration

Activity level:
Beginner

Time frame:
6 weeks

Participants:
Unlimited

Materials Needed

- One computer with email access (Web access is optional)

Students record and compare signs of spring across the United States.

OBJECTIVES

- Students identify signs of spring.

- Students compare signs of spring and dates seen across the U.S. (or worldwide)

PREREQUISITES

None

PROCEDURE

Note: This project is best done between February and May.

1. Post Call for Collaborators soliciting partner classrooms. Look for partners from different latitudes.

2. Working in pairs, have students go outside to take notes on signs of spring once a week for four weeks. Ask: What do you see this week that you didn't see last week? Have students record their observations in their "field notebooks." (Have younger students note one new observation to report to you. Record all observations in a class field notebook.)

3. Have classrooms compile and post their data to the project coordinator via email. The project coordinator then shares all data with participating classrooms.

4. For younger students: Using a wall map, help students locate partner classrooms. Review the observations, noting similarities and differences across latitudes.

   For older students: Have students create a summary of each classroom's observations with dates. Cut and tack onto a wall map.

5. Help students interpret the data. Ask: What differences do you notice between northern and southern schools? How are the signs similar between sites? How do the signs move south to north?

6. Classrooms share their analysis via email.

FOR OLDER STUDENTS

If you have Web access, students can post and compare data about common sightings, such as the American robin or monarch butterflies, at Journey North (*http://www.ties.k12.mn.us/%7Ejnorth*).

TIMELINE

Week 1   Post Call for Collaborators soliciting participants.

Weeks 2-5 Make observations and share data with all participants.

Week 6   Analyze and share results.

ART AND LITERATURE EXTENSION

Have students create an illustrated nature diary! In blank books, students can draw and notate the signs of spring. Include poetry and quotes from literature (or have students write their own). Students will have a wonderful record of the project and the unfolding of spring. *The Nature Notes of an Edwardian Lady* by naturalist Edith Holden is a beautiful example that you could share with students.

SPRING FLING

Have plenty of field guides available for students to identify plants and animals from your area.

TIP

TRADING TEMPS

Subject:
Science, Mathematics, Social Studies

Grade level:
Grades 3-8

Activity type:
Web Collaboration

Activity level:
Beginner

Time frame:
4 Weeks

Participants:
Unlimited

Materials Needed

- One computer with email/Web access
- Spreadsheet software
- Large laminated world map
- Thermometer mounted outside school building in shade

Students compare temperatures around the globe by latitude to determine how temperature is affected by proximity to the equator.

OBJECTIVES

- Students explore the relationship globally between temperature and latitude.
- Students acquire basic skills such as predicting, collecting, graphing, computing means, and analyzing data.
- Students practice conversion from Celsius to Fahrenheit.
- Students learn basic world geography.

PREREQUISITES

None

PROCEDURE

Note: This project is best done during March, when the equinox occurs.

1. Post a Call for Collaborators looking for partners from different latitudes to compare temperatures. (To time this with the equinox, post the Call for Collaborators in mid-February.)

2. Working in pairs, ask students to hypothesize how latitude generally effects daily temperature and length of day. How would this be affected by the equinox? Record their hypotheses.

3. Have students from participating classrooms around the world take temperature readings every day for a week between 11:00 am and 1:00 pm local time, and register time of sunrise and sunset for each day. If you have Web access, you can find sunrise and sunset times for U.S. cities at *http://tycho.usno.navy.mil/srss.html*.

4. Classrooms compile and post their data to the project coordinator via email. The project coordinator then shares all data with participating classrooms.

5. Have students calculate for each city:
   - Mean temperature in Fahrenheit
   - Mean temperature in Celsius
   - Mean hours of daylight

   Note: Have students create their own Celsius to Fahrenheit conversion chart for easy reference.

From an activity by Cynthia Addison, teacher, Stevens Institute of Technology, Hoboken, New Jersey.

6. Have students enter all data onto spreadsheets. Spreadsheets should have 5 columns: name of city, latitude, mean temperature in Celsius, mean temperature in Fahrenheit, and hours of daylight.

7. Students test their original hypotheses by organizing the data by latitude and analyzing the results. Anomalies in temperature data can be investigated by taking global satellite and radar images off the Web for the U.S. at Weather by Intellicast (*http://www.intellicast.com/weather/intl/worldsat.gif*) and for other countries at (*http://cirrus.sprl.umich.edu/wxnet/radsat.html*) for the days the temperature recording was taking place. (When data related to the equinox shows anomalies, request additional information from the Ask a Scientist site at *http://www.cedarnet.org/aska/scientist/index.html.*)

8. Share your analyses with partner classrooms via email.

FOR YOUNGER STUDENTS

Have younger students write their data directly on the laminated wall map. It will help them spot trends related to latitude.

FOR OLDER STUDENTS

Make this project more sophisticated by adding the variables of proximity to water and elevation to the data set. How is temperature affected by these variables?

TIMELINE

Week 1	Post Call for Collaborators soliciting participants.
Week 2	Email procedures and introductions of students to all registered schools.
Week 3	Take measurements and share data with all participants.
Week 4	Analyze and share results.

TRADING TEMPS

"Our knowledge of the world has been increased. We not only know the names of places in the U.S., Canada, Europe, South America, and other parts of Australia, but we know a little of the way of life in those areas." —Student, Mareeba School, Australia.

TIP

RATING RAINFALL

Subject:
Science, Mathematics,
Geography

Grade level:
Grades 4-8

Activity type:
Web Collaboration

Activity level:
Beginner

Time frame:
5 weeks

Participants:
Unlimited

Materials Needed

- One computer with email access
- Spreadsheet software
- Wall map
- Rain gauge mounted outside the classroom

Students compare rainfall across the U.S. by longitude.

OBJECTIVES

- Students learn about weather patterns.
- Students acquire basic skills such as predicting, collecting, graphing, computing means, and analyzing data.
- Students learn basic U.S. geography.

PREREQUISITES

None

PROCEDURE

1. Post a Call for Collaborators soliciting partner classrooms. (You'll need students from different longitudes.)
2. Working in pairs, ask students to hypothesize how one's longitude might affect rainfall. Help them develop their hypothesis by showing them a U.S. map. What do they notice about the placement of deserts? Where are the forests? Record their hypotheses.
3. Have students from participating classrooms around the country record daily rainfall for a designated period of 2 weeks.
4. Classrooms compile and post their data to the project coordinator via email. The project coordinator shares all data with participating classrooms.
5. Students calculate mean rainfall for each day for each city.
6. Students enter all data onto spreadsheets. Spreadsheets should have 3 columns: name of city, longitude, and mean rainfall.
7. Students test their original hypotheses by organizing the data by longitude and analyzing the results.
8. Classrooms share their analysis via email.

TIMELINE

Week 1	Post Call for Collaborators soliciting participants.
Week 2-4	Take measurements and share data with all participants.
Week 5	Analyze and share results.

TIP Have students create flags for their data and post directly on the laminated wall map. It will help them spot trends.

THE GEN(IE) IN THE BOTTLE

Students explore recessive and dominant gene traits by conducting a national survey on characteristics.

OBJECTIVES

- Students research dominant and recessive gene traits.
- Students analyze, interpret, and report on data.

PREREQUISITES

None

PROCEDURE

1. Have students research dominant and recessive gene traits and create a survey to test the traits on a large sample. Include questions about at least 3 dominant and 3 recessive genes in your survey.
2. Conduct an email survey of other students across the U.S. by posting the survey for other classrooms (offer to share all data with respondees).
3. Once the results are in, help students design a database (either manually or online using spreadsheet software) and compile data.
4. Have students analyze data.
5. Present data in class using graphs, bar charts, and pie charts.

FOR YOUNGER STUDENTS

Elementary students can modify this activity by surveying students on a fun genetic trait such as the ability to curl your tongue.

TIMELINE

Week 1	Students research dominant versus recessive genes.
Weeks 2-5	Conduct email surveys.
Week 6	Compile data.
Week 7	Analyze data.

This activity was suggested by Jane Clarke, former research associate, Cellcor, Inc., Newton Massachusetts.

Subject:
Science, Mathematics

Grade level:
Grades 7-12

Activity type:
Web Survey

Activity level:
Beginner

Time frame:
10 weeks

Participants:
Unlimited

Materials Needed

- One computer with email/Web access
- Database or spreadsheet software (optional)

WEATHER WEEK

Subject:
Science, Mathematics,
Social Studies

Grade level:
Grades 2-6

Activity type:
Web Collaboration

Activity level:
Beginner

Time frame:
4 weeks

Participants:
25-30 classrooms

Materials Needed

- One computer with email access (Web access is optional)
- Thermometer
- A weathervane (can be made)
- Spreadsheet software (optional)

During a designated week, students around the world collect and share daily temperature, cloud type, precipitation, and wind direction data.

OBJECTIVES

- Students acquire basic skills such as predicting, collecting, graphing, computing means, and analyzing data.
- Students practice conversion from Celsius to Fahrenheit.
- Students learn basic world geography.
- Students apply weather concepts.

PREREQUISITES

Ability to identify cloud types: cirrus, cumulus, and stratus

PROCEDURE

1. Post a Call for Collaborators looking for partners to compare weather data. (See registration form in Appendix B.)

2. Have students from participating classrooms around the world take weather data every day for a week between 1:30 and 2:30 pm. Students should record:

- **Temperature:**
Attach your thermometer to a stick or yardstick so that it can be placed 3 feet off of the ground in a shady spot. Record the temperature each day between 1:30 and 2:30 p.m.

- **Cloud Types:**
During the same hour, observe the clouds to determine the predominate cloud type: cumulus, cirrus, or stratus.

- **Precipitation:**
Record the type of precipitation: None, rainfall, mist, snow, sleet, freezing rain, other (please list).

- **Wind Direction:**
This can be accomplished with a commercial or "homemade" weather vane to determine the direction of the wind. The wind direction is the direction the wind is coming from. (For example a northeast wind blows from the northeast.)

(See the weather data form in Appendix B.)

From an activity by Cindy Cooper, teacher, Mt. Ulla and Hurley Elementary School, Mt.Ulla and Salisbury, North Carolina. Additional input provided by Kathy Pulliam, also a teacher at Mt. Ulla Elementary. This project was inspired by the National Geographic Weather in Action project.

3. Classrooms compile and post their data to the project coordinator via email. The project coordinator then shares all data with participating classrooms.

4. Have students in pairs enter all data onto spreadsheets and graph. Students will need to convert all temperature readings to Fahrenheit. (Each student will have his or her own data set.)

5. Have student pairs analyze and compare the results. What patterns emerge? How is weather a function of latitude? How is it a function of longitude? Can you guess where the class is located from the data? What clues might help you do this? Trace a front as it moves across the country!

6. Share your analyses with partner classrooms via email.

TIMELINE

Week 1 Post Call for Collaborators soliciting participants.

Week 2 Email procedures and introductions of students to all registered schools.

Week 3 Take measurements and share data with all participants.

Week 4 Analyze and share results.

WEATHER WEEK

The Web has many excellent weather resources, including additional activities you can do in your classroom. Check out the Weather Channel (*http://www.weather.com*); CNN's Weather Page (*http://www.cnn.com/WEATHER/index.html*) and their European Weather Page (*http://www.cnn.com/WEATHER/ Europe/region_map.html*); and NOAA's Weather Page (*http://www.esdim.noaa.gov/weather_page.html*). Links to other weather sites can be found at Weather Information Superhighway (*http://thunder.met.fsu.edu/~nws/wxhwy.html*).

TIP

PRIMARY PRODUCTIVITY

Subject:
Science, Biology, Chemistry, Mathematics

Grade level:
Grades 10-12

Activity type:
Web Collaboration

Activity level:
Beginner

Time frame:
4 weeks

Participants:
Unlimited

Materials Needed

- One computer with email/Web access
- Spreadsheet software
- Large laminated world map
- One clear bottle
- One black bottle (or a clear bottle painted black)
- DO_2 (dissolved oxygen) test kit
- Anchor
- Buoy
- Line

Students compare the primary productivity of the Atlantic/Caribbean ocean by latitude to determine how productivity is affected by proximity to the equator (or angle of the sun).

OBJECTIVES

- Students will have a deeper understanding of photosynthesis and its role in ocean ecology.
- Students learn about properties of water and light.
- Students explore relationship globally between primary productivity and latitude.
- Students acquire basic skills such as predicting, collecting, graphing, computing means, and analyzing data.
- Students learn basic world geography.

PREREQUISITES

Access to the Atlantic ocean

PROCEDURE

1. Post a Call for Collaborators looking for partners from different latitudes to compare primary productivity in the Atlantic/Caribbean ocean.

2. Explain properties of light and water to your class (specifically light reflection and absorption).

3. Explain primary productivity, the role of phytoplankton, and the process of photosynthesis in the ocean:

$$6\ CO_2 + 6\ H_2O \xrightarrow[\text{sunlight and nutrients}]{\text{(yields)}} C_6H_{12}O_6 + 6O_2$$

Tell students that there are significant differences in the photosynthetic activity in the oceans. Ask what factors might contribute to this (for example, depth; type of plant matter: phytoplankton, cyanobacteria, benthic microalgae, benthic macroalgae, seed plants, symbiotic algal cell, etc.; light availability, etc.). Explain that phytoplankton (including cyanobacteria) account for more than 95 percent of the primary productivity in the ocean. This experiment will measure the oxygen production of the phytoplankton at the surface over a fixed period of time at various locations to see if any trends emerge related to latitude.

4. Working in pairs, ask students to hypothesize how latitude might effect primary productivity. Circulate among the groups, asking: What affects productivity? How does latitude affect the position of the sun? How might this affect photosynthesis? Record their hypotheses.

PRIMARY PRODUCTIVITY

5. Have students from participating classrooms do the following experiment to measure photosynthetic activity.

The Experiment

Note: Inform participating classrooms that this experiment needs to take place within a designated time period (no more than a week), between 10:00 am and 2:00 pm on a sunny day.

 a. Collect a sea water sample from the surface (via boat or wading) of a fixed volume (all partners must use the same volume).

 b. Test the sample for its Do_2 (dissolved oxygen) content. Record the results.

 c. Split the sample evenly between a bottle that is clear (allowing light to penetrate) and one that does not allow light to penetrate. (You can paint a clear bottle black or wrap it in tin foil.)

 d. Tie the bottles together. Attach to a flotation devise and anchor. Return the bottles to the surface. Leave for 2-4 hours. (This period can be altered; however, it's important that this time period remain fixed between sites and span the noon hour. For meaningful results, the time period should not exceed 8 hours).

 e. Collect the samples. Again test for Do_2 (dissolved oxygen) in both bottles. Record the results.

 f. Have students compute and record the net change in oxygen levels for both bottles. (Due to respiration, the dark bottle should show a net loss. The light bottle should show a net gain.)

 g. Ask students: Given that there has been some oxygen loss (respiration) in the dark bottle and some oxygen gain (photosynthesis) in the light bottle, how will we compute the actual oxygen gain from photosynthesis only? (Students should realize that they have already computed the loss from respiration through the dark bottle. Deducting the respiration loss from the light bottle's total oxygen gain will then yield the oxygen gain from photosynthesis.)

 h. Have students compute the oxygen gain (gross photosynthesis).

6. Classrooms compile and post their data to the project coordinator via email. The project coordinator then shares all data with participating classrooms.

7. In small groups, have students create a spreadsheet that shows the gross photosynthesis for all sites by latitude. Have them choose an appropriate graphing method to display the results.

8. In small groups, students test their original hypothesis by analyzing the results.

Sites in the tropics (nearest the equator) should have the highest productivity. Why? (The angle of the sun at noon is perpendicular, so little light is reflected, compared with other sites where a less or greater than 90 percent angle causes more reflection. Reflected light is lost to the system.)

**PRIMARY
PRODUCTIVITY**

Anomalies in data can be investigated by requesting additional information from the Ask a Scientist site (*http://www.cedarnet.org/aska/scientist/index.html*).

7. Share your analyses with partner classrooms via email.

TIMELINE

Week 1 Post Call for Collaborators soliciting participants.

Week 2 Email procedures and introductions of students to all registered schools.

Week 3 Take measurements and share data with all participants.

Week 4 Analyze and share results.

TIP   Kits for testing dissolved oxygen are available through the LaMotte Company at (800) 344-3100.

A BIRD IN THE HAND?

Students record and compare the spring migration pattern of the American robin.

OBJECTIVES

- Through field research, students learn about spring migration patterns for common birds (specifically the American robin).

- Students acquire basic skills such as predicting, collecting, graphing, and analyzing data.

- Students learn about isotherms by exploring the relationship of sightings to temperature.

PREREQUISITES

None

PROCEDURE

Note: This project is best done between February and May.

1. Post Call for Collaborators soliciting partner schools around the U.S. (You'll need schools across latitudes.)

2. Students from participating classrooms around the U.S. record daily temperatures and their first sighting of the American robin.

3. Classrooms compile and post their data to the project coordinator via email. The project coordinator then shares all data with participating classrooms. (If you have Web access, you can post your data and find other data to include in your study through Journey North at *http://www.ties.k12.mn.us/~jnorth/critters/robin/*.)

4. Students graph the temperature changes by latitude, marking the date the robin is first observed.

5. Working in pairs, students analyze the results. Discuss the function of isotherms. Have students compute average temperatures by city. Does the robin travel with the isotherm? Given massive mortality rates during migration, why is it that the robin takes such an extreme journey? What function does migration have?

   If you have Web access and need help interpreting your results, see the Journey North's site (address above) for its Ask an Expert feature. Or have students hone their researching skills using the Web. See The Birds of America site at *http://compstat.wharton.upenn.edu:8001/~siler/birdlinks. html* for links to all sorts of interesting information about birds.

6. Classrooms share their analysis via email.

Subject:
Science, Mathematics, English

Grade level:
Grades 7-12

Activity type:
Web Collaboration

Activity level:
Beginner

Time frame:
6 weeks

Participants:
Unlimited

Materials Needed

- One computer with email access (Web access is optional)
- Spreadsheet software
- Thermometer mounted outside classroom in the shade

A BIRD IN THE HAND?

TIMELINE

Week 1   Post Call for Collaborators soliciting participants.

Week 2-5   Take measurements and share data with all participants.

Week 6   Analyze and share results.

ENGLISH EXTENSION

Have students read Rachel Carson's *Silent Spring*. Use it as a launching point to explain basic principles of ecology. Explain how the book started the movement to outlaw DDT. Discuss: Why do we need birds? What do they add to our lives? What environmental threats exist locally? How might we address it? Have students write a response in their journals.

TIP   This project can be modified to track other local migratory birds and/or animals. Journey North's home page (*http://www.ties.k12.mn.us/%7Ejnorth*) includes migratory data on the bald eagle, caribou, loggerhead sea turtles, the common loon, monarch butterflies, the northern oriole, peregrine falcon, and humpback whales.

A WHALE'S TALE

Students virtually trace the Atlantic migration of a humpback whale from the breeding grounds of the Dominican Republic to the feeding grounds of Maine.

OBJECTIVES

- Students will research the life of humpback whales locally.
- Students will learn about the life history traits of a humpback whale.
- Students will learn how to use Web and other research tools.
- Students will learn how to create a timeline.
- Students will paint and draw whales.

PREREQUISITES

None

PROCEDURE

1. Post a Call for Collaborators soliciting partner classrooms. (You'll need students from different latitudes along the Atlantic seaboard from the Dominican Republic to Maine.) See the Call for Collaborators in Chapter 3 for an example.

2. Working in pairs, have students use the Web and other resources to research humpback whales. They will need to know:

   - When humpbacks are in local waters
   - What humpbacks do daily in local waters
   - Where humpbacks are headed when they leave your local waters

3. Have students from participating classrooms from around the country send postcards via email from Hugh the Humpback Whale describing what Hugh does during his time in their waters. (You can collect all of your students' postcards into one file to send from your class, dated the approximate day and month that Hugh would be in your area.)

4. Share all email postcards with partner classrooms.

5. Have students organize the postcards chronologically (by date when Hugh is in that locale).

6. Split students into pairs to read a portion of the postcards, creating a timeline for where Hugh is and what he is doing during that month.

7. Have each pair present their section of the timeline and sample postcards to the class chronologically.

8. Mark Hugh's migration route on a wall map, flagging the months he is in each particular area.

Subject:
Science, Geography, Language Arts, Art

Grade level:
Grades K-8

Activity type:
Web Simulation

Activity level:
Intermediate

Time frame:
5 weeks

Participants:
Unlimited (along Atlantic Seaboard from the Dominican Republic to Maine)

Materials Needed

- One computer with email/Web access
- Wall map
- Art supplies

A WHALE'S TALE

9. Have students (again in original pairs) write and illustrate the portion of the story of Hugh's life that their timeline covered.

10. Gather together all of the stories chronologically and bind into a book.

11. Copy the entire story for each child and have students each create his or her own cover for their *Whale's Tale*.

TIMELINE

Weeks 1-2   Post Call for Collaborators soliciting partners. Research whales.

Week 3   Postcards are due to project coordinator.

Week 4   Create timeline.

Week 5   Create storybook.

TIP   If you are lucky enough to live in an area with a whale watch, combine this activity with a field trip to see the mighty giants up close. Supplement this activity with videos on whales from National Geographic and picture books for young nonreaders. Readers 4th grade and older will enjoy *Whalesong* by Robert Siegel, a novelette about the life of a mythical whale named Hruna.

BAKING BREAD

Students research bread, tracing its components to their source.

OBJECTIVES

- Students learn about bread and its components.
- Students practice communication skills.
- Students develop Web research skills.

PREREQUISITES

None

PROCEDURE

1. Download bread recipes for the children from the following Web site: *http://www.fatfree.com/recipes/breads-yeast/*. Then choose a simple recipe to make if you have a kitchen facility or bring in a loaf to share with your class.

2. Ask: What are the basic ingredients in bread? With the children, break down those ingredients to their most basic parts. What is flour made from? How? Where does wheat come from? If necessary, help younger students research these questions using the Web.

3. Post a Call for Collaborators on the Web looking for a partner classroom from a wheat farming community to conduct interviews of farmers. (Your partner classroom will gain valuable experience interviewing and writing about wheat farming and harvesting.)

   Note: You can also do this as a Web Mentor Activity by looking for an agricultural expert via Ask an Expert (*http://www.askanexpert.com/askanexpert*).

4. Have students in pairs generate a list of questions for the partner classroom about the wheat growing/harvesting process.

5. Email questions to your partner class for response. They can research the answers by interviewing local farmers. Allow 2 weeks for their responses.

6. Using the Web, have students research the milling process. How does wheat become flour? Share what you learn with your partner classroom.

7. Create a display for your school on bread, including the interviews with farmers done by your partner and any other interesting items you find in your research. Decorate the display with magazine photos of bread, farming, and baking. Shellac sample bread that students bake and include in the display.

Subject:
Science, Social Studies

Grade level:
Grades 3-7

Activity type:
Web Resource, Web Mentor

Activity level:
Intermediate

Time frame:
7 weeks

Participants:
1 classroom from a farming community (or an agricultural expert)

Materials Needed

- One computer with email/Web access

BAKING BREAD

FOR OLDER STUDENTS

Have older students use the Web to research other interesting information about bread. What nutritional value does bread hold? In what cultures is bread significant in ceremony? What role does yeast play?

TIMELINE

Weeks 1-2   Research bread components and post Call for Collaborators for participants.

Weeks 3-4   Prepare questions for partners and post.

Weeks 5-6   Partners respond.

Week 7   Create the bread display.

SOCIAL STUDIES EXTENSION

Try this activity partnering with international classrooms. Have each partner contribute recipes, folk tales, and holiday traditions associated with bread. Then hold a culminating festival featuring each classroom's contribution where parents and community members can sample breads from around the world.

TIP   Plan this activity for the fall and have your partner classrooms from the heartland send you a stalk of recently harvested wheat. Have the children separate the kernel from the chaff and discuss the milling process.

PLENTY OF FISH IN THE SEA?

Students research where their local fish comes from and communicate with a classroom from a fishing community to learn more about fishing practice and stocks.

OBJECTIVES

- Students learn about fishing practice.
- Students practice communication skills.
- Students develop Web research skills.

PREREQUISITES

None

PROCEDURE

1. Ask: Where do the fish we eat in this community come from? What about fresh-water fish? What about ocean fish (if applicable)? Choose one fish to research. Trace the fish back to its distributor and, finally, its point of origin. If necessary, help younger students research this question using the local grocery store as a source.

2. Post a Call for Collaborators looking for a partner classroom from a fishing community.

   Note: You can also do this as a Web Mentor Activity by looking for an agricultural expert via Ask an Expert (*http://www.askanexpert.com/askanexpert*).

3. Have students in pairs generate a list of questions they have about the fishing process for the partner classroom.

4. Email questions to your partner class for response. Allow 2 weeks for their response. (Partner classrooms can research the questions by interviewing local fishermen.)

5. Using the Web and your partner classroom as a resource, help students research the state of your designated fish stock. Are there "plenty of fish" in the sea? What rules govern fishing and why? How have the fish stocks changed over time? Why? What can you do about it?

TIMELINE

Weeks 1-2 Research fish origin and post Call for Collaborators for participants.

Weeks 3-4 Prepare questions for partners and post.

Weeks 5-6 Partners respond.

Subject:
Science, Social Studies

Grade level:
Grades 3-8

Activity type:
Simulation

Activity level:
Intermediate

Time frame:
6 weeks

Participants:
1 classroom from a fishing community

Materials Needed

- One computer with email/Web access

TIP   Does your region have any local resources that travel great distances to other places? Help students research the answer to this question, and if possible, send a sample to your partner classroom as a thank you. Perhaps they would want to research more about your resource!

GROUNDHOG WATCH

Students in different locations around the globe measure and compare their shadow's length.

OBJECTIVES

- Students explore the relationship globally between the sun's position in the sky (or shadow length) and latitude.
- Students acquire basic skills such as predicting, collecting, graphing, and analyzing data.
- Students practice metric conversion.
- Students learn basic world geography.

PREREQUISITES

None

PROCEDURE

1. Bring paired students outside at two different times during a sunny day (morning and afternoon) to trace their shadows with chalk and measure them. How has the shadow changed from morning to afternoon?

2. Ask students to explore together what affects their shadow's length.

3. **For younger students:** Once they have established that a shadow's length has something to do with the position of the sun's light, conduct the following demonstration:

    Cover a table or desk with drawing paper. Place a standing object on the table or desk and slowly arch a lit lamp over the object to simulate a rising and setting sun. Stop at regular intervals along the arch and let students take turns drawing the outline of the shadow cast by the object, as shown below.

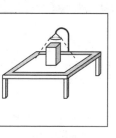

For older students: Give student pairs pushpins, a lamp, and a rubber ball to explore and hypothesize how latitude generally affects a shadow's length. Would there be a difference between a person's shadow length in North America versus someone's shadow length in South America at the same time?

Subject:
Science, Mathematics, Art

Grade level:
Grades 3-12

Activity type:
Web Collaboration

Activity level:
Intermediate

Time frame:
4 weeks

Participants:
Unlimited

Materials Needed

- One computer with email access
- Large laminated world map
- Rubber balls (one per student pair)
- Several lamps (one per student pair is ideal)
- Push pins
- Standing objects (one per student pair)
- Chalk
- Tape measure(s)

GROUNDHOG WATCH

Using the rubber ball as a globe, with push pins representing people in different hemispheres and a lamp held representing the sun, students can hold the ball in a single place and turn it on its axis. Record their hypotheses on chart paper.

4. Post a Call for Collaborators soliciting partner schools around the world (northern and southern hemispheres).

5. Have students from participating classrooms around the world measure their shadows at a designated time (adjusted for their time zone) every day over the course of a week. Explain that students working in pairs can outline their partner's shadow with chalk and then measure its length at the greatest distance.

6. Have classrooms compile and post their data to the project coordinator via email. Share data with participating classrooms.

7. Assign students in pairs to plot one classroom's data showing daily shadow lengths. How does shadow length change day to day? Have students compute average shadow length for their assigned school.

   Note: Older students can create their own metric conversion chart for easy reference. Convert data for younger children.

8. Locate all participating classrooms on a large laminated wall map and note average shadow lengths with an erasable marker.

9. Have students test their original hypothesis by organizing the data by latitude and analyzing the results. Ask: What trends do you notice?

10. Have participating classrooms share their analyses via email.

TIMELINE

Week 1	Solicit partners and begin inquiry into topic.
Week 2	Email procedures and introductions of students to all registered schools.
Week 3	Take measurements and share data with all participants.
Week 4	Analyze and share results.

ART EXTENSION

Using colored chalk, have younger students create a self-portrait from their shadow's outline. Older students can use large format chart paper, trace their shadows, and then paint or color their self-portrait.

TIP   Schedule this activity for Groundhog Day. Then compute the percentage of students who saw their shadow versus those who did not. What is *your* groundhog's prediction? Ask partner schools to track their spring weather and report back. Then compare to national weather statistics. How accurate was *your* groundhog?

TUNE INTO TIDES

Students in different locations around the globe measure and compare the height of high and low tide.

OBJECTIVES

- Students explore the relationship of tides to latitude.
- Students acquire basic skills such as predicting, collecting, graphing, computing averages, and analyzing data.
- Students practice metric conversion.
- Students learn basic world geography.

PREREQUISITES

None

PROCEDURE

1. Post a Call for Collaborators soliciting partner schools around the world. (You'll want participants from both the southern and northern hemispheres.)

2. Have students from participating classrooms around the world record high and low tides for their area over a full month. (Local newspapers publish tide charts.)

3. Have classrooms compile and post their data to the project coordinator via email. The project coordinator then shares all data with participating classrooms.

4. Assign student pairs to convert metric measurements (if necessary) and plot one classroom's data showing the day by day tide heights. Bring the students back together. What patterns do they see? Are the patterns consistent across sites?

5. Have students locate and mark participating classrooms on a large wall map, making note of the latitude of each classroom.

6. Have students combine their data for a designated day onto one larger graph using chart paper. Plot the data by latitude and analyze the results. How does latitude affect tide height?

7. Returning to the month's data supplied by partner classrooms, compute the average difference between high and low tide for each location.

   (When data shows anomalies, request additional information from the Ask a Scientist site: *http://www.cedarnet.org/aska/scientist/index.html*).

8. Share analysis with partner classrooms via email.

Subject:
Science, Mathematics

Grade level:
Grades 4-8

Activity type:
Web Collaboration

Activity level:
Intermediate

Time frame:
8 weeks

Participants:
Unlimited

Materials Needed

- One computer with email access
- Large laminated world map

TUNE INTO TIDES

FOR OLDER STUDENTS

Coordinate your data collection around one complete phase of the moon. Have students investigate the relationship between the moon's phases and the height of the tides by latitude. What is happening? Assign students to diagram moon, sun, and earth positions as the moon moves through its phases and affects the tides.

TIMELINE

3 months
prior: Post Call for Collaborators soliciting participants.

Week 1   Email procedures and introductions of students to all registered schools.

Weeks 2-6 Take measurements and share data with all participants.

Weeks 7-8 Analyze and share results.

FIELD TRIP EXTENSION

Celebrate low tide by bringing your students to the beach for a tide pool hunt. Arrange a scavenger hunt for younger students. Older students can learn to use a field guide and identify marine animals and plants they find, classifying them into kingdom, phylum, class, and order. How do the shapes and lengths of various seaweeds relate to where they live? Why? What adaptations do the animals have that make it possible for them to live in the intertidal zone?

PLANT A TREE

Students learn about the effects of deforestation on the environment and rally support for a national tree planting campaign.

OBJECTIVES

- Students learn about deforestation.
- Students learn basic ecological principles and conservation practice.
- Students practice persuasive writing.
- Trees are planted across the country.

PREREQUISITES

None

PROCEDURE

1. Have students in small cooperative groups research deforestation using the Web and other library resources.
   For all students:
   - What values do trees and forests have?
   - How do we use trees?
   - What is deforestation and how does it affect the environment?

   For older students:
   - What is the history of deforestation?
   - What has been done to address it?
   - What are the issues?
   - Who are the different stakeholders?
   - What is each stakeholder's perspective on deforestation?
   - What are each stakeholder's positions and interests? (Positions are what each stakeholder is demanding. Interests are *why* they need them—the underlying need being addressed by the demand.)

2. Using the facts learned in their research, have students write a persuasive document, enlisting support for a national tree planting campaign.

3. Have students peer-edit the persuasive documents.

4. Choose one essay to post to several sites soliciting schools to partner with in a national tree planting campaign. Ask schools to commit to planting a minimum number of trees. Supply a timeline with a target date for planting. You'll need to be flexible about the coordination since every school will have its own challenges around this project. Ask partners to photograph their tree planting day.

Subject:
Science, Social Studies, Language Arts, Conflict Resolution, Service Learning

Grade level:
Grades 4-12

Activity type:
Social Action

Activity level:
Intermediate

Time frame:
10 weeks

Participants:
Unlimited

Materials Needed

- One computer with email/Web access
- Seedling trees (for planting)
- Camera (for photographing event)

PLANT A TREE

5. Plan your local tree planting campaign. (Brainstorm with students possible fundraising sources for the tree planting, a site for the planting, etc.)

6. Have partners report on their progress 2 weeks before the tree planting event. Share ideas and strategies that emerge with all partners.

7. Hold and photograph your tree planting event!

8. Collect photos from all partners and statistics on numbers of trees planted. Email to all partners the total number of trees planted in the campaign.

9. Mark the tree planting on a large wall map with one green flag per ten trees planted.

10. Create a scrapbook from all of the tree plantings. If possible, photocopy the scrapbook for all participants.

TIMELINE

Weeks 1-2   Research deforestation.

Week 3   Write persuasive essays and solicit partners.

Weeks 4-9   Fundraise and plan tree planting event.

Week 10   Hold tree planting.

TIP   Plan this project to coincide with Arbor Day in April. Invite parents, town residents, the press, and local officials to an official tree planting ceremony on Arbor Day. Share any press clippings, etc., with partners.

AN ENVIRONMENTAL CHALLENGE

Students identify an environmental problem in their town or city and work with a scientist to devise a plan of action to address the problem.

OBJECTIVES

- Students learn about local ecology.

- Students learn ecological principles and conservation practice.

- Students learn about local politics and the democratic process.

PREREQUISITES

None

PROCEDURE

1. Have students research your local ecology. (How healthy are your local waterways? How is waste being disposed of in your area? Does your town spray to eliminate pests? Survey how residents dispose of toxic waste such as used motor oil, etc.) If possible, invite a local official into the classroom to present an overview of the issues to students.

2. From the results of their study, have students choose one environmental problem to address.

3. Post a Call for Collaborators in an Ask a Scientist site (*http://www. cedarnet.org/aska/scientist/index.html*) or a Web site that features links to other experts including scientists (*http://njnie.dl.stevens-tech.edu/ curriculum/aska.html*) looking for a volunteer expert(s) who can help your students address this problem.

4. Have students in small cooperative groups further research the selected problem, addressing the following questions:

   - What is the history of the problem?

   - What has been done to address it?

   - What are the issues?

   - Who are the different stakeholders in the problem?

   - What is each stakeholder's perspective on the problem?

   - What are each stakeholder's positions and interests? (Positions are what each stakeholder is demanding. Interests are *why* they need them—the underlying need being addressed by the demand.)

   Note: Interviewing or inviting a local politician and other stakeholders in the issue into your classroom is an effective way to get this information.

5. Have students write a comprehensive report on the problem, outlining the issues and any questions they have for your volunteer expert.

Subject:
Science, Social Studies, Language Arts, Conflict Resolution, Service Learning

Grade level:
Grades 6-12

Activity type:
Web Mentor

Activity level:
Intermediate

Time frame:
8 weeks

Participants:
None

Materials Needed

- One computer with email/Web access

- Back issues of your local newspaper (optional)

- Access to town records (optional)

AN ENVIRON-MENTAL CHALLENGE

6. Post the report to your volunteer expert asking for their general advice in effectively addressing the problem. (Your expert can help shed light on the scientific issues that inform the problem.)

7. In cooperative groups, assign students the task of outlining a plan to address the issue. The plan must effectively address the interests of the various stakeholders.

8. Post the plans to your volunteer expert for feedback.

9. Make any necessary adjustments to your plan.

10. Discuss as a class an implementation strategy for your plan including a timeline. Can your plan be published in the local newspaper? Who do you need behind your plan in order to implement it? Who can you enlist to help? Can this class implement the plan? If not in its entirety, what part of the plan can this class implement?

11. Implement the plan.

TIMELINE

Weeks 1-2   Research your local ecology.

Weeks 3-4   Research the identified problem.

Weeks 5-6   Develop a plan to address the problem.

Weeks 7-8   Implement plan.

GREEN

http://www.igc.apc.org/ green/green.html

The Global Rivers Environmental Education Network has excellent water quality testing resources available for teachers.

Watershed Education Resources

http://www.igc.apc.org/ green/resources.html

This site provides links to other water quality education resources.

TIP   For more practice for your students with conflict resolution techniques, use *Elementary Perspectives: Teaching Concepts of Peace and Conflict* (for elementary students), *Conflict Resolution in the Middle School* (for middle school students), and *Making Choices, Part I* and *Part II* (for high school students). These resources are all available through Educators for Social Responsibility, 23 Garden Street, Cambridge, MA 02138 (800) 370-2515.

TIP   Fold a unit on water quality into this project. Have students test a local waterway for temperature, pH, dissolved oxygen, biochemical oxygen demand, nitrates, total dissolved solids (TDS) and salinity, turbidity, and total coliform bacteria. For an example of what such a project could look like online, take a look at Grand Traverse Bay K-12 Water Quality Monitoring Program (*http://traverse.lib.mi.us/schools/gtbwi/bay.htm*), a school-based water-quality monitoring project in northern Lake Michigan.

TIP

Water quality test kits are available through the LaMotte Company at (800) 344-3100. Lactose broth tubes for testing total coliform bacteria can be purchased separately through Connecticut Valley Biological Supply at (800) 628-7748.

SPOTTED OWL OR LOGGERS?

Subject:
Science, Social Studies, Conflict Resolution, English

Grade level:
Grades 9-12

Activity type:
Simulation

Activity level:
Intermediate

Time frame:
6 weeks

Participants:
1 classroom

Materials Needed

- One computer with email/Web access

Students learn more about this controversial topic by taking both sides of the issue in an online debate with students from a logging community.

OBJECTIVES

- Students learn more about a controversial topic.
- Students learn about differing perspectives in a conflict.
- Students learn about the Endangered Species Act and its effect on a local community.
- Students learn about logging and its effect on endangered species.

PREREQUISITES

None

PROCEDURE

1. Post a Call for Collaborators to solicit a partner classroom for an online debate on the spotted owl protection in the Pacific Northwest. A classroom from a logging community in the Pacific Northwest is preferred.

2. Have students in small cooperative groups from both classrooms research the protection of the spotted owl and its effect on the logging community in the Pacific Northwest.

   - What is the history of the conflict?
   - What has been done to address it?
   - What are the issues?
   - Who are the different stakeholders?
   - What is each stakeholder's perspective on the issue?
   - What are each stakeholder's positions and interests? (Positions are what each stakeholder is demanding. Interests are *why* they need them—the underlying need being addressed by the demand.)

3. Using the facts learned in their research, have students frame a question and in small groups prepare for an online debate. (The question will be something like "Should logging be stopped in the Pacific Northwest to protect the spotted owl?") Your class will be taking the position of "Yes." Your partner class will be taking the position of "No."

   Suggested small group process for preparing for the debate:
   a. Prepare a list of the relevant issues on both sides of the argument.
   b. For each issue, identify both the positions and interests.
   c. Prepare rebuttals for the other side's arguments.

   d. Decide on the most persuasive arguments to use in an opening argument.

   e. Prepare opening argument and review key issues.

4. Begin the debate by exchanging opening arguments via email with your partner classroom. Then, taking turns between students and between classrooms, email the following:

   a. Rebuttal

   b. Cross-examination

   c. Rebuttal

   d. Cross-examination

   e. Rebuttal

   f. Cross-examination (repeat until each student has had a turn)

5. Anonymously poll all students (including the partner classroom) on their individual positions on the debate.

6. Reverse positions on the issue and hold another debate. (The partner classroom now argues "Yes" and your classroom argues "No.") Repeat steps 3 and 4.

7. Anonymously poll all students again on their individual positions on the debate. Facilitate a discussion: How have your views been affected by the debate? Did anyone change his or her mind? Why? How did it feel to argue the other point of view? What did you learn?

8. Share what you've learned with your partner classroom.

9. Optional Assessment: Students can peer-evaluate the debate using speaker points. Each student is given a score from 1 to 30 (with 30 being the highest). The scores are then added up and the team with the highest score wins. Explain that the assignment will be judged on the following criteria:

- Effectiveness of persuasive arguments
- Use of supporting facts.

TIMELINE

   Weeks 1-2 Research the issue and prepare arguments.

   Weeks 3-4 Hold first debate.

   Weeks 5-6 Hold second debate.

ENGLISH EXTENSION

Have students write an unbiased magazine-length article about the issue, presenting both sides of the story. Clip other articles of this nature for students to model.

Social Studies

8

- Letters from Felix
- A Peace Chain
- Visiting the National Parks
- Lunches Around the World
- A Global Service Project
- Find Your True Home
- Across the U.S. in 1772
- Heroes in Our Midst
- Tell Me Your Story
- Global Connections
- A Nation Torn in Two
- U.S. Immigration
- World War II History Textbooks Project
- A Perspective on Bosnia
- Was the A-Bomb a Necessary Evil?
- Our Village
- Family Project Center

LETTERS FROM FELIX

Students read *Letters from Felix*, a book about a bunny that travels around the world and writes letters about where he is visiting. Children from all over collaborate writing their own letters pretending Felix has visited their home.

OBJECTIVES

- Students learn about U.S. and world geography.
- Students practice communication skills.

PREREQUISITES

None

PROCEDURE

1. Solicit partner classrooms (grades 3 and up) to write letters about Felix's visit to their home.
2. Read *Letters from Felix* by Annette Langean and Constanza Droop to the children (or have older children read the book themselves).
3. Optional: Paint bunny prints on the floor showing Felix's path through your classroom. Bring in a stuffed Felix bunny.
4. Have students dictate or write their own letter about Felix's visit to your classroom to share with the partner classrooms.
5. Collect all of the stories via email and share with partners.
6. Read the letters to the children daily and mark their origins on a wall map.
7. Create your own *Letters About Felix* book!

TIMELINE

Week 1 Post Call for Collaborators soliciting participants.

Week 2 Read *Letters from Felix*.

Week 3 Write your own letter about Felix's visit.

Week 4 Exchange letters.

Subject:
Geography, Language Arts

Grade level:
Grades K-4

Activity type:
Web Simulation

Activity level:
Beginner

Time frame:
4 weeks

Partners:
Unlimited

Materials Needed

- One computer with email access
- *Letters from Felix*, by Annette Langean and Constanza Droop

Allyson Marsh

Have children take turns bringing Felix the bunny home! Send Felix and a notebook home in a totebag. Children can then write a letter in the notebook about Felix's visit. Read the letters to the class the next day.

TIP

This activity is a popular Internet project for elementary children. Its origin is unknown. This was submitted by Allyson Y. Marsh, teacher, Southwest R-V Elementary, Washburn, Missouri.

A PEACE CHAIN

Subject:
Conflict Resolution,
Language Arts, Social
Studies

Grade level:
Grades K-12

Activity type:
Cooperative Challenge

Activity level:
Beginner

Time frame:
Ongoing

Partners:
10 classrooms

Materials Needed

- One computer with
  email access

Students create a peace chain around the world by cooperatively writing about times they have nonviolently resolved a conflict.

OBJECTIVES

- Students learn ways to nonviolently respond to conflict.

- Students are recognized for their conflict resolution skills.

- Students learn about other cultures.

PREREQUISITES

Kisses for Everyone? (Chapter 2)

PROCEDURE

1. Post a Call for Collaborators looking for 10 participant classrooms around the world for peace email chain letter. Give a 2-week deadline for responding.

2. Have your classroom begin by asking one student to write about a time that he or she responded nonviolently to conflict. Create an order for each student in your classroom to respond.

3. Have the next student in order respond to the first's essay with his or her own essay. They must begin their essay, however, using something from the previous person's essay as a launching-off point. (For example, they might begin with, "I too have had really bad fights with my sister. One that was particularly bad that I resolved nonviolently involved. . .") The second essay needn't be about the same topic.

4. Email your classroom's essays to the list of participants with written instructions on how to continue the chain to 10 more classrooms (with a deadline), keeping your classroom's email address at the bottom of the list.

5. Watch as the essays flood in! Are their similarities between the essays? Are there differences? What have you learned from other students' abilities to resolve conflict peacefully?

6. Mark on a wall map where the essays come from.

7. Create a scrapbook from the collection of essays and illustrate.

TIMELINE

Ongoing

This project was inspired by Kids' Conscious Acts of Peace, a joint project of Ben & Jerry's, Educators for Social Responsibility (ESR), and the Corporation for Public Broadcasting. For more information on Kids' Conscious Acts of Peace, call ESR at (800) 370-2515.

You'll find that children love to resolve conflicts. But you'll need to give them the tools to do so. Curricula for building conflict resolution skills in your students is available from Educators for Social Responsibility, 23 Garden Street, Cambridge, MA 02138 (800) 370-2515.

TIP

VISITING THE NATIONAL PARKS

Subject:
Geography, Science

Grade level:
Grades 3-6

Activity type:
Web Resource

Activity level:
Beginner

Time frame:
One class period

Partners:
None

Materials Needed

- One or more computers with Web access
- Large map of United States with locations of national parks shown
- Resource books and guides to national parks

Students research information on the Web about national parks in various locations, and compare plant and animal life based on the geography.

OBJECTIVES

- Students learn about the varied geography within our country.
- Students learn to use the Web to find information.
- Students work cooperatively.

PREREQUISITES

None

PROCEDURE

1. To prepare, create a set of bookmarks for the national parks. If access to the Web is limited, save the Web pages on your hard disk, so students can use them.

2. Present introductory lessons about the national park system and about different types of terrain. Highlights would include:

   - Importance of national parks
   - Brief history of the national park system and how it started
   - Map showing locations of national parks
   - Discussion of different climates and major geographical features

3. Assign each student to work with a partner. Using map and list of parks, have each pair choose a national park to research.

4. Have each pair of students work 10-15 minutes on the computer to read the information about their national park. Meanwhile, other students use other resource materials in classroom to find information.

5. After each pair of students has worked on the computer and has used resource materials within the classroom, pass out checklist sheets to students (see Appendix B for checklist template). These help students focus on certain types of information and organize their information. Review checklists with students.

6. Students work on computers in 15-minute blocks to locate information, while using checklists. Other students use other resource materials.

From an activity by Sue Miller, technology specialist, Lexington High School, Lexington, Massachusetts.

LUNCHES AROUND THE WORLD

Students research and compare nutrition, cost, and appeal of school lunches across the country.

OBJECTIVES

- Students learn about other schools.
- Students learn to gather and organize information.
- Students work cooperatively.

PREREQUISITES

None

PROCEDURE

1. Organize students into teams of 2-4 members each.
2. Each team is responsible for one week of menus from its school and a week of menus from another school.
3. Students locate information about menus from other schools on the Web (see Web66 at *http://web66.coled.umn.edu/schools.html* to get a list of school Web sites). Students could limit their search to middle schools or include elementary and high schools.
4. Each team prepares a presentation of its information in a table or spreadsheet format. For an example, see Figure 8-1.
5. Each team analyzes their data, rating the schools' lunches in 3 categories:
   1. Nutritional value
   2. Cost
   3. General appeal
6. Facilitate a discussion: What were the most common items? What were the least common? What cultural differences did you find? What do those differences reveal about the values of the school?
7. The class compiles the data, announcing a winner in the Lunches Around the World search, in each of the categories surveyed and overall.
8. Have students individually email the winning schools, telling them of their award and the reasons why they were selected.

TIMELINE

Weeks 1-2 Collect data on school lunches.

Week 3   Students compile data.

Week 4   Students analyze data and discuss.

Week 5   Announce winner.

Adapted from an activity by Sue Miller, technology specialist, Lexington High School, Lexington, Massachusetts.

Subject:
Social Studies, Mathematics, Life Skills

Grade level:
Grades 5-8

Activity type:
Web Research

Activity level:
Beginner

Time frame:
5 weeks

Partners:
None

Materials Needed

- One computer with email/Web access

Menu	Grain	Fruit/Veg	Protein	Fat	Cost
Monday	Pizza				
	Salad				
	Fruit				
	PB & J				
	Milk				
	Ice Cream				
Tuesday	Pasta Salad				
	Veggie Sticks				
	Milk				
	PB & J				
	Cookies				
Wednesday	Mac & Cheese				
	Carrots				
	PB & J				
	Milk				
Thursday	Hot Dogs				
	French Fries				
	Carrots				
	Fruit				
Friday	Pizza				
	Salad				
	Cookies				
	Milk				

FIGURE 8-1
Sample School Menu Spreadsheet

A GLOBAL SERVICE PROJECT

Students team with the world community to address a mutually agreed-upon problem.

OBJECTIVES

- Students conduct a survey.

- Students design a service learning project.

PREREQUISITES

None

PROCEDURE

1. Have students in small groups prepare a questionnaire for an email survey of other students in the world to research global issues. Have students brainstorm possible questions: What is your single most pressing concern for the world? On what issue might young people make the greatest difference?

2. Bring the groups together and record all questions. As a class, vote on the questions to be included on your survey. Prepare the survey.

3. Post the survey to several project sites. Allow 4 weeks for participants to complete your survey. Invite responding classrooms to join in a service learning project that addresses the top concern.

4. Once the results are in, have students design a service learning project for the world community that addresses this problem. (They might decide on a clothing or food drive for a world organization or hold a fundraiser to support a cause like AIDS research or the environment.) The project must include objectives, a timeline (allowing generous amounts of times for other schools to participate), and a closing event that all schools will do on the same day.

5. Share the plan with all participating classrooms for feedback.

6. Incorporate participating classrooms' feedback.

7. Implement the plan. Keep in regular contact with your partner classrooms throughout the implementation, sharing accomplishments and reminding of any upcoming milestones.

8. Take pictures at your culminating event. Have partner classrooms share results and photos.

9 Create a final report for all partners outlining the results of your collective effort. Thank all participants for their important contributions.

Subject:
Service Learning, Character Education, Conflict Resolution, Diversity Education, English, Social Studies

Grade level:
Grades 3-12

Activity type:
Social Action

Activity level:
Beginner

Time frame:
7 weeks to ongoing

Partners:
Unlimited

Materials Needed

- One computer with email

A GLOBAL SERVICE PROJECT

TIMELINE

Week 1   Design survey.

Weeks 2-5   Post survey.

Week 6   Design service learning project.

Week 7/
ongoing   Implement project and share with partners.

ENGLISH EXTENSION

Have students write a press release about your project. Submit it and a few select photos to local and national news sources such as the AP and UPI newswires.

FIND YOUR TRUE HOME

Students explore the Web, researching various cities and towns in which they might like to live.

OBJECTIVES

- Students are introduced to the Web.
- Students practice research skills.
- Students learn about another community in the U.S.
- Students learn important life skills such as creating criteria for thinking about where they might want to live.

PREREQUISITES

None

PROCEDURE

1. Explain that this lesson will familiarize students with the Web. Have students outline criteria for where they might like to live. What lifestyle would they like to have?

2. In what community might they find such a lifestyle? Have students choose from a wall map a city or town in the U.S. in which they think they would like to live.

3. Using City Link (*http://usacitylink.com/*), City Net (*http://www.city.net/*), and Map Quest: the Interactive Atlas (*http://www.mapquest.com/*) have students research the city they would like to live in.

4. How much will an average apartment cost in their city? (Have students go to Apartment Search at *http://www.rent.net.*) Have students find an apartment in which they would like to live.

5. How far is their new city from where they live now? Use HomeBuyer's Fair (*http://www.homefair.com/*) to calculate the distance.

6. Is a newspaper online for their city, state, or a place nearby? If so, what can they learn about the community to which they plan to move? (Use Online Newspapers at *http://www.webwombat.com.au/intercom/newsprs/ index.htm.*) Does their community meet the criteria as outlined earlier? If not, what community might? (Other questions to explore include: What is the city known for? Are there any major businesses or universities in the city? Are there any books, stories, or novels about the city?)

Subject:
Social Studies, Life Skills, Language Arts, Art

Grade level:
Grades 4-12

Activity type:
Web Resource

Activity level:
Beginner

Time frame:
2 class periods

Partners:
None

Materials Needed

- One computer with Web access per student
- Wall map

From an activity by Nancy Skomars Davis, computer and English teacher, Advanced Technologies Academy, Las Vegas, Nevada.

FIND YOUR TRUE HOME

TIMELINE

Classes 1-2 Have students research their city.

ENGLISH EXTENSION

Create a culminating activity for this unit. Assign students to put together a travel brochure for their city complete with postcards, maps, excerpts from a local paper, and other interesting details about their community. Post the travel brochures in a public place for interested travelers.

TIP Use this activity to introduce the Web to your students. By giving them the sites they need to visit and showing them some of the interesting up-to-date resources available, you'll have shown your students what is available on the Web in a fun, nonthreatening way.

ACROSS THE U.S. IN 1772

Drawing from their local history, students across the country research and write accounts of a day in the life of a fictional character in 1772. The accounts are then published in a booklet and shared via email or published on a Web site (optional) to create a profile of one day across the United States.

OBJECTIVES

- Students learn local and U.S. history.
- Students acquire research skills using various tools including the Web.

PREREQUISITES

None

PROCEDURE

1. Post a Call for Collaborators soliciting partner classrooms to collaboratively create a booklet about a fictional character from their area in 1772 (one classroom per each U.S. time zone).

2. Break students into small groups to research local 18th century history using library and Web resources. Have students identify and research at least 6 topics that interest them (diet, housing, transportation, children's roles, games, regional vocabulary, etc.). Narrow the areas for research for

Subject:
History, Social Studies, Geography, Language Arts, Art

Grade level:
Grades 5-12

Activity type:
Web Collaboration

Activity level:
Beginner

Time frame:
9 weeks

Partners:
6 classrooms (at least one from each U.S. time zone)

Materials Needed

- One computer with email access

From the C.L. Smith School in San Luis Obispo, California.

Patricia Foote with student

ACROSS THE U.S. IN 1772

younger children to 2-3 areas. Good sources of information include local newspapers and town and church records.

3. Participating classrooms write a fictional narrative describing their activities on a particular day in 1772. Students chronicle their day in 3 segments: morning, afternoon, and late evening. Have each student:

   - Write his or her name at the top of the response

   - Label each paragraph with the time of day and put a return at the end of the paragraph. (See the sidebar "A Day in the Life of a Chumash Girl" for an example.)

4. Have classrooms compile all of the profiles into one document and submit to the project coordinator via email.

5. Compile all profiles by geographic region to share with all participating classrooms via email.

6. Create a booklet of all the accounts organized by state and geographic region for the students to read.

FOR YOUNGER STUDENTS

Have younger students research and write about a day in the 1920s or '30s. Invite older community members (or children's grandparents) into class to be interviewed. Then help students write and draw their profiles.

TIMELINE

Week 1   Post Call for Collaborators soliciting up to 6 participants (1 per time zone).

Weeks 2-3 Email procedures to all registered schools.

Weeks 4-8 Allow 1 month for schools to respond and for compilation of results.

Week 9   Post profiles to all participants.

ART EXTENSION

Partner with an art class and publish a book of the profiles. Have participating classrooms supply original art or research authentic graphics and photographs to include.

"We learned about famous people, like Thomas Jefferson, Ben Franklin, and Daniel Boone, as well as everyday people like slaves, Native Americans, southern ladies, and boys and girls. We even learned about the life of a buffalo on that day." —A student participant, C.L. Smith School, San Luis Obispo, California.

June 1, 1772

In the morning, my mom and I are out collecting berries, nuts, acorns, and other things as usual. When we come back, we grind the nuts. Then we get a clam shell and taste the mix. This time, it is a little bitter! We women get the best job because we get to taste the food before anyone else in the tribe.

Before I know it, it is afternoon time. I play with my brother and sisters. We play this game where you have a long bone and a rock. The way you play it is by hitting the rock to the end of the field. Guess what! I just made a goal. We always play for hours and hours because it is a fun game to play especially when you have lots of people to play with. I even like it more when the ladies and the boys want to challenge us. We say, "OK, but you're going to get beat again!" They say, "We don't care! You're going to lose this time." Then it is time for dinner.

A Day in the Life of a Chumash Girl

HEROES IN OUR MIDST

Subject:
Social Studies, Language Arts, Conflict Resolution

Grade level:
Grades 5-12

Activity type:
Cooperative Challenge, Web Publishing

Activity level:
Beginner

Time frame:
5 weeks

Partners:
Unlimited

Materials Needed

- One computer with email access
- Chart paper/chalkboard

Students work collaboratively with another classroom to identify heroes in their respective communities to interview and profile in a Web site.

OBJECTIVES

- Students identify characteristics of a hero.
- Students learn interviewing skills.
- Students practice writing in the biography genre.

PREREQUISITES

Kisses for Everyone? (Chapter 2)

PROCEDURE

1. Post a Call for Collaborators soliciting partner schools.

2. Assign students to read short stories or non-fiction biographies about heroes (the *UTNE Reader* visionary profiles, articles in the local newspaper, etc.).

3. In journals, have your students identify and profile any person (living or dead) whom they consider a hero.

4. Discuss: What is it about your hero you most admire? What are the qualities of a hero? Ask for a show of hands: How many of you know your hero? How many of you don't? Do you have to be famous to be a hero?

5. Have students identify a local hero. (They may need some help with this. Suggest possibilities or offer back issues of a local newspaper as a source.)

6. Prepare students to interview their hero. Discuss with students what makes a biography interesting. What would we want to include in a biography? What type of questions solicit good information? (Discuss the difference between open-ended and closed questions.) On chart paper or the chalkboard, record all answers.

7. Have students practice interviewing each other.

8. Have students interview and then write biographies of their heroes.

9. Have students peer-edit their biographies.

10. Exchange the biographies via email with partner classrooms. Discuss: How are the heroes featured similar? How are they different? What personal qualities are common to all heroes featured?

11. Publish the biographies in booklet form or on the Web (see "Creating a Web Site" in Chapter 3).

This activity was suggested by Jay Altman, former co-director, Summersbridge, New Orleans, Louisiana.

TIMELINE

Week 1   Post Call for Collaborators soliciting partner. Write initial biographies.

Weeks 2-3 Identify and interview local heroes.

Week 4   Write and edit biographies.

Week 5   Publish biographies.

HEROES IN OUR MIDST

TELL ME YOUR STORY

Subject:
Social Studies, History, Language Arts

Grade level:
Grades 5-12

Activity type:
Keypals

Activity level:
Beginner

Time frame:
5 weeks

Partners:
1 senior citizen per student

Materials Needed

- One computer with email access

Students interview senior citizens from a different culture (U.S. or world), then together write and publish their biographies.

OBJECTIVES

- Students learn about the 1920s and '30s.
- Students learn about another culture.
- Students learn interviewing skills.
- Students practice writing in the biography genre.

PREREQUISITES

None

PROCEDURE

1. Students post a message to SeniorNet (*http://www.seniornet.org/ cgi-bin/WebX*) soliciting volunteers of a different culture, ethnicity, or race. The volunteer will be interviewed by the student for a biography.

2. Have student pairs brainstorm questions to ask their senior partners about their lives. What would they most like to be asked about *their* lives?

3. Have students refine their questions by practice-interviewing one another.

4. Bring the groups together to debrief. What questions were most stimulating? What were least? (Distinguish between open- and closed-ended questions.)

5. Have each student create his or her own questionnaire. Have partners review the questionnaires and make suggestions.

6. Email questionnaires to the senior partners.

7. Download answers and schedule students at the computer in 5-minute time periods to email any additional questions to their senior partner.

8. Have students write biographies.

9. Have students peer-edit their biographies.

10. Email the biographies to the senior partners for fact-checking and editorial suggestions.

11. Publish the biographies in booklet form or on the Web (see "Creating a Web Site," Chapter 3). Have students share their biographies with the class.

12. Email or send a copy of all the biographies to all senior partners with a thank-you letter from the student partner.

TIMELINE

Week 1 Post message soliciting senior citizen partners (one per student). Develop questionnaire.

Week 2 Email questionnaire to senior partners with 2-week deadline.

Week 4 Write and edit biographies.

Week 5 Publish biographies.

TELL ME YOUR STORY

TIP

Have students read and analyze biographies before beginning this project. Focus this activity by organizing it around a theme you have been studying. If you have just finished a unit on the history of Native Americans in the U.S., for example, have students profile native elders. Or if you're planning a unit on aviation, kick it off by interviewing retired pilots.

GLOBAL CONNECTIONS

Subject:
Social Studies, Geography, Language Arts, Computer Technology, Diversity Education

Grade level:
Grades 3-9

Activity type:
Keypals

Activity level:
Intermediate

Time frame:
9 weeks

Partners:
1 student per student (from a country of the student's choosing)

Materials Needed

- One computer with email/Web access
- Large laminated wall map

Students research a country through the Web and through partnering with another student from that country.

OBJECTIVES

- Students learn about world geography.
- Students practice communication skills.
- Students develop Web research skills.
- Students challenge stereotypes.

PREREQUISITES

None

PROCEDURE

1. Have each child identify a country to study. Mark the country's location on a large laminated wall map.

2. Post a Call for Collaborators to international bulletin boards looking for participants in the designated countries. (*IECC-projects@stolaf.edu* is an excellent place to post a Call for Collaborators for international partners.)

3. Teach the children the basics of email etiquette. Explain the importance of beginning an email message with an introduction. Pair students and have them practice writing introductions about themselves to use later as their first message to participants.

4. Help students research their country using the Web (schedule computer time in 15-minute intervals) and other library resources. To look up other schools that might have a home page, check out Web66 (*http://web66.coled.umn.edu*).

5. Have students write essays about what they imagine a day in the life of their partner would be like and vice versa. Exchange essays with partners. Have them respond with their own essays.

6. Hold a discussion: How accurate were your ideas about your partner's life? What was different from what you thought? What was similar? How is their life different from yours? How is it similar? Where did your ideas about the other country come from? How were those ideas biased in one way or another? Why?

7. Allow students to continue their keypal relationships. Have students collect their letters and responses in a keypal journal.

From an activity by Janice Friesen, teacher, Russell Boulevard Elementary School, Columbia, Missouri.

FOR YOUNGER STUDENTS

Have younger students do this as a whole-class activity, choosing one country to research. Research Web sites in advance, write addresses on index cards, and provide students time in pairs to explore the sites. Compose the essays together and support children with the technical aspects.

TIMELINE

Week 1   Identify countries to research and post Call for Collaborators. Allow 4 weeks for a response.

Weeks 2-4 Research countries using the Web and other resources.

Week 5   Prepare essays and post to partners.

Weeks 6-9 Partners respond.

ART EXTENSION

Using the Web, research indigenous art for your partner countries. Have students draw and paint responses to the art. Then create a scrapbook that includes all of the letters and artwork, or publish the results on the Web.

A NATION TORN IN TWO

Subject:
History, Language Arts, Mathematics, Conflict Resolution

Grade level:
Grades 5-12

Activity type:
Web Survey

Activity level:
Intermediate

Time frame:
6 weeks

Partners:
Civil War states only

Materials Needed

- One computer with email/Web access

Students explore the U.S. Civil War, researching the events before, during, and after the war through the perspectives of both Northerners and Southerners.

OBJECTIVES

- Students research the U.S. Civil War.
- Students analyze, interpret, and report on data.
- Students critically analyze conflict.
- Students enhance their information processing skills through the use of a variety of technology tools.

PREREQUISITES

None

PROCEDURE

1. Break students into small groups to briefly research the Civil War using the Web and library resources. Students are to find controversial topics about the war to address in an opinion survey. Assign each group a period of the war:

   - Events leading up to the war (1 group)
   - The war itself (multiple groups)
   - The aftermath of the war (1 group)

   Some excellent Web sites to use as resources on the Civil War include:

   - U.S. Civil War Center (*http://www.cwc.lsu.edu/civlink.htm*)
   - Dakota State University Civil War Resources (*http://www.dsu.edu/~jankej/civilwar.html*)
   - Rutgers Civil War Resources (*http://www.libraries.rutgers.edu/rulib/socsci/hist/civwar-2.html*)

2. Each group is responsible for providing one question per student in the group about their area of inquiry for an opinion survey that will be sent to all project participants. (Note: Students must also provide a range of survey answers that participants will choose among.)

3. As a class, review and refine the suggested questions creating the survey to be sent to both Northern and Southern project participants. Encour-

---

From an activity by Heather Swift, media specialist, and Greg Smith, social studies teacher, Erine Middle School, Akron, Ohio.

age participants to include a 2-3-line justification for their answer. (See the sample questionnaire from Erwine Middle School in the sidebar "A Nation Torn in Two: Remembering the Civil War".)

4. Define the states that participated in the Civil War, distinguishing Confederate from Union states. Post a Call for Collaborators looking for project participants from those states. Attach the survey with a deadline. Offer that all participants will receive the results of the survey for discussion in their classrooms. (The survey results should provoke interesting discussion.)

5. Have each student in your classroom research and answer the questions on the survey. Students must provide justification for their answers to each question in writing.

6. Once the results of the survey are in, help students design a database (either manually or online using spreadsheet software) and compile data, computing percentages for the responses comparing Northern and Southern school responses.

7. Have students in small groups analyze the compiled data. What differences, if any, were there between Northern and Southern responses? What might those differences be attributed to? How did those differing perspectives contribute to the war?

8. Bring the students together. Have each small group report on their assignment. Facilitate a group discussion.

A NATION TORN IN TWO

Perspectives

"You are using the wrong name. A civil war occurs when two groups fight for control of one government. The South wanted to do the same thing the colonists did in 1776—start a government. That is the reason the Confederacy put George Washington on its Great Seal." —A project participant from Tennessee.

"My great-great-great-grandpa, Sampson Yeargin, also a Tennesseean, is reported to have hid out in the cellar while troops searched the house for him. His wife, Rebecca, sat in a rocking chair above where the cellar door was and rocked away while the troops searched his house. As far as we know, he did not serve in the army on either side." —A participant from Oklahoma.

A Nation Torn in Two: Remembering the Civil War

Survey from Erwine Middle School, Akron, Ohio

1. Who do you feel started the war (North or South)?

2. What did the South fight for?

3. What do you think the North was fighting for?

4. Do you feel the South had a right to secede from the Union?

5. Do you think that the war could have been avoided? If so, how?

6. What are your feelings about the compromises of 1820 and 1850? Did they lead to the war or just prolong it?

7. How did the war affect the South?

8. How did the war affect the North?

9. Do you have bad feelings against the North for the Civil War?

10. Describe what you think this country would have been like if the South had won the war.

11. How did the war affect your grandparents' or ancestors' lives?

12. How do you feel about Abraham Lincoln?

13. Was Lincoln the best choice in the election of 1860?

14. Do you think that he should be considered one of our nation's greatest Presidents?

15. How do you think the death of Lincoln affected the post-Civil war era?

16. Do you think that John Wilkes Booth did the South a favor by assassinating Lincoln?

17. Why did the South have slavery?

18. How do you feel about slavery?

19. If you had been alive during the Civil War, would you have been for or against slavery? Why?

20. Were there lots of Southerners at the time of the war who disagreed with slavery?

21. Do you feel that the ending of slavery was worth a war?

22. Do you think that Harriet Tubman was a heroine?

23. Do you think that abolitionists like W.L. Garrison, John Brown, and Frederick Douglass should be considered heroes?

24. Do you think that men like these caused the war?

Explore bias in polling with students before they construct **TIP**
their survey. Bias, as defined by the *American Heritage
Dictionary*, means to influence in a particular, typically unfair,
direction. Using the sample survey, have students examine each
question as it is constructed. Is the question biased or
unbiased? How might the bias affect the outcome? How could
the question be rewritten to be less biased? Apply this same
analysis to your classroom's survey before posting it to the
Web.

U.S. IMMIGRATION

Subject:
History, Language Arts, Music, Art, Foreign Languages

Grade level:
Grades 8-12

Activity type:
Web Resource, Keypals

Activity level:
Intermediate

Time frame:
6 weeks

Partners:
3-6 classrooms

Materials Needed

- One computer with email/Web access (preferably 1 workstation per 3 students)

The Genealogy Home Page
http://www.genhomepage.com/

This genealogy page contains great links to other relevant sites.

Students collaboratively research immigration to the United States during the 19th and 20th centuries.

OBJECTIVES

- Students learn about the origins and contributions of various ethnic peoples who immigrated to the U.S. in the late 19th and early 20th centuries.

- Students gain an awareness of their own past through intergenerational research and research with peers.

PREREQUISITES

None

PROCEDURE:

1. Have students choose a country from their ethnic heritage or an area of interest to research. They will be researching the immigration patterns to this country during the late 19th and early 20th centuries.

2. Cooperatively group students who are researching the same countries or regions of the world.

3. Post a Call for Collaborators looking for partner ESL (English as a Second Language) classrooms in countries of students' choosing to jointly research that country's pattern of immigration to the U.S. in the late 19th and 20th centuries. Note: This is an excellent opportunity for everyone involved to practice language skills.

4. Pair each student in a cooperative group with a student from the appropriate partner classroom as a keypal.

5. Have each cooperative group in your classroom meet to develop 10 questions to research about the immigration patterns to the U.S. in the late 19th and early 20th century. Some possible questions include: Who came? Why did they come? What were they leaving? Where did they go when they got here and what did they do? How were they treated? How did their culture affect American culture?

6. Along with their keypals, have students research their questions using the Web, the library, and email as resources. There are numerous Web sites to help with genealogical research.

7. Have students present their findings in research paper format. Optional: Have students include personal ethnographies in their research papers.

From an activity by Desmond Connolly, history teacher, Eleva Strum Schools, Strum, Wisconsin.

8. Have cooperative groups meet to share, discuss, and peer-edit their papers.

9. Have students share their papers via email with their keypals.

10. Facilitate a discussion about the U.S. as a melting pot. What does that metaphor suggest? What are the ramifications of the U.S. as a melting pot? Discuss people who chose to emigrate of their own free will versus those who did not.

U.S. IMMIGRATION

TIMELINE

Week 1   Select countries and solicit partners.

Weeks 2-5 Students research.

Weeks 6-7 Students draft, rewrite, and submit papers.

MULTICULTURAL EXTENSION

Use this activity as a launching pad to research your own area's pattern of immigration. What peoples have moved to your town or city over its history? How were they treated? What groups have had power when? What groups did not? Why?

Students can use email to intergenerationally interview both Americans who immigrated and citizens currently living in the selected country who may have known people who emigrated.

TIP

WORLD WAR II HISTORY TEXTBOOKS PROJECT

Subject:
History, Social Studies, Diversity Education, Conflict Resolution

Grade level:
Grades 9-12

Activity type:
Web Collaboration

Activity level:
Intermediate

Time frame:
12 weeks

Partners:
One classroom per designated country

Materials Needed

- One computer with email/Web access
- Chart paper or chalkboard

Jon Brokering

Students research and compare how events of World War II are treated in various countries' school textbooks through linking with another classroom from that country.

OBJECTIVES

- Students learn about the events of World War II.
- Students explore cultural stereotypes.
- Students delve into issues of revisionist history.
- Students use the Web to explore issues of public policy.

PREREQUISITES

None

PROCEDURE

1. Have students in small groups identify countries with which they want to partner to explore how World War II is treated in their countries' textbooks. What issues do they want addressed?

2. Bring the groups together and on the board or chart paper outline the project, including the desired countries to participate and the issues to be addressed. Some potential issues include:

   - How are Germans/Japanese/British/Americans portrayed in each country's textbooks (positively, negatively, aggressor, victim)?
   - What aspects of the Pacific War are emphasized or de-emphasized and how might this be a result of government policy?
   - How is the topic of the atomic bomb dealt with?
   - How is history taught in each classroom?
   - How are history textbooks written and adopted in each classroom? What role does the government play?
   - How have textbooks' handling of this topic changed over time?

3. Post a Call for Collaborators to international bulletin boards looking for participants in the designated countries. (*IECC-projects@stolaf.edu* is an excellent place to post a Call for Collaborators for international partners.)

4. Have partner classrooms and your own classroom research the answers to the outlined issues using the Web and other available library resources. Break students into small groups, assigning an issue for each group to address.

From an activity by Jon M. Brokering, Faculty of Policy Studies, Chuo University, Japan.

5. Share all information with participating classrooms.

6. In small groups, have students interpret the data, comparing each country's response on their assigned issue.

7. Have each small group do a presentation on their issue.

8. Hold two discussions:

   - Explore the different perspectives of each country on the events of the war. Ask: What differences were there between countries' treatments of the war? Why? What are the issues? Who are the different stakeholders in the issue? What is each stakeholder's perspective? What are each stakeholder's positions and interests? (Positions are what each stakeholder is demanding. Interests are *why* they need them—the underlying need being addressed by the demand.)

   - Explore the role of history in our society. Ask: What is truth? In what ways does our society value truth? In what ways does it not? How do we acquire our knowledge about the past? In the interest of serving truth, what would be the best way of acquiring our knowledge about the past?

WORLD WAR II HISTORY TEXTBOOKS PROJECT

TIMELINE

Weeks 1-4   Identify countries and issues to research and post Call for Collaborators for participants. Allow 3 weeks for a response.

Weeks 5-9   Research issues using the Web and other resources.

Week 10   Share results with partners.

Weeks 11-12 Interpret results. Have group presentations and discussions.

Supplement this activity with actual historical documents, diaries/memoirs, newspaper accounts, and films about World War II. Discuss each mode of recorded history and its relative credibility as a source.

TIP

A PERSPECTIVE ON BOSNIA

Subject:
History, English, Art

Grade level:
Grades 9-12

Activity type:
Web Resource, Keypals

Activity level:
Intermediate

Time frame:
6 weeks

Partners:
Unlimited

Materials Needed

- One computer with email/Web access
- Chart paper

Students create a portrait of the civil war in Bosnia by partnering with students affected by the war and by using the Web as a resource.

OBJECTIVES

- Students learn about the Serbo-Croatian civil war.
- Students acquire research skills using various tools, including the Web.

PREREQUISITES

None

PROCEDURE

1. Students research the war in Bosnia using library and Web resources. (See *http://www.iht.it/arte/bih/links.htm* for links to interesting sites.) They must include first-hand accounts in their portraits, as well as information in a variety of media (artwork, photographs, newspaper accounts, etc.).

2. Post a Call for Collaborators looking for students affected by the civil war to partner with. (*IECC-projects@stolaf.edu* is an excellent place to post a Call for Collaborators for international partners.)

3. Working in small, cooperative groups of 2-3 students, students outline topics that they would like their portrait of the war to cover (give students some examples to begin with: the war's effect on foods you eat or on your friendships, etc.).

4. Bring the groups together for a large group session. On chart paper, record all of the small groups' ideas. As a class, create an outline of topics for the portrait.

5. Again, in the original small groups, parcel the topics between students for further research (each student should have at least one topic of his or her own). Schedule students on the computer in 15-minute intervals for research. Encourage students to use primary documents (and use Bosnian students as a resource).

6. Have students write up their topics, illustrating them with original photographs or artwork supplied by the Bosnian students.

7. Have each group do an oral presentation of their topic.

8. Combine the reports into one big book. Exhibit publicly in your school.

TIMELINE

Week 1	Research the war and outline topics.
Weeks 2-4	Small group research.
Week 5	Small group presentation.
Week 6	Create book.

A PERSPECTIVE ON BOSNIA

Have students also read *Zlata's Diary*, by Zlata Fliapovic, a moving diary of a teenage Bosnian girl.

TIP

WAS THE A-BOMB A NECESSARY EVIL?

Subject:
History, Social Studies,
Government, Conflict
Resolution

Grade level:
Grades 9-12

Activity type:
Simulation

Activity level:
Intermediate

Time frame:
6 weeks

Partners:
1 classroom

Materials Needed

- One computer with
  email/Web access

Japanese and U.S. students learn more about this controversial topic by taking both sides of the issue in an online debate.

OBJECTIVES

- Students discover the significance of differing perspectives in a conflict.
- Students learn about the bombing of Hiroshima and Nagasaki.

PREREQUISITES

None

PROCEDURE

1. Post a Call for Collaborators to solicit a partner classroom from Japan for an online debate on whether or not the U.S. should have dropped the A-bomb on Hiroshima and Nagasaki.

2. Have students in small cooperative groups from both classrooms research the issue.

   - What were the events leading up to the dropping of the A-bomb on Hiroshima and Nagasaki?
   - Why was the bomb dropped?
   - What were the effects of this action?
   - Who are the different stakeholders in the issue?
   - What is each stakeholder's perspective on the issue?
   - What are each stakeholder's positions and interests? (Positions are what each stakeholder is demanding. Interests are *why* they need them—the underlying need being addressed by the demand.)

3. Using the facts learned in their research, have students frame a question and in small groups prepare for an online debate. (The question will be something like, "Should the U.S. have dropped the bomb on Hiroshima and Nagasaki to end World War II?") Your class will be taking the position of "Yes." Your partner class will be taking the position of "No."
   Suggested small group process for preparing for the debate:
   a. Prepare a list of the relevant issues on both sides of the argument.
   b. For each issue, identify both the positions and interests.
   c. Prepare rebuttals for the other side's arguments.
   d. Decide on the most persuasive arguments to use in an opening argument.
   e. Prepare opening argument and review key issues.

4. Begin the debate by exchanging opening arguments via email with your partner classroom. Then, taking turns between students and between classrooms, email the following:

   a. Rebuttal

   b. Cross-examination

   c. Rebuttal

   d. Cross-examination

   e. Rebuttal

   f. Cross-examination (repeat until each student has had a turn)

5. Anonymously poll all students (including the partner classroom) on their individual positions on the debate.

6. Reverse positions on the issue and hold another debate. (The partner classroom now argues "Yes" and your classroom argues "No.") Repeat steps 3 and 4.

7. Anonymously poll all students again on their individual positions on the debate. Facilitate a discussion (or have students address in a journal): How have your views been affected by the debate? Did anyone change his or her mind? Why? How did it feel to argue each point of view? What did you learn?

8. Share what you've learned with your partner classroom.

9. Optional Assessment: Students can peer-evaluate the debate using speaker points. Each student is given a score from 1 to 30 (with 30 being the highest). The scores are then added up and the team with the highest score wins. Explain that the assignment will be judged on the following criteria:

   - Effectiveness of persuasive arguments

   - Use of supporting facts

TIMELINE

Weeks 1-2 Research the issue and prepare arguments.

Weeks 3-4 Hold first debate.

Weeks 5-6 Hold second debate.

WAS THE A-BOMB A NECESSARY EVIL?

TIP

This is understandably an emotionally charged topic to debate. Discuss with the teacher of the partner classroom how to handle the topic. Involve students in establishing ground rules for the debate.

TIP   For more practice for your students with conflict resolution techniques, use *Elementary Perspectives: Teaching Concepts of Peace and Conflict* (for elementary students), *Conflict Resolution in the Middle School* (for middle school students), and *Making Choices, Part I* and *Part II* (for high school students). These resources are all available through Educators for Social Responsibility, 23 Garden Street, Cambridge, MA 02138 (800) 370-2515.

OUR VILLAGE

Students profile school personnel, community members, parents, grandparents, and others for their school's Web site. This is a good activity for involving parents.

OBJECTIVES

- Community members are acknowledged for their important role in schools.

- New students and their families are provided with a way to learn more about the greater school community.

- A sense of community is built around the central role of schools.

- Students learn interviewing skills.

- Students practice writing in several genres: biography, poetry, etc.

- Students creating drawings, photographs, and a musical score for their site.

PREREQUISITES

None

PROCEDURE

1. Involve your entire school district in this project. Develop a team of lead teachers (at least one from each school) to pull the project together. Have each lead teacher develop a cross-disciplinary team of teachers in his or her school to implement the project. Be sure to involve teachers from all racial and ethic groups represented by your school.

2. Introduce students to the African proverb, "It takes a village to raise a child." In journals, have students respond to the saying. Do they agree or disagree with it? What villages do students feel they belong to? Why? What constitutes a community? How are communities important in schools? How have communities made a difference in their lives?

3. Working in pairs, have students identify 5 individuals from their "village" or community who have had an impact on their lives. They should include people from their neighborhood, from the school, and from the larger community. Have each student share how this person has had an impact on his or her life. Then have children paraphrase why their partner chose his or her particular individuals.

4. Each child will have to select from their individuals one to interview and profile. As a group, have the children together develop criteria for the selection. Suggest diversity as a criteria if it does not come up. You'll not only want a representative selection from your community racially and

Subject:
Social Studies, History, Language Arts, Art, Music

Grade level:
Grades K-12

Activity type:
Community Connection, Web Publishing

Activity level:
Advanced

Time frame:
6 weeks

Partners:
None

Materials Needed

- One computer with email/Web access

- An Internet Service Provider that offers space on their Web server

OUR VILLAGE

ethnically, but you'll also want to profile individuals from a wide variety of roles (firefighters, librarians, grandparents, shop owners, teachers, etc.).

5. Prepare students for their interviews. Brainstorm good questions together. Have students practice interviewing one another.

6. Have children interview their individuals and write profiles. The profiles can be in the form of prose, poetry, etc. They should also ask their community member to respond in writing to "What I cherish most about this community is. . ."

7. Have students peer-edit their profiles.

8. Send the profiles to community members for fact-checking and response.

9. Publish the profiles on your school's Web site or create a Web site for this purpose (see "Creating a Web Site," Chapter 3). Have students include photographs, original drawings, and (if possible) music to create a portrait of their village.

FOR YOUNGER STUDENTS

Elementary children can do a modified version of this project. Using a tape recorder, have students tell you about a special person in their life and draw or paint a portrait. Add these audiotracks and drawings to the Web site. Then choose one or two people selected by the children to be interviewed by the class. Upper elementary students can write about the interview and post their profiles to the Web site. For lower elementary students, audio or videotape the interviews and include in the Web site.

TIMELINE

Week 1   Explore the concept of the village and identify a community member per student to interview.

Week 2   Interview community member.

Weeks 3-4 Write and edit profiles.

Weeks 5-6 Create Web site.

TIP   Involve parents in the development of your Web site. Ask for volunteers to serve as Webmaster. Schedule parents for this duty in shifts.

FAMILY PROJECT CENTER

Students create on the school's Web site a Family Project Center where parents can find ideas for educational projects they can do with their children. This is a good activity to involve parents.

OBJECTIVES

- Parents are encouraged and supported in providing educational enrichment for their children.
- Parents are shown they are valued and important members of the school community.
- Students apply concepts learned in class to enrichment activities at home.
- Students become more fully invested in the classroom as co-creators of the curriculum.

PREREQUISITES

None

PROCEDURE

1. Explain the project: Students and teachers together will create a place on the school's Web site where families can find ideas for educational enrichment projects they can do with their children. The center will be updated on an ongoing basis with ideas to link to the current curriculum.

2. In small groups, have students brainstorm educational enrichment projects that could be included in a family project center. They can draw from projects for school that they have done at home, projects they have seen on TV or in books, etc. Help each group get started by making a few suggestions (families could take an inventory of how much water they use and for what; build a miniature Japanese garden; research the growth rate of a sunflower; visit a local museum or library, etc.).

3. Bring students together and record all ideas for projects on chart paper or the board. What subject areas and grade level does each idea serve?

4. As a class, develop criteria for projects to be included in the family project center.

5. Again in small groups, have students evaluate each idea on the criteria set forth, scoring one point for each criteria met.

6. Bring the students together and add the scores for each idea. The top scoring ideas will be included in the family project center.

7. Have each student select one project idea and write a detailed description for the family project center. Students may need some help researching their project.

Subject:
Social Studies, Math, History, Language Arts, English Art, Music

Grade level:
Grades K-12

Activity type:
Community Connection, Web Publishing

Activity level:
Advanced

Time frame:
4 weeks/ongoing

Partners:
None

Materials Needed

- One computer with email/Web access
- An Internet Service Provider that offers space on their Web server

FAMILY PROJECT CENTER

8. Organize the projects by level and subject area and publish to your school's Web site or create a Web site for this purpose (see "Creating a Web Site" in Chapter 3).

9. With students, compose a letter to send home to parents explaining the purpose of the family project center and giving any necessary instructions.

10. Update the family project center throughout the year, adding projects that link with your current curriculum. Create a place where parents can go specifically for these current projects. Be sure to include a "freshness date" giving parents a deadline when the project will no longer be relevant to your current curriculum.

TIMELINE

Week 1   Brainstorm and select projects for inclusion.

Week 2   Students write up projects.

Weeks 3-4 Create the Web site.

TIP   Be sure to provide this information in two forms: on the Web and sent home as a hard-copy packet to families that do not have access to the Web. Remember to provide timely updates on projects that link to your curriculum.

Appendixes

Lesson Plan Index

ACTIVITY TYPE

Community Connection

Cooperative Challenge

Keypals

Multimedia

Simulation

Social Action

Web Collaboration

Web Mentor

Web Publishing

Web Resource

Worksheets

THE COST OF LIVING ROLE PLAY CARDS

You are a computer software engineer making $70,000 a year in Boston. You have a spouse who is a student. Your combined student loan payments are $575 a month. You have $20,000 saved and would like to move and buy a house in the midwest.

You are a car mechanic with a spouse and two children living in northern Texas. You make $24,000 a year and own your own home worth $80,000. You have $68,000 more to pay on your mortgage. You have $8,000 in savings. You love to scuba dive and would like to live closer to the ocean.

You are a nature photographer just starting out in your career. You are debt-free, but currently unemployed. You have a savings account of $1,400.

You are an actor who has done mostly industrial work, but would like to break into theatre. You currently make an average of $28,000 a year and live in a suburb of Minneapolis, Minnesota. There is little theatre work in Minnesota.

THE COST OF LIVING ROLE PLAY CARDS

You and your spouse own a popular restaurant in your small town. You have lived in that town with your three children all of your life and would like to move somewhere different. You think that you might like to sell your restaurant and manage a restaurant owned by someone else in a warm climate. You've been told that your business is worth $180,000. After paying off debt, you expect to have about $80,000.

You are a reporter for the *New York Times*, but have grown tired of the rat race. You own a 1-bedroom condominium in New York City worth $240,000, of which you still owe $200,000. You have a savings account of $14,000.

You are a marine biology graduate student, about to finish your Ph.D. and look for your first job. You pay approximately $500 a month in student loans. You have a $2,000 savings account.

You are a computer technician who makes $28,000 a year and lives in a small town. You've inherited your home, which is worth $90,000. You've always wanted to live in a big city and try your hand at writing novels. Where should you move?

THE COST OF LIVING ROLE PLAY CARDS

You own an organic farm that makes a modest income. Because of a building boom in your rural area, your land is now worth $250,000. You would like to sell your farm and own a small florist business in a more culturally stimulating area.

You have just finished high school and would like to move away from your home town and save money for the purchase of a home or to possibly attend community college. Your goal is to save $10,000 in three years. You've worked summers helping out in a local bank. You think you might like to find a job as a bank teller, but know that you will have to move to do so.

PRIMETIME: SAMPLE QUESTIONNAIRE

We appreciate your participation in our project. Attached are the grocery shopping list, nutritional survey, and recycling questionnaire that you will need to complete and return to us. If you have questions, comments or concerns about the material or the project, please contact me at: *(insert your email address)*

- -

GROCERY SHOPPING LIST

Send students (individually, in teams, or as a class) to the supermarket and calculate the AVERAGE PRICE for each of the items on the shopping list.

IMPORTANT Please use regular retail prices, not sale or promotional prices. It would also help us out a great deal if you could make your shopping list look as much like ours as possible. Thank you.

Item/Quantity	*Average Price*
Spaghetti (1 pound)	
Bananas (1 pound)	
Hamburger (1 pound, 80% lean)	
Rice (1 pound)	
Oranges (5-pound bag)	
White flour (5-pound bag)	
Whole milk (1 gallon)	
Potatoes (5-pound bag)	
Corn (16-oz. can)	
Peanut butter (12-oz. jar)	
Whole chicken (1 pound)	
Apples, red delicious (1 pound)	
Sugar, white (5-pound bag)	
Butter (1 pound)	
Local currency (if not in U.S. $)	

FIVE-DAY NUTRITIONAL SURVEY

Please make a copy of this template for each student and use one master copy to enter your class totals. Have each student record the number of servings from each food group they ate.

Enter the AVERAGE NUMBER OF SERVINGS your whole class ate from each of the food groups each day on the master copy. (Your class will need to do some addition and division to determine this data.) Again, it would help us out a great deal if you could make your master copy look as much like ours as possible. Thank you.

Name/School Name: _____

Food Groups (MDSR)**	Average Number of Servings/ Day				
	M	T	W	Th	F
Fruit (2)	( )	( )	( )	( )	( )
Vegetables (3)	( )	( )	( )	( )	( )
Grains (6)	( )	( )	( )	( )	( )
Dairy (3-4)	( )	( )	( )	( )	( )
Meats (2-3)	( )	( )	( )	( )	( )

**Minimum daily servings recommended*

RECYCLING QUESTIONNAIRE

Please survey your class to determine the extent to which they and their family attempt to recycle and preserve the environment. Please check or fill in the blank as appropriate. Thank you.

1. Does your community have a recycling program? ☐ yes ☐ no

2. Do you and your family recycle? ☐ yes ☐ no

3. Does your school recycle? ☐ yes ☐ no

    a. How many bags of trash does your school generate in a day? _____

    b. What percentage of this trash is recycled? _____%

Again, thank you for participating in PrimeTime. If we can return the favor at any time in the future, please let us know.

WEATHER WEEK

REGISTRATION FORM

Teacher's Name: _____

School: _____

Subject(s) / Grade: _____

City, State, Country_____

Global Address: _____
(Latitude and Longitude—Degrees and Minutes)

Email Address: _____
Please include a short introductory paragraph about your class and their expectations for doing this project.

This information will be forwarded to the other participants.
Send registration via email to the project coordinator:

WEATHER DATA FORM

School Name: _____

City, State, Country_____

Global Address: _____
(Latitude and Longitude—Degrees and Minutes)

Weather from 1:30 - 2:30 pm:

	Monday	Tuesday	Wednesday	Thursday	Friday
Temp. (F)					
Clouds					
Precipitation					
Wind					
Direction					

Temperature should be measured in a shady spot with the thermometer 3 feet above the ground. Please specify Fahrenheit or Celsius.

Clouds: None, cumulus, cirrus, or stratus

Precipitation: None, rainfall, mist, snow, sleet, freezing rain, other (please list)

Wind direction: The direction the wind is blowing from. If no wind, put none.

VISITING THE NATIONAL PARKS

NATIONAL PARKS CHECKLIST

Students _____

_____

_____

Name of national park _____

Location (city, state) _____

GEOGRAPHY

Land (check all that apply):

☐ Mountain

☐ Hills

☐ Caves

☐ Desert

☐ Other _____

Water and Moisture

☐ River_____

☐ Streams

☐ Ocean_____

☐ Swamps_____

☐ Salt marshes_____

☐ Fresh water marshes_____

☐ Large lakes_____

☐ Small lakes or ponds_____

☐ Other forms of water _____

☐ Rainfall (high, medium, low, none) _____

☐ Amount of rain per year _____

Land Cover

☐ Forest

☐ Meadows

☐ Prairies

☐ Desert plants

☐ None

Continued on following page

Plants: List 5 of the most common plants, for example: pine trees, wildflowers, cactus, deciduous trees, and so on.

_____

_____

_____

_____

_____

Land Animals: List five of the most common land animals found in your park:

_____

_____

_____

_____

_____

Aquatic Animals: List five of the most common aquatic animals found in your park:

_____

_____

_____

_____

_____

Birds: List five of the most common birds found in your park:

_____

_____

_____

_____

_____

Top Sites by Subject Area

I asked teachers about their favorite sites—the ones they come back to again and again. The following list includes the top sites from teachers across the country. You'll find links to all the sites listed here at *http://www.bedrockbarn.com/pages/sites.htm*.

The sites represented here are a small fraction of the resources available to your classroom through the Web. It won't be long before you'll have your own list of top sites!

OF INTEREST TO ALL

Library of Congress
http://marvel.loc.gov/homepage/

What do I need to say about the benefits of having the Library of Congress available at your fingertips? An excellent resource, includes photos from the Civil War, samples of African music, links to sites featuring Latin and Greek literature classics, anything you'd need to know about our government, and much, much more.

CNN
http://www.cnn.com

Access to up-to-the-minute news.

Education World
http://www.educationworld.com

Features the top 10,000 education sites where you can search by keyword, topic, or check out award-winning sites.

Newspapers Online
http://www.intercom.com.au/intercom/newsprs/index.htm

Local newspapers that are available online.

I'm grateful to the many teachers who contributed to this appendix. A special thanks goes to Nancy Skomars Davis, an English and computer teacher at the Advanced Technologies Academy in Las Vegas, Nevada, for providing so many interesting sites for the English section.

ART

Art Treasures
http://sgwww.epfl.ch/BERGER/index.html

Art from the far and near east.

Artserv
http://rubens.anu.edu.au/

Award-winning site from the Australian National University, includes more than 16,000 images, as well as art tutorials for students. Best for the secondary level.

Time Life Photo Sight
http://pathfinder.com/photo/sighthome.html

From Time-Life's famous archives.

Web Museum, Paris
http://sunsite.unc.edu/wm/

Tour Paris and visit this collection of famous paintings.

The Refrigerator Art Contest
http://www.seeusa.com/refrigerator.html

This award-winning site features children's art. Students can submit art for a weekly contest. The 5 best pictures are displayed, and the Internet audience votes on what picture goes to the "Hall of Fame."

Ansel Adams
http://bookweb.cwis.uci.edu:8042/SlicedExhibit/NoCal.html

An Ansel Adams exhibition featuring the photographer himself talking about his work.

Crayola Art Site
http://www.crayola.com/art_education/

A terrific site including classroom activities, contests, etc.

Art Deadlines
http://rtuh.com/adl

A call for entries for competitions of student-submitted art.

ENGLISH

The Online Books Page

http://www.cs.cmu.edu/Web/books.html

An index of thousands of online books and other documents, updated regularly.

Elements of Literature

http://fur.rscc.cc.tn.us/OWL/ElementsLit.html

For definitions of literary terms.

Online Writing Lab

http://www2.rscc.cc.tn.us/~jordan_JJ/OWL/owl.html

Features information on correct usage, avoiding sexist language, and links to other resources for writing help.

St. Cloud's University Literacy Online

http://leo.stcloud.msus.edu/

For help with writing for younger students.

Carnegie-Mellon's English Server

http://english-www.hss.cmu.edu/

For literature links.

Building Blocks to Reading

http://www.macconnect.com/~jrpotter/ltrain.spm/

Activities to encourage a child's love of reading.

Word Play

http://homepage.interaccess.com/~wolinsky/word.htm

A great site to check out if you're into words.

Teachers and Writers Collaborative

http://www.twc.org/tmmain.htm

A source for finding professional writers.

American Literature Survey Site

http://www.en.utexas.edu/~daniel/amlit/amlit.html

Students can discuss great works online and view other students' works.

ArthurNet

http://reality.sgi.com/employees/chris_manchester/guide.html

A guide to Arthurian sites on the Web.

The Camelot Project

http://rodent.lib.rochester.edu/camelot/cphome.htm

A database of Arthurian texts, images, and more.

Where in the World Is Roger?

http://www.gsn.org/gsn/proj/rog/index.html

For elementary students. Follow Roger as he travels all over the world in his truck named Bubba.

FOR STUDENTS

KidsWeb

http://www.npac.syr.edu/textbook/kidsweb

A digital library for kids, with links to art, drama, science, social studies, games, and other resources, as well as other digital libraries.

Girl Talk

http://www.worldkids.net/clubs/CSIS/

A moderated bulletin board for girls on a variety of discussion topics.

Cyber Sisters

http://wwwworldkids.net/clubs/csis

Great links to home pages of special interest to girls.

Cyberspace Middle School

http://www.scri.fsu.edu/~dennisl/CMS.html

Great places for middle school students to visit, including NASA, the Smithsonian, and more.

LANGUAGES

Languages for Travelers
http://www.travlang.com/languages/index.html
A guide to more than 35 languages, from Afrikaans to Zulu.

MATH

The Math Forum
http://forum.swarthmore.edu/
The Geometry Forum features a problem of the week, an ask-an-expert forum (Ask Dr. Math), an Internet hunt, and has great additional resources.

The Virtual School
http://www.webcom.com/~vschool
Weekly algebra problems are posted.

Fun with Numbers
http://www.newdream.net/~sage/old/numbers/
What the name suggests!

Math Projects
http://www.ed.hawaii.edu
A source of excellent math projects.

MEDIA LITERACY

Video Placement Worldwide
http://www.vpw.com/
Provides videos and other classroom materials free of charge.

Modern Educator Resource Center
http://www.modern.com/
Offers free and loaned videos, plus other helpful resources.

The Discovery Channel School
http://school.discovery.com/
Media literacy tips, resources, and much more.

MUSIC

ClassicalNet
http://www.classical.net
An introduction to classical music, containing biographies, history, and guides to classical recordings.

The Piano Education Page
http://www.unm.edu/~loritaf/pnoedmn.html
Information about playing and learning piano. Includes hints on software and finding the right teacher.

CD Link
http://www.voyagerco.com/cdlink/
A sound application for browsers, and for playing audio CDs on CD-ROM drives.

Music from Favorite Artists
http://www.music.sony.com/Music/MusicIndex.html
A guide to music links, video information, samples, and more.

Music Education Online
http://www.geocities.com/Athens/2405/index.html
Music education lesson plans, plus great links to other resources.

SOCIAL STUDIES

MECC Interactive Explorer Series
http://www.mecc.com/ies.html
The MECC Interactive Explorer Series includes MayaQuest, where students explore ancient ruins while connected to classrooms around the world, and Oregon Trail Online, a 6-week online experience where classrooms—set up as wagons—team up across the country to traverse the trail.

Public Policy

http://www.pitt.edu/~ian/ianres.html

A Web library of public policy sites. Links to good public policy information by the University of Pittsburgh.

Visit the United Nations

http://www.un.org/

The U.N.'s home page. Includes a daily list of documents issued by the U.N.

Formerly Classified Government Documents

http://www.doe.gov/html/osti/opennet/opennet1.html

Includes links to previously classified documents regarding nuclear weapons.

Citylink

http://www.Neosoft.com/citylink

Visit any U.S. city with a home page.

Underground Railroad

http://www.npca.org/walk.html

Retrace the Underground Railroad from Maryland to Canada.

SCIENCE

Global Monitoring

http://www.globe.gov/

This is an excellent resource for monitoring the environment internationally.

National Science Foundation

http://www.ehr.nsf.gov

Offers incredible projects you can join, hooks up with real scientists, etc.

NASA

http://img.arc.nasa.gov/current-projects.html

A list of NASA's projects you can join. Also see *http://quest.arc.nasa.gov/index.html* for an overview of resources. For interesting images from NASA, see *http://pds.jpl.nasa.gov/planets/*. Also check out NASA's spacelink at *http://spacelink.msfc.nasa.gov/*.

NOAA on Tap

http://www.gsn.org/gsn/cu.noaa.html

Scientists from the Office of Ocean Resources Conservation and Assessment (ORCA) and the National Oceanic and Atmospheric Administration (NOAA) sponsor CU-SeeMe video-conferencing for high schools worldwide.

Possibilities for Science

http://kendaco.telebyte.com:80/billband/Possibilities.html

A Magellan 4-star site that looks at the use of the Internet in the science classroom.

Arctic Project

http://ics.soe.umich.edu/ed712/IAPIntro.html

Explore the Arctic alongside famous explorers.

The Discovery Channel Online

http://www.discovery.com

Award-winning Web programming offered around different themes: history, nature, science, people, exploration, technology, etc.

The Why Files

http://whyfiles.news.wisc.edu

The National Institute for Science Education looks at science issues behind the headline news. Updated bi-weekly.

Earth & Sky

http://www.earthsky.com

A radio show on general topics of science interest, accompanied by classroom activities. Classroom materials and schedule available through the Web site.

Solar System

http://bang.lanl.gov/solarsys/

Tour the solar system!

Nineplanets

http://www.seds.org/nineplanets/nineplanets

Learn more about the planets in our solar system.

Ask the Scientist Videoconferences

http://space.rice.edu/

Select "videoconferences" for a full list of CU-SeeMe conferences available online on topics related to space.

Frog Dissection

http://george.lbl.gov/ITG.hm.pg.docs/dissect/

See a virtual frog dissection from every angle imaginable.

Explore the Heart

http://sln2.fi.edu/biosci/heart.html

Everything you might want to know about the human heart, and more.

Weather Quiz

http://water.dnr.state.sc.us

Southeast Regional Climate Center offers a weather quiz on their educational page.

Weather Links

http://www.geog.okstate.edu/weather/weather.htm

All sorts of links to interesting weather sites.

Exploratorium

http://www.exploratorium.edu/

San Francisco's science museum offers interactive science exhibits.

Science and the Environment

http://www.voyagepub.com/publish/voyage.htm

Voyage Publishing offers current news on the environment that can be used to supplement your curriculum

Dinosaur Exhibit

http://www.hcc.hawaii.edu/hccinfo/dinos/dinos.1.html

A dinosaur exhibit complete with expert narration.

Froggy Things

http://www.cs.yale.edu/HTML/YALE/CS/HyPlans/loosemore-sandra/froggy.html

Pictures and frog sounds from frogs all over the world.

Environmental Education

http://www.igc.org/igc/econet/index.html.

Excellent environmental resources available for teachers.

FOR MORE INFORMATION

Cohen, E.G. (1994). *Designing Groupwork: Strategies for the Heterogeneous Classroom.* New York: Teachers College Press.

Ellsworth, J. H. (1994). *Education on the Internet.* Indianapolis, Indiana: Sams Publishing.

Gardner, Howard (1993). *Multiple Intelligences: The Theory in Practice.* New York: Basic Books.

Kreidler, W.J. (1990). *Elementary Perspectives: Teaching Concepts of Peace and Conflict.* Cambridge, Massachusetts: Educators for Social Responsibility.

Kreidler, W.J. (1994). *Conflict Resolution in the Middle School.* Cambridge, Massachusetts: Educators for Social Responsibility.

Leshin, Cynthia B. (1995). *Internet Adventures.* Phoenix, Arizona: Xplora Publishing.

Lieber, C.M. (1995). *Making Choices: Part I.* Cambridge, Massachusetts: Educators for Social Responsibility.

Robin, B., Keeler, E., and Miller, R. (1997). *Educator's Guide to the Web.* New York: MIS: Press.

Rohnke, K. (1984). *Silver Bullets: A Guide to Initiative Problems, Adventure Games, and Trust Activities.* Hamilton, Massachusetts: Project Adventure.

Serim, F. & Koch, M. (1996). *NetLearning: Why Teachers Use the Internet.* Sebastapol, California: Songline Studios, Inc., and O'Reilly & Associates, Inc.

Williams, B. (1995). *The Internet for Teachers.* Foster City, California: IDG Books Worldwide.

Index

More Titles from O'Reilly

Songline Guides

NetResearch: Finding Information Online

By Daniel J. Barrett
1st Edition February 1997
200 pages, ISBN 1-56592-245-X

NetResearch teaches you how to locate the information you need in the constantly changing online world. You'll learn effective search techniques that work with any Internet search programs, present or future, and will build intuition on how to succeed when searches fail. Covers America Online, CompuServe, Microsoft Network and Prodigy, as well as direct and dial-up Internet connections.

NetSuccess: How Real Estate Agents Use the Internet

By Scott Kersnar
1st Edition August 1996
214 pages, ISBN 1-56592-213-1

This book shows real estate agents how to harness the communications and marketing tools of the Internet to enhance their careers and make the Internet work for them. Through agents' stories and "A day in the life" scenarios, readers see what changes and what stays the same when you make technology a full partner in your working life.

NetLearning: Why Teachers Use the Internet

By Ferdi Serim & Melissa Koch
1st Edition June 1996
304 pages, Includes CD-ROM
ISBN 1-56592-201-8

In this book educators and Internet users who've been exploring its potential for education share stories to help teachers use this medium to its fullest potential in their classrooms. The book offers advice on how to adapt, how to get what you want, and where to go to get help. The goal: To invite educators online with the reassurance there will be people there to greet them.

NetTravel: How Travelers Use the Internet

By Michael Shapiro
1st Edition April 1997
312 pages, Includes CD-ROM
ISBN 1-56592-172-0

NetTravel is a virtual toolbox of advice for those travelers who want to tap into the rich vein of travel resources on the Internet. It is filled with personal accounts by travelers who've used the Net to plan their business trips, vacations, honeymoons, and explorations. The author gives readers all the tools they need to use the Net immediately to find and save money on airline tickets, accommodations, car rentals, and more.

Net Law: How Lawyers Use the Internet

By Paul Jacobsen
1st Edition January 1997
254 pages, Includes CD-ROM
ISBN 1-56592-258-1

From simple email to sophisticated online marketing, *Net Law* shows how the solo practitioner or the large law firm can turn the Net into an effective and efficient tool. Through stories from those who've set up pioneering legal Net sites, attorney Paul Jacobsen explains how lawyers can successfully integrate the Internet into their practices, sharing lessons "early adopters" have learned.

shopPBS

from the comfort of your own computer chair

http://www.pbs.org/shop

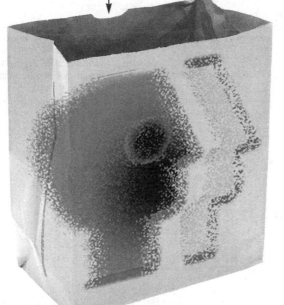

Now your favorite PBS videos and products are just a mouse click away with shopPBS.

At this special cyber shop you'll find a video collection with more than 200 titles, a bookshelf that includes the acclaimed book *NetLearning: How Teachers Use the Internet* and other fun items like the lovable Wishbone doll. Best of all, ordering is done online with secure credit card transactions!

For a fun-filled shopping adventure, make your next online stop shopPBS.

http://www.pbs.org/shop

PBS ONLINE® (http://www.pbs.org) is the premier choice for unique and compelling interactive content developed specifically for the Internet.

IF PBS DOESN'T DO IT, WHO WILL?   http://www.pbs.org/shop

SONGLINE™

S T U D I O S

Songline Studios specializes in developing innovative, interactive content for online audiences.

Songline Studios mission is to create online programs that allow audiences to experience new people, places, and ideas in unique ways that can only be accomplished through the Web. "Users are not just looking for information online but are searching for rewarding experiences. We are focused on creating these experiences," notes Dale Dougherty, president and CEO of Songline Studios.

THE MEANING OF "SONGLINE"

Songline Studios derives its name from the Australian aboriginal concept of using songs to guide people through unknown territories. These oral maps or "songlines" depict events at successive sites along a walking trail that traverses through a region. This is evocative of Songline Studios' mission: to create resources and guides for online audiences as they seek out and experience new territories and new communities on the Internet.

You can visit the many online and print properties created by Songline Studios through their Web site located at *http://www.songline.com*

SONGLINE GUIDES

The Songline Guides book series connects people with their communities of interest on the Internet. They are non-technical guides, featuring the experiences of specific community members who are also early Internet adopters. These stories help the reader focus on what he or she might expect to gain from being online. Songline Guides can be found at your local bookstore or can be ordered directly from O'Reilly & Associates by calling **1-800-998-9938** or send an email message to **order@ora.com**. Look for Songline Guides for Realtors, Parents and other communities of interest in the near future.

For more information about Songline Studios, call 1-800-998-9973 or send email to: *info@songline.com*

How to stay in touch with O'Reilly

1. Visit Our Award-Winning Web Site

http://www.oreilly.com/

★ "Top 100 Sites on the Web" —*PC Magazine*
★ "Top 5% Web sites" —*Point Communications*
★ "3-Star site" —*The McKinley Group*

Our web site contains a library of comprehensiveproduct information (including book excerpts and tables of contents), downloadable software, background articles, interviews with technology leaders, links to relevant sites, book cover art, and more. File us in your Bookmarks or Hotlist!

2. Join Our Email Mailing Lists

New Product Releases

To receive automatic email with brief descriptions of all new O'Reilly products as they are released, send email to:
listproc@online.oreilly.com
Put the following information in the first line of your message (*not* in the Subject field):
subscribe oreilly-news

O'Reilly Events

If you'd also like us to send information about trade show events, special promotions, and other O'Reilly events, send email to:
listproc@online.oreilly.com
Put the following information in the first line of your message (*not* in the Subject field):
subscribe oreilly-events

3. Get Examples from Our Books via FTP

There are two ways to access an archive of example files from our books:

Regular FTP

- ftp to:
  ftp.oreilly.com
  (login: anonymous
  password: your email address)
- Point your web browser to:
  ftp://ftp.oreilly.com/

FTPMAIL

- Send an email message to:
  ftpmail@online.oreilly.com
  (Write "help" in the message body)

4. Contact Us via Email

order@oreilly.com
To place a book or software order online. Good for North American and international customers.

subscriptions@oreilly.com
To place an order for any of our newsletters or periodicals.

books@oreilly.com
General questions about any of our books.

software@oreilly.com
For general questions and product information about our software. Check out O'Reilly Software Online at **http://software.oreilly.com/** for software and technical support information. Registered O'Reilly software users send your questions to: **website-support@oreilly.com**

cs@oreilly.com
For answers to problems regarding your order or our products.

booktech@oreilly.com
For book content technical questions or corrections.

proposals@oreilly.com
To submit new book or software proposals to our editors and product managers.

international@oreilly.com
For information about our international distributors or translation queries. For a list of our distributors outside of North America check out:
http://www.oreilly.com/www/order/country.html

O'Reilly & Associates, Inc.
101 Morris Street, Sebastopol, CA 95472 USA
TEL   707-829-0515 or 800-998-9938
          (6am to 5pm PST)
FAX   707-829-0104

Titles from O'Reilly

WEB
Advanced Perl Programming
Apache: The Definitive Guide
Building Your Own Web Conferences
Building Your Own Website™
CGI Programming
    for the World Wide Web
Designing for the Web
Designing Sound for the Web
Designing with Animation
Designing with JavaScript
Dynamic HTML:
    The Definitive Reference
Frontier: The Definitive Guide
Gif Animation Studio
HTML: The Definitive Guide,
    2nd Edition
Information Architecture
    for the World Wide Web
JavaScript: The Definitive Guide,
    3nd Edition
Mastering Regular Expressions
Netscape IFC in a Nutshell
Photoshop for the Web
Shockwave Studio
WebMaster in a Nutshell
WebMaster in a Nutshell,
    Deluxe Edition
Web Navigation:
    Designing the User Experience
Web Security & Commerce

PERL
Learning Perl, 2nd Edition
Learning Perl for Win32 Systems
Perl5 Desktop Reference
Perl Cookbook
Perl in a Nutshell
Perl Resource Kit—UNIX Edition
Perl Resource Kit—Win32 Edition
Programming Perl, 2nd Edition
Web Client Programming with Perl

JAVA SERIES
Database Programming with
    JDBC and Java
Developing Java Beans
Exploring Java, 2nd Edition
Java AWT Reference
Java Cryptography
Java Distributed Computing
Java Examples in a Nutshell
Java Fundamental Classes Reference
Java in a Nutshell, 2nd Edition
Java in a Nutshell, Deluxe Edition
Java Language Reference, 2nd Edition
Java Native Methods
Java Network Programming
Java Security
Java Threads
Java Virtual Machine

SYSTEM ADMINISTRATION
Building Internet Firewalls
Computer Crime:
    A Crimefighter's Handbook
Computer Security Basics
DNS and BIND, 2nd Edition
Essential System Administration,
    2nd Edition
Essential WindowsNT
    System Administration
Getting Connected:
    The Internet at 56K and Up
High Performance Computing,
    2nd Edition
Linux Network Administrator's Guide
Managing Internet Information
    Services, 2nd Edition
Managing IP Networks
    with Cisco Routers
Managing Mailing Lists
Managing NFS and NIS
Managing the WinNT Registry
Managing Usenet
MCSE: The Core Exams in a Nutshell
MCSE: The Electives in a Nutshell
Networking Personal Computers
    with TCP/IP
PalmPilot: The Ultimate Guide
Practical UNIX & Internet Security,
    2nd Edition
PGP: Pretty Good Privacy
Protecting Networks with SATAN
sendmail, 2nd Edition
sendmail Desktop Reference
System Performance Tuning
TCP/IP Network Administration,
    2nd Edition
termcap & terminfo
Using & Managing PPP
Using & Managing UUCP
Virtual Private Networks
Volume 8: X Window System
    Administrator's Guide
Web Security & Commerce
WindowsNT Backup & Restore
WindowsNT Desktop Reference
WindowsNT in a Nutshell
WindowsNT Server 4.0
    for Netware Administrators
WindowsNT SNMP
WindowsNT User Administration

GRAPHICS & MULTIMEDIA
Director in a Nutshell
Photoshop in a Nutshell
QuarkXPress in a Nutshell

UNIX
Exploring Expect
Learning VBScript
Learning GNU Emacs, 2nd Edition
Learning the bash Shell, 2nd Edition
Learning the Korn Shell
Learning the UNIX Operating System,
    4th Edition
Learning the vi Editor, 5th Edition
Linux Device Drivers
Linux in a Nutshell
Linux Multimedia Guide
Running Linux, 2nd Edition
SCO UNIX in a Nutshell
sed & awk, 2nd Edition
Tcl/Tk Tools
UNIX in a Nutshell, Deluxe Edition
UNIX in a Nutshell, System V Edition
UNIX Power Tools, 2nd Edition
Using csh & tsch
What You Need To Know:
    When You Can't Find Your
    UNIX System Administrator
Writing GNU Emacs Extensions

WINDOWS
Access Database Design
    and Programming
Developing Windows Error Messages
Inside the Windows 95 File System
Inside the Windows 95 Registry
VB/VBA in a Nutshell: The Languages
Win32 Multithreaded Programming
Windows95 in a Nutshell
Windows NT File System Internals
Windows NT in a Nutshell

USING THE INTERNET
AOL in a Nutshell
Bandits on the Information
    Superhighway
Internet in a Nutshell
Smileys
The Whole Internet for Windows95
The Whole Internet:
    The Next Generation
The Whole Internet
    User's Guide & Catalog

ANNOYANCES
Excel97 Annoyances
Office97 Annoyances
Outlook Annoyances
Windows97 Annoyances
Word97 Annoyances

SONGLINE GUIDES
NetLaw   NetResearch
NetLearning   NetSuccess
NetLessons   NetTravel

PROGRAMMING
Advanced Oracle PL/SQL
    Programming with Packages
Applying RCS and SCCS
BE Developer's Guide
BE Advanced Topics
C++: The Core Language
Checking C Programs with lint
Encyclopedia of Graphics File
    Formats, 2nd Edition
Guide to Writing DCE Applications
lex & yacc, 2nd Edition
Managing Projects with make
Mastering Oracle Power Objects
Oracle8 Design Tips
Oracle Built-in Packages
Oracle Design
Oracle Performance Tuning,
    2nd Edition
Oracle PL/SQL Programming,
    2nd Edition
Oracle Scripts
Porting UNIX Software
POSIX Programmer's Guide
POSIX.4: Programming
    for the Real World
Power Programming with RPC
Practical C Programming, 3rd Edition
Practical C++ Programming
Programming Python
Programming with curses
Programming with GNU Software
Pthreads Programming
Software Portability with imake,
    2nd Edition
Understanding DCE
UNIX Systems Programming for SVR4

X PROGRAMMING
Vol. 0: X Protocol Reference Manual
Vol. 1: Xlib Programming Manual
Vol. 2: Xlib Reference Manual
Vol. 3M: X Window System User's
    Guide, Motif Edition
Vol. 4M: X Toolkit Intrinsics
    Programming Manual,
    Motif Edition
Vol. 5: X Toolkit Intrinsics Reference
    Manual
Vol. 6A: Motif Programming Manual
Vol. 6B: Motif Reference Manual
Vol. 8 : X Window System
    Administrator's Guide

SOFTWARE
Building Your Own WebSite™
Building Your Own Web Conference
WebBoard™ 3.0
WebSite Professional™ 2.0
PolyForm™

O'REILLY™

TO ORDER: **800-998-9938** • **order@oreilly.com** • **http://www.oreilly.com/**
OUR PRODUCTS ARE AVAILABLE AT A BOOKSTORE OR SOFTWARE STORE NEAR YOU.
FOR INFORMATION: **800-998-9938** • **707-829-0515** • **info@oreilly.com**

International Distributors

UK, EUROPE, MIDDLE EAST AND NORTHERN AFRICA (EXCEPT FRANCE, GERMANY, SWITZERLAND, & AUSTRIA)

INQUIRIES
International Thomson Publishing Europe
Berkshire House
168-173 High Holborn
London WC1V 7AA
United Kingdom
Telephone: 44-171-497-1422
Fax: 44-171-497-1426
Email: itpint@itps.co.uk

ORDERS
International Thomson Publishing Services, Ltd.
Cheriton House, North Way
Andover, Hampshire SP10 5BE
United Kingdom
Telephone: 44-264-342-832 (UK)
Telephone: 44-264-342-806 (outside UK)
Fax: 44-264-364418 (UK)
Fax: 44-264-342761 (outside UK)
UK & Eire orders: itpuk@itps.co.uk
International orders: itpint@itps.co.uk

FRANCE
Editions Eyrolles
61 bd Saint-Germain
75240 Paris Cedex 05
France
Fax: 33-01-44-41-11-44

FRENCH LANGUAGE BOOKS
All countries except Canada
Telephone: 33-01-44-41-46-16
Email: geodif@eyrolles.com
English language books
Telephone: 33-01-44-41-11-87
Email: distribution@eyrolles.com

GERMANY, SWITZERLAND, AND AUSTRIA

INQUIRIES
O'Reilly Verlag
Balthasarstr. 81
D-50670 Köln
Germany
Telephone: 49-221-97-31-60-0
Fax: 49-221-97-31-60-8
Email: anfragen@oreilly.de

ORDERS
International Thomson Publishing
Königswinterer Straße 418
53227 Bonn, Germany
Telephone: 49-228-97024 0
Fax: 49-228-441342
Email: order@oreilly.de

JAPAN
O'Reilly Japan, Inc.
Kiyoshige Building 2F
12-Banchi, Sanei-cho
Shinjuku-ku
Tokyo 160-0008 Japan
Telephone: 81-3-3356-5227
Fax: 81-3-3356-5261
Email: kenji@oreilly.com

INDIA
Computer Bookshop (India) PVT. Ltd.
190 Dr. D.N. Road, Fort
Bombay 400 001 India
Telephone: 91-22-207-0989
Fax: 91-22-262-3551
Email: cbsbom@giasbm01.vsnl.net.in

HONG KONG
City Discount Subscription Service Ltd.
Unit D, 3rd Floor, Yan's Tower
27 Wong Chuk Hang Road
Aberdeen, Hong Kong
Telephone: 852-2580-3539
Fax: 852-2580-6463
Email: citydis@ppn.com.hk

KOREA
Hanbit Media, Inc.
Sonyoung Bldg. 202
Yeksam-dong 736-36
Kangnam-ku
Seoul, Korea
Telephone: 822-554-9610
Fax: 822-556-0363
Email: hant93@chollian.dacom.co.kr

SINGAPORE, MALAYSIA, AND THAILAND
Addison Wesley Longman Singapore PTE Ltd.
25 First Lok Yang Road
Singapore 629734
Telephone: 65-268-2666
Fax: 65-268-7023
Email: daniel@longman.com.sg

PHILIPPINES
Mutual Books, Inc.
429-D Shaw Boulevard
Mandaluyong City, Metro
Manila, Philippines
Telephone: 632-725-7538
Fax: 632-721-3056
Email: mbikikog@mnl.sequel.net

CHINA
Ron's DataCom Co., Ltd.
79 Dongwu Avenue
Dongxihu District
Wuhan 430040
China
Telephone: 86-27-83892568
Fax: 86-27-83222108
Email: hongfeng@public.wh.hb.cn

ALL OTHER ASIAN COUNTRIES
O'Reilly & Associates, Inc.
101 Morris Street
Sebastopol, CA 95472 USA
Telephone: 707-829-0515
Fax: 707-829-0104
Email: order@oreilly.com

AUSTRALIA
WoodsLane Pty. Ltd.
7/5 Vuko Place, Warriewood NSW 2102
P.O. Box 935
Mona Vale NSW 2103
Australia
Telephone: 61-2-9970-5111
Fax: 61-2-9970-5002
Email: info@woodslane.com.au

NEW ZEALAND
Woodslane New Zealand Ltd.
21 Cooks Street (P.O. Box 575)
Waganui, New Zealand
Telephone: 64-6-347-6543
Fax: 64-6-345-4840
Email: info@woodslane.com.au

THE AMERICAS
McGraw-Hill Interamericana Editores, S.A. de C.V.
Cedro No. 512
Col. Atlampa 06450
Mexico, D.F.
Telephone: 52-5-541-3155
Fax: 52-5-541-4913
Email: mcgraw-hill@infosel.net.mx

SOUTH AFRICA
International Thomson Publishing South Africa
Building 18, Constantia Park
138 Sixteenth Road
P.O. Box 2459
Halfway House, 1685 South Africa
Telephone: 27-11-805-4819
Fax: 27-11-805-3648

O'REILLY™

O'Reilly & Associates, Inc.
101 Morris Street
Sebastopol, CA 95472-9902
1-800-998-9938

Visit us online at:
http://www.ora.com/
orders@ora.com

O'REILLY WOULD LIKE TO HEAR FROM YOU

Which book did this card come from?

_____

Where did you buy this book?
- ❏ Bookstore
- ❏ Direct from O'Reilly
- ❏ Bundled with hardware/software
- ❏ Other _____

- ❏ Computer Store
- ❏ Class/seminar

What operating system do you use?
- ❏ UNIX
- ❏ Windows NT
- ❏ Other _____

- ❏ Macintosh
- ❏ PC(Windows/DOS)

What is your job description?
- ❏ System Administrator
- ❏ Network Administrator
- ❏ Web Developer
- ❏ Other _____

- ❏ Programmer
- ❏ Educator/Teacher

❏ Please send me O'Reilly's catalog, containing
  a complete listing of O'Reilly books and
  software.

Name _____   Company/Organization _____

Address _____

City _____   State _____   Zip/Postal Code _____   Country _____

Telephone _____   Internet or other email address (specify network) _____

Nineteenth century wood engraving
of a bear from the O'Reilly &
Associates Nutshell Handbook®
Using & Managing UUCP.

BUSINESS REPLY MAIL
FIRST CLASS MAIL   PERMIT NO. 80   SEBASTOPOL, CA

Postage will be paid by addressee

O'Reilly & Associates, Inc.
101 Morris Street
Sebastopol, CA 95472-9902